A Cellarful of Marmalade

MARGARET HUBBARD

RED PINAFORE PRESS

Published by Red Pinafore Press

Illustrated by Susan M Turmeau

'A Cellarful of Marmalade' is a work of fiction. It is the story of a house. Many of the characters were and are real people, while others have been invented. Some indeed are both; real with fictionalised additions to their stories. The characters who could be identified have all agreed to their sections of the story.

To family, friends and acquaintances from whom I have learned that regardless of time and distance a home lives within us.

Chapter One

Beth lay wrapped in her quilt, her body warm and snug, her mind cold and frightened. Her gaze went beyond the window. Would the world outside look as it had yesterday?

The sun was shining, the trees swaying with a gentleness of breathing. The river beyond was gleaming. She shifted onto her elbow to see the garden. Vivid green from all the winter rain, the grass released from its long winter sleep had begun its annual re-birth. Scattered randomly across the grass grew the daffodils. Last week she was busy and had only glanced at them as she hurried by. They had not yet bloomed, she recalled, or thought she recalled. Were they mere green shoots then, or had she just not paid attention? Now determined to be noticed, they were announcing the arrival of spring. She looked closer. In the flower border edging the path, a primrose and a primula had suddenly emerged. Purple, yellow, bold colours she liked. Nature did not come back stealthily every year. It arrived in colours to be reckoned with.

Like the flowers, she too surged with life at the coming of

spring. January 1st meant nothing. A new year began when the flowers came up. A new year of adventures lay ahead.

But not this year. Life had just suddenly stopped.

She turned her attention to the room. She looked at each feature, and each piece of furniture, slowly and deliberately. She liked this room. She had designed it very carefully, choosing the off-white wardrobes with their simple lines, the green carpet (an extension of the grass, she always said) and the furniture – some pieces bought; other pieces, which had been in her family for years, kept for the memories.

The more she looked, the more she realised it was not she who had designed this room. The charm of the room was in large part because of its rather quirky shape. The long two-door cupboard under the eaves, where she and her brother had chased each other when they were small, belonged in the mind of a nineteenth-century architect. It seemed a great pity she did not know the name of the person who had designed what to children had been a wonderful wet-weather playground. She and her brother could hide behind, and even in, the boxes resident in that cupboard. Shrieking with laughter, they chased each other round and round the oval shape created by both sides of the long wall and the doors, one at each end. The family dog usually joined in this frantic game, although he never quite understood that when you were 'tagged' you became the chaser, and the run then took off in the opposite direction. Amidst the tangle of legs in which he often found himself caught, no serious damage was done. It certainly did not deter him from the fray.

On the mantelpiece above the fireplace, she had placed photographs of her parents, her aunt, her grandfather alongside treasures of no particular value gathered over seventy years. She often wandered into their remembered stories, but today it was the mantelpiece which drew her attention. It was elegant, a mantelpiece for the master bedroom of a wealthy Victorian merchant. For how many decades had she dusted round these fire brackets? Had she ever looked at them? Today she did. She got out of bed and looked at them. Whose hands had crafted them, she wondered. Had they been made to the craftsman's own design, twisting the metal at his own forge? Had he ever seen them in their intended setting, where they had held the fire safely quartered for one hundred and fifty years? Did he ever imagine a woman would look at them so many years later? Like the flowers and the trees, they seemed solid and eternal.

Crouching beside the fire brackets, she closed her eyes. Had this room in the past experienced the misery she was feeling now? It must have. This house had stood so many decades. Pain does not belong to one person and one time. It binds us across continents and centuries.

Restless, she crossed to the window again. The sun danced across the flowers. The long, dark winter was over. Hers was just beginning.

She had known this house all her life, and she loved it. At the end of her childhood she had gone away and built a life and a career amidst the bright lights, but had always come 'home' to see her parents. In time she came back to live here. She recalled when she was about forty looking over the wall, and imagining a different family, not hers, strangers happily playing in the garden. The sharpness of the pain of that imagined loss left her breathless. It was no different now.

As a child at school, Beth had been drawn to history. It was an adventure story. As an adult, she could see beyond the facts to the humans behind them. How people felt, and the choices they made to embark on certain courses of action, seemed to vary little century after century. People did not change as quickly as did the world around them. This room she loved must have known other people who had loved it too. It must also have seen desolation and fear.

Some years earlier, she had become interested in who had lived in the house before her family. This had come about in rather a roundabout way, quite by chance. Her mother, Mina, had lost her husband and her sister in the same month, and Beth had cast about to find something that would help her to withstand this devastation. Her mother's phrase that she was 'the lone standing stone' terrified Beth. In her late seventies, there was no one left who had known Mina when she had been young. She had become twofold isolated; in bereavement, she was bereft also of her own past. Beth watched her mother's loneliness, but in her forties as she was then, had not the empathy of understanding that only years and circumstance can bring.

There had always been a mystery surrounding her mother's grandmother, and as the months of widowhood went on, Mina talked more and more of her lost granny. It was as if to heal the loss of those she had known, she had reached back to connect into an earlier generation. In an attempt to give her mother comfort, Beth wanted to find the 'missing Jane,' and, to that end, learned the methods of family research.

Over the months and years that followed, Beth and her mum embarked on tracing the records, and then visiting where her family had lived in the century before her mother had been born. Liverpool, Gateshead, Barrow, Govan, Dewsbury became sought-after destinations for holiday trips. The excitement when they successfully tracked down a name in a document, an address with the original house still standing, a plot in a pauper's grave! As the family connections grew, these people of the past became as real to them as the living.

Beth smiled as she recalled her mother at the age of seventy-nine, sprinting across a cemetery in Liverpool, as she bore down on a stone in a faraway corner.

'It's here. It's here!' she had declared triumphantly, her eyes shining.

And then there was the day in Dewsbury when they had located an address from over a century before. They stood looking at the house until the door opened, and a friendly voice asked what they were doing.

'I'm looking at where some of my family lived many, many years ago,' announced Mina.

This conversation lead to a cup of tea, and then a tour of the house, only marginally structurally altered in all that time. There was a thrill of excitement in touching the walls their ancestors had touched. Until this point they had been names on documents; now they were people with real lives.

These were happy days.

One day Beth had thought, 'If people can have a family tree, can not a house?' and so the two of them set off again, researching the people who had lived in the house Beth was standing in. With the house as the focus, there were few new places to visit, but the adventure they were on together was just the same. They both loved the house, and felt they were in some way bringing it back to life.

A family tree grew for the house. The people who were on the branches of the tree before Beth had been born had all stood in this room at some point. Of that, she was sure. Invisible presences, they were here. They were ghosts whose presence could be sensed by the walls, the fire brackets and the old apple tree in the garden.

Through her research, she knew who had lived here. No kings and queens, dukes and earls; just ordinary people living ordinary lives, each one rich in his or her own uniqueness. The house had borne witness to them all. Beth listened as its story began.

Chapter Two

The house had been built in the late 1860s. It was lived in, briefly, by a wealthy merchant, Mr Leitch, who had been a hatter in Glasgow. He then built a second house just along the road, renting this one to a gardener and his family, a family who had known pain. Hugh Weir was a widower before he was forty. His daughter Mary ran the house, and brought up her younger siblings. Over the wall in the adjoining cottage was another family, a family whole of father, mother and three children.

Beth wondered what Hugh and his daughter looked like. Did she remind him of his dead wife, Christina, when she had been sixteen? Mary had already lost her mother two years by then. Had her father in his grief been able to comfort her? Beth thought not. They lived at a time when grief was hidden. Beth pondered how lucky she was to live in a world where expressing it was acceptable... if a person could. She had learnt that isolation and pain are silencers, regardless of the norms of society.

She began to create Mary in her mind. Dark-haired, rosy-cheeked, a comely lass. She watched Mary climb the stairs carrying firewood, her plain brown dress needing cleaned – tomorrow's task. Boiling water, big zinc bath, trampling clothing dirty from the work in the fields.

Perhaps Mary longed to go elsewhere, to have a life beyond the small village. Many young girls of her time went to the cities, or boarded the ships she could see sailing down the river on their way across the ocean. She may have looked forward to a home of her own, children of her own, or have dreamed of a different way of life, not yet clear to her, but beyond the boundaries of what she could see lying ahead; the inherited duty of running the household, looking after her father, her siblings and a lodger essential to the family economy.

Had Mary stood here in this room, where her mother had slept, and felt her life too had stopped?

Beth knew from her research Mary's life had not stopped here, that she had drawn the attention of a young man who lived nearby. He had come recently to the village, working as a labourer building the big houses, to which the city merchants were increasingly coming on holiday. From there he had progressed to building the little school about half a mile along the road. She passed it every day as she went for her messages.

One Sunday morning at church, he smiled to her. Her heart quickened and she returned the smile. The next Sunday, she took more care of her appearance than usual. Once in her pew she sat anxious, fearful he was no longer in the village, but had gone back to the city. And then in he came. He seemed to be looking to where she had sat the previous week. They did not smile, but their eyes spoke silently. Months later, they recalled that moment; they both knew they had seen beyond the outer layer to the very essence of the other. Years later, they developed the habit of leaving the pew at different times, and as he went out, he always turned to look back towards her, for them both to relive that first moment again.

As the days of spring lengthened, Mary walked each day for her messages, passing the little school and watching it grow. How wonderful, she thought, that children, boys and girls, would go to school and learn to read and write. She herself would like to be able to read. Her brother would be one of the first pupils at the school, and she wondered if he would be able to teach her once he had mastered his letters. There would be no material change in her life by being able to read and write, but she somehow knew that it would enrich her. It would allow her to enter a world she was not part of – the world of books and learning. It would take her beyond the closed life of the village, even if she herself never left it, and in these thoughts the chains of her life fell away. She was no longer isolated in her little world, but part of something older, wider, new.

One morning in autumn he said to her, 'What are you thinking about?' Peter had been watching her from the school building he was working on.

She was startled. She had not realised how long she had been standing thinking, nor that he had seen her and come down from the roof to talk to her. His voice was warm, and although she felt herself to know him, it was the first time she had heard him speak.

'I want to learn to read,' she blurted out. 'I hope my little brother will be able to teach me.'

There was a pause, and then Peter said slowly, 'I can teach you if you wish.'

'Can you read? How did you learn?'

'The minister, where I lived before I came here, taught me. I am learning my trade as a joiner, but I also wanted to read. I want to understand ideas. Robert Burns was a gardener's son, and his father insisted he learned to read. I am a gardener's son, and my father wanted this for me too.' He paused and added shyly, 'I think reading should also be for girls.' He watched for her reaction. 'Would you like me to teach you?'

'Yes, very much, but I must ask my father.'

Once again the look that passed between them said more than words.

'Peter, will you get back here and get on with the job?' came a voice from the roof.

He smiled. 'Let me know what your father says.'

Mary walked on, alive with the new adventure that was no longer just a dream. She would learn to read. This young man would teach her.

She walked to the shops, she collected her messages and she walked back to her house by a different route. She did not want to pass the school and see him just yet. She needed time to think.

Once home she lit the fires, washed the first pile of clothes and turned over in her mind different ways of speaking to her father. He was a kind man and since the death of his wife, he relied on his daughter. He himself could not read. How was he going to agree to her learning a skill which could take her beyond the household which depended on her?

By the time she had made the dinner and finished her evening chores, she was no closer to knowing how to approach her father than she had been as she had walked up the road. But something had changed; reading had become real, and she was determined. This was something she would not let slip through her fingers.

By the next evening, she was no clearer. As she put the soup on the table, she was aware her father was slightly different with her. Could he guess what was in her mind? Once the smaller children were in bed, and the lodger had gone out courting, her father suddenly said, 'I hear you want to learn to read. And I hear you have found yourself a teacher.'

She glanced at him, afraid of what was coming. 'How did you know?'

'Nae secrets in villages, especially when I ken the faither of the teacher.'

'Will you let me?' She held her breath. In this moment

isolation hung.

He smiled. 'I will, but on one condition. I learn too. I fancy being able to read, and anyway where would you go to learn? Ye canna be alone with yon young man. Ye need someone wi' you, and who better than your auld faither?'

And so the lessons began. They had to be in summer, because paraffin for lamps was expensive. Hugh borrowed a slate from the minister, and chalk from the kitchen of the big house where he worked. Father and daughter pored over letters as they were combined into words, and by the autumn they could read. Long complex sentences would take longer, but they had mastered the code.

By the time the nights were dark, Mary and Peter were preparing for their future together. It would be difficult to leave her father and siblings, so the solution was simple. Peter would move in once they were married. Spring came again, and the young couple walked on the hills behind the house. In the garden the daffodils blossomed, and beyond, the river glistened. As soon as it was warm enough to sit outside, there were Mary, Peter and Hugh reading aloud to each other, one at a time. Hugh was able to borrow books from the house where he worked. Peter had finished building the school, and had moved on to building another house. He found a way of borrowing books from the packing cases when they arrived from the city – they would be only temporarily missed! By then too, there was a local newspaper, of which the little group read every word.

Here were three adults living in the same house, linked by the life rituals of birth and marriage. But they were also linked by their reading, which led them into exploration of other worlds of earlier times and faraway lands. The very effort to master this new skill bound them to unknown people in different places and different times, people who had also yearned to know.

The reading, of course, extended into discussion of what they read. Each new idea was carefully examined, and through this exploration the links of the threesome strengthened. The household chores no longer seemed so wearisome. As her father and husband went to work, so Mary did her work, while all the time turning over whatever demanded debate.

One autumn day, she was making jam. She had gathered the brambles from the hedgerows and the apples from the tree in the garden. She had cut them up and put them into the metal pan which had belonged to her grandmother. In went the water and the sugar, and then the pan was placed on the open fire. Mary knew from experience she had to watch the boiling as it was taking place, constantly turning the pan to distribute the heat evenly. She then had to stir. This was a task she had always seen as a waste of her precious time. Just sitting stirring was not to her liking. But no longer. She relished it. She banked the fire, she sat on the little stool constructed at the exact height for this task, and she stirred. She had much to think on.

Their recent reading, *Robinson Crusoe*, had turned on the meaning of isolation. Was it being alone; or was it a state of being, inside one's own mind? She was never alone in a busy household, but she had felt isolation. As she stirred, she tussled with why she no longer felt this. Was it her growing closeness to Peter, or was it discovering she had a connection through the ideas in the books to people she did not know, but who had felt as she felt? She hardly dared to believe this, and yet when she veered away from this new world of ideas, her sense of isolation returned in double strength.

The jam was ready to come off the heat. Now came the tricky part. It had to be strained through cloth to separate the liquid from the pulp. Mary used a very old piece of muslin passed down the years. Peter had watched her do this, and devised an easier way for her to pour. He had constructed a square of sticks and nailed the muslin onto them. This was attached to a stand. She could pour without risk of being burned. Out of habit she still poured carefully, and then, as she blended the liquid and the pulp in each earthenware jar, her thoughts returned to the castaway they had been reading about. From long gone centuries, she considered monks who had chosen to live on islands alone. And then in her own century, there were lighthouse keepers.

Hermits, she concluded, are alone, but they are not lonely. Nor are they isolated beyond the physical sense. They are connected to the experience of every other person who searches out being alone, whether for a few hours, a few days or a lifetime. The connection of shared experience empties isolation of loneliness.

Jam making and philosophy opened up a new world.

Tidying up one morning, Mary found a pencil on the floor. Instead of putting it where it belonged, she found herself looking for paper. An old bill was all she could find, but that would have to do. Abandoning her chores, she sat at the table and began to form a sentence, and then another and another. She read them over, crossed out words, re-wrote and re-wrote until she had a short piece of writing she liked.

As she lay on the grass, she watched the stars sprinkled – no, spread across – no, come alive. Is there a Mary up there watching Earth? Does it rain where you are?

She stopped. She had run out of paper.

That evening, Peter found the piece of paper. He did not say a word, but a few days later he came home with an exercise book found amidst the discarded packing boxes where he was working.

'I know you have been writing on scraps of paper. This will be better.' With it was a shiny new pencil.

Month after month into the green exercise book went descriptions and snippets of story, the work of someone thrilled with the experiment of writing her own words. Into the back of the book went recipes she used only occasionally; sloe and apple pie or blackberry juice.

Hugh found a new world, too. When Mary and Peter had

married, he moved out of the bedroom he had shared with his wife. He had dreaded this moment. The nights were the time of most severe loneliness. He remembered the joy of the early nights of his marriage, and it was as torture to give up the room in which what were now memories had once been alive. Now it was the room for Mary and Peter to build their lives, and he fervently wished them all he had known. He missed Christina desperately, but through the exchange of ideas with his daughter and his son-in-law he had found a new calm. He had begun to talk of his loss, and just as his daughter had done, had come to realise isolation had more to do with disconnection than with being physically alone.

In a busy household, being alone was often a challenge. He solved that with long walks in the hills above the house. There he could walk and remember without pain. He walked along talking to his wife, telling her of Mary and Peter, and of their reading. Occasionally, after checking there was no one else around, he would pick up a stick and teach her letters by marking them on the path. He sometimes thought he heard her laughing with him at his funny stories of the people he worked for. Often he would look at these people who gave him his orders, but never did he find in their eyes the energy he knew in the people he loved. They were trapped in the isolation of their behaviour and their wealth; lonely, unable to break free to welcome new challenges and new ideas.

As Beth pondered on the people who had lived in this room more than a century before, there grew in her an awareness that isolation was about being separate from the flow of life of what has gone before, what is around us now and what is to come. She felt a strange connection to Hugh and Christina, Mary and Peter. When they had looked out of the window every morning, they had seen the same hills on the horizon. They too had experienced joy and sorrow in this room. And in this she found an odd comfort. Alone in the bedroom, the emptiness Beth had felt on waking had begun to lessen.

The door to the cupboard under the eaves was slightly ajar, and as she turned, something caught her eye. It was a metal pan. Her grandmother had used it for making jam, and then her mother for making marmalade. Beth too used it for the annual marmalade making, carefully using every bit of the oranges, flesh and peeled skin, and then grinding them through a very old mincing machine. Beth momentarily wondered if the pan and the mincing machine had been in the house when her grandmother had come here. Perhaps they went as far back as Christina and Mary. They certainly looked as if they might. How many hands had stirred ingredients in that pan? Sitting there on a shelf in the cupboard, it had its own story.

As she moved away from the window towards the bathroom, she smiled to herself. Now that was a space in the house that Hugh and Christina, Mary and Peter did not know. Her own parents had installed it almost a century after the house was built.

She looked again at the fire brackets. Yes, they had seen all that had passed. In the playground under the eaves, she stored sheets and a gramophone. Perhaps Hugh and Christina, and then Peter and Mary stored bedding there too. But an old gramophone! That, like the bathroom, came later.

Chapter Three

Beth went down the stairs, which had been designed by the anonymous architect. She had always liked the elegance of the bottom step. It was not squared off, but rather gently curved at its edges, as if flowing into the rooms on each side.

She made her breakfast, and yes, that was different. How would Mary have liked a cooker, a toaster and an electric kettle? Perhaps not at all. Beth had read of a cook in a very grand house, who had resigned on the spot when she was told the kitchen was getting new cooking utensils! She could only work with her half-century-old models.

She sat down with her one plate and one cup at the kitchen table, a table which had been in the house for more than half a century. It was one of the old-style tables, with very deep drawers, a dumping ground and a treasure trove for 'everything which might one day come in useful,' as the family mantra went.

Cooking for one can be lonely. She remembered when she was divorced, and experienced this for the first time. One cup, one plate, and no one to share the morning silence with. She had been alone. She had been isolated. She had been lonely. And she had been afraid, afraid that this misery would never pass. As time went on, she had found ways round this. Listen to the radio. Reconfigure the room. Sit in a different place. Time passed. She was still alone, still isolated, but the loneliness shrank into the shadows. It would sometimes reappear when least expected, catching her off-balance, but even this she learned how to manage. In time, the gap was filled. She was still alone. She was still isolated eating her morning meal on her own, but she was not lonely. Being alone, being isolated, was not loneliness.

When her mother had died the aloneness, the loneliness, the isolation were familiar enemies. From three decades earlier, she resurrected the strategies to survive.

On this strange morning, once she had poured her second cup of coffee, she sat looking, really looking at this room she knew so well. At the window was the sink. It had never changed location, as the most ancient of drains was below the kitchen-sink window. Beth remembered a time when the sink had been porcelain. Modernity had required an upgrade to stainless steel, itself now in place for more than twenty years. If her parents had kept the porcelain sink, it would have been high fashion now.

She could recall when there was only a cold-water tap. Then her parents had acquired a gadget called a geyser, which was lit by a match; it must have been powered by gas. On igniting it, a trickle of cold water gradually became a trickle of hot water. This too was superseded by a back boiler. Behind the coal fire sat a water tank. The fire heated the water. The result was no hot water on hot summer days, and rather scary noises in winter when the fire had been on all day. The water burbled and gurgled as it boiled behind the fire. And then, when the central heating arrived, lo and behold a combi boiler! At the turn of a tap, hot water gushed forth.

The kitchen had a recess, which in its earliest time may have been for storage, or may have housed a bed. Certainly, the kitchen was a warm place to be. When Beth and her brother were ill, their mother made up a bed for them in this recess, so that she could keep her eye on her sick child, and go about her chores at the same time. Beth loved lying on the floor in that recess bed. She was on a level with the fire and the dog. He cuddled up beside her. Perhaps a treat for him too.

Under the stair was another funny little cupboard for children to hide in. Coal, logs, paper: all the necessities to keep the fire going lived in there.

Her thoughts turned to all the people who had sat in this kitchen, and after breakfast she fetched the folder containing the notes for the house family tree.

Mary's siblings, and then her children, attended the school – the records state this clearly. As a family unit they went to church just along the road – other records provided this information.

Each night in winter Peter, Mary and Hugh gathered round the fireside to regale the rest of the family with the events of their day, and of course the village gossip. That fire was the heart of the house. It was then, and it had continued to be ever since. A later fire surround had been put in, but the shape of the nest and the chimney had been the place of heating and cooking for so many decades.

Unlike most of the inhabitants of the village, the Weirs had gone to the extravagance of paraffin to read by, once they had discovered books. Night after night, the adults supervised the small children striving with their reading homework in this room. A literate working-class household was not unusual in Scotland.

Books! Beth could not imagine life without them. For as long as she could remember she had sat by that fireside, reading everything that came her way. Stories, adventures, travels to faraway places, biographies, history – books had opened the door to the world.

She turned to the census returns further on in the century.

By 1881, Hugh and his family had moved to a larger house

along the road. Hugh had been very reluctant to leave, and for months had refused to even discuss it as a possibility. He just wanted time to stand still. In the end, and as the family expanded, he knew the move had to happen, but that didn't stop him harbouring a hope that somehow, one day, he would come back.

Alone in the house on census night, there was just one resident. A housekeeper, born, the records state, further north.

Isabella Thomson's story was that of many unmarried women of their time. The family who had built the house needed somewhere for the family matriarch in need of permanent help. It was not the role of the lady of the house to provide that; her social life would have been restricted, quite aside from the fact that looking after old people can be both demanding and dirty. And it went without saying that if the lady of the house were to undertake looking after an elderly parent herself, might that not have suggested a limited income? Housekeepers were employed to take care of elderly relatives, often not in the family home. Holiday homes were the ideal solution.

Of course, when the old lady died, the housekeeper was out of a job and a home.

On the night the census was taken, the old lady was not in the house. Isabella enjoyed having the house to herself. Private space was a rare commodity in the nineteenth century.

In the parlour, the architect had created something very beautiful. Plaster of Paris centre roses around light hangings were standard, but a centre lily of the valley, the detail of which was picked up in the cornice, was very distinctive. In the bay window sat a grand, circular table.

On this rare night of having her time entirely to herself, Isabella drew the curtains. She bent over the fire in the kitchen to make her meal, and then, borrowing clothes from her employer's wardrobe, she dressed in the elegance she saw daily, but would never have. She carried her food to the parlour and dined in fine style. She already had the parlour fire blazing, and after she had eaten, she arranged herself graciously in one of the armchairs. She lit the paraffin lamps, comfortable in the silence of her momentary imagined world. Alone, isolated, and freed from demands for one delicious night.

When the person appointed to gather the facts for the census had asked her age, she had simply said, 'Fifty.' She saw, rather than felt the pity, and she smiled. She knew she had few years ahead of her and even fewer choices, but she had pride.

Very early on, she had known she could not follow the path expected of a young woman. As her friends were courting and looking towards marriage, she knew this could not be her destiny. To have taken this path would have been a betrayal of who she knew herself to be. She could barely explain her feelings to herself, far less to anyone else, but she knew what was not for her. She knew what she wanted, and she knew she could not have it, and in privacy and silence, she had shaped her life. She had earned her living, looking after old person after old person. She was trusted by every employer she had ever worked for. She had carved out a life for herself in comfortable houses with lovely gardens. In the parlour she sat proud.

Looking up to the lily of the valley, she traced the life in its leaves and shapes. No two sections were identical. Each had been handmade separately, and in their individuality they were alive and dignified.

Shortly after this night the old lady she looked after died, and Isabella Thomson moved on to care for another elderly person. As she packed away the clothes of her former employer, she stroked the satin of the dress she had worn during her evening of grandeur.

By the time she was leaving, Hugh Weir had recently remarried, and was looking for a new home. His new wife, Sheena, could not be expected to live in the house run by his daughter. The strains were beginning to show as the weeks passed, and a suitable house had not become available. One morning, Hugh overheard that his 'home' was once again available for renting. His heart quickened as he told Sheena this wonderful piece of news, but what he saw in her eyes was uncertainty, bordering on fear. Panic gripped her at the idea of moving into the home where his first family had been born, while at the same time she knew she could not resist. Younger than him by quite a few years, she had not the confidence to voice her anxiety. He would be a good husband, and she told herself she would manage.

Hugh was not a callous man. He had seen her reaction. Suddenly he too was torn. He had dreamed of coming back since the day he had left, and could not turn away from this opportunity. At the same time he did not want Sheena to suffer, and hoped that in time when she was running their home, she too would come to love it. Hugh could not shake off the fleeting notion that the house welcomed and cherished those whom it protected.

Their first child, Jack, was born in the upstairs bedroom where Mary had come into the world some twenty years before. The little boy grew up as another brother and sister came along. Jack, like his father, loved the house. As soon as he was able to crawl, up the stairs he would go, and then yell to be brought back down again, just to repeat the game hour after hour.

One day he hid in the big cupboard under the eaves. He kept quiet and waited. The main door had been left open, and once the family realised Jack had disappeared, the search was on. He still kept quiet, and then as the silence grew, he realised he was alone in the house. Everyone had gone out and forgotten about him. It did not occur to him that they were frantically searching. Forlorn, he came out of the cupboard and made his way to the top of the stairs. How was he going to get down? He had watched how his parents went up and down stairs, but knew his legs could not reach. Nor could he stretch to the handrail to hold on. He decided to slither down backwards. Onto his tummy he rolled, and then edged himself step by step backwards. One step; success. Step two; success. The steps were wooden but had old pieces of carpet, leftovers from the grand house where Hugh Weir worked, nailed onto every second one. Gripping his way down, he slithered over the pink step, and then the blue one, and with only a few stairs to go, the ones with pictures on them, he managed to reach the bottom.

Then what? No one had come back. He had been abandoned because he had hidden. Onto the step outside the door, he toddled. Choking back tears, eyes shut, fists tight, he pleaded for them to come home to him and promised in return never to hide again.

His mother appeared first, and when she saw the bundle of misery on the doorstep, she was too relieved to be angry. She tried to prise from him where he had been, but to no avail. Only as the afternoon passed into evening, and her husband asked if she knew why the carpet pieces on the stairs had been torn loose, did they begin to fit the story together.

For many a long month, Jack kept his eye on his parents. Hiding was not such a good game after all. And no longer was the constant stair-crawling.

The garden of the house was large, and in order to eke out the family income, the ground was put to use. Grass and daffodils had no place in a kitchen garden. Part of Hugh's wages was a supply of seeds. Onions, leeks, lettuce, potatoes were raised. The whole family was engaged in the work of the garden, once the daily work was over. Mary and Peter and their growing family living just along the road spent much of their time visiting Grandad.

When Beth looked out of the window, she imagined a glimpse of the little children from another century busy in the garden, part of a family bound not only by genetics, but by the land on which they worked.

The village had grown by this time. Hugh had seen enormous change in his lifetime. When he was a child, it had been simply a few farms along the hillside, each tenant farm stretching from the top of the hill to the river. This gave every farmer sparse upland ground which was an ideal location for the sheep, and good growing ground further down. Cutting across the downward run of each farm ran a horizontal path, linking the farmhouses spaced along the hillside. Along this path, life flowed. People went to market; the village had no shops.

For centuries markets in rural communities were vital, and not only to the economy. They were places where people could go seeking a husband or a wife, to meet and exchange ideas, discuss new methods of farming, and for the enduring pleasure of gossip. Taverns were always a draw as they did not exist beyond the market towns. Market days meant a holiday, laughter, new people to talk with, meeting up with family who worked on slightly more distant farms, and the longed for thrill of romance. A ribbon previously bought and stored was woven through washed-in-the-burn hair. A shirt was brought out of hiding and aired. Shoes were brushed. Market days were dazzling, with the shimmer not in the ribbons and the new shirts, but in the excitement on the faces.

The isolated life of each farm was broken for a day.

Cattle were driven along this path to the nearest town, and because the village was on a peninsula, in the interest of speed, from time to time cattle had to be swum across the narrows. Centuries earlier, the problem of how to persuade the animals into the water had been solved by the 'swimming cow'. Owning a swimming cow was big business, its owner hiring out his cow to lead the other animals across the water. They generally followed. Reluctant ones learned the hard way.

Along the path, the village population went to church. The nearest was five miles away, and this round trip of ten miles was done twice every Sunday. The tenant farmers and their families trudged along in their heavy boots carrying their church shoes. On rainy days, the bundle they carried contained dry clothes to keep them comfortable during the two-hour service.

During Hugh's lifetime, all of this had changed. Glasgow had become a very wealthy city, and the merchants wanted holiday homes. This little community of hill farms was ideal. Close enough to the city to make it possible for the merchants to commute, here was a beauty spot of hillside and estuary widening out to the sea. The rich acquired land, and the farms shrank.

First came the architects to design grand houses along the shoreline. And then came the builders from the city. The local population did not know how to build grand mansions, but they knew how to earn a living from the workforce – after all, they had to be fed. They watched as the builders set about their task.

The carriage houses went up first, as a place to store the equipment, and also as a place for the workforce to live. Some found accommodation in the hill farms. Beth recalled finding at the ruins of one of them a wall which had been cemented. It was not in the usual intricate dry stone dyking pattern of traditional stone houses. Clearly, the builders had paid for accommodation in kind!

As the houses neared completion, the long gardens were laid out. Each had its croquet lawn. As with the building, this work could not be done by the local farmers. Gardeners, like Hugh Weir's father, having learned their craft in other parts of Scotland, had followed the work.

By the time Hugh had married for the second time, the builders and the gardeners had moved into the community as a significant workforce servicing the grand houses on the shoreline. In time, many of the tradesmen built houses of their own, smaller and on the hillside along the old path. They built two-storied houses, one storey to live in, and one to rent out as summer lets. The village was the place to be seen holidaying, and if someone wanting to be here could not afford to build, renting for a month was a pretty good substitute.

The shops had developed from basic provisioning by enterprising grocers and butchers from across the river. Shoemakers, dressmakers and even a wine merchant arrived once the wealthy had taken up residence.

A pier had been built and a regular steamer service carried provisions, people and the mail. In the morning, and when the evening steamer came in each day, carriages were driven to the pier to transport their owners.

Two churches, and then a third and a fourth, had been built, removing the long Sunday walk. In winter only two of the churches were open, but in summer they were all open. There were two ministers of different sects, while the other two seasonal churches had visiting pastors. On Sunday morning, the whole village was on the move. From the big houses came the owners in their carriages, followed by the staff walking behind.

The little community was no longer isolated. It was bustling with activity in summer, and in winter after the holiday visitors had gone home, it hibernated.

Beth wondered how the long-time residents felt about this. Of course, there were those who benefitted from the grand houses. A proportion of the staff in these houses came with the families; they were the servants in the city, and moved as the family moved. But for many, the houses provided a wage even in winter. The buildings had to be protected against the weather. They had to be repaired, and for the gardeners there was work to be done year-round.

And through the dark months, the community could lie still, and let the land sleep until the daffodils came up again.

Chapter Four

Beth finished her breakfast and went outside to sit in the spring sunshine. The old wooden bench was in need of repair, but she was loathe to do this, as her grandfather had made it decades before. She could see him still, hammering it together. He was a sheet metal worker to trade, and had forged the frame where he worked in Glasgow. He had brought it in sections to this garden in the early 1950s, just when her parents had taken over the house. Sourcing and cutting the wooden planks he had had help with, but the frame was his. How had he managed to make it resist over sixty years of rain in the west coast of Scotland, she wondered; where was the rust? She found a corner where the wood had withstood the ravages of time, and her mind wandered back to sitting there with him playing the spelling games of her childhood. If she lingered too long in the warmth of this memory, it would become, she knew from experience, tinged by the sadness that he was gone when she was just fourteen. That caught her breath for a moment; she realised that she had lost her grandfather at the age Mary Weir had lost her mother. Almost a hundred years came in between, but the pain and the loss were the same. Patterns of life cross the centuries.

She turned to look at the house. It was in three sections. Mr Leitch had built a two-storey section for himself and his family, a section below this for the servants, and a coach house with accommodation for a small coach, the horses and the coach driver. Once he had moved to the second house he built along the road, he rented out the first house to the Weirs, but only the main section. The other two parts he retained for his use when he arrived with horses, coach and servants.

It certainly was an odd shape. Firstly, it did not face the river. It sat gable end on to the water. When Mr Leitch had bought the land, a cottage stood on the adjacent piece of ground. He was not going to have his grand house, his statement of economic success, side by side with a cottage, so he built in such a way that he turned his back on it, by raising the back wall of his house as close to the cottage as possible. With this scheme in mind, he made sure that he dwarfed it. The house shut out not only its view, but much of its light.

Although the house had been built in three distinct sections, the architect had managed to make it appear as one. There was the main house where Beth lived. The door to the servants' house underneath was tucked away, almost as a secret with its own waiting-to-be-discovered charm. On the roadside was the section for the coach, the coachman and the horses.

Hugh and Sheena brought up their family in the main section of the house for almost a decade. Sheena had tried, and almost managed, to make it her own, but the ghost of Christina could not be entirely kept at bay.

One summer evening Hugh said to her, 'I have long known how hard this has been for you. I loved Christina. We were young together, with all the wild excitement of our youth. But she left me a long time ago. She has remained in the years we had together. She belongs to a time in my life which has gone.

'Since then, I have grown to love your quiet strength. I see it every day you live in this house. I have been thinking for a while, and now I am ready. I would not hurt you by speaking of this until I was sure. But now I think you and I should grow old, together, somewhere else. Would you like to do that?'

Sheena had no words. She knew what it meant to him to leave this house, and he was willing to do this for her. She took his toughened hands in hers, and with the tiniest of movements nodded her head. Then she looked at this man she had cared for, and who had cared for her, until they had grown into an adult love, and she smiled.

Days rolled on, and still she could not speak about it. He took the lead, telling her he had found a house for rent only a mile away. He would miss his garden, but, well, he would just create another.

Jack was furious. He raged and he ranted. He argued with the decision. It had no logic. His parents could not explain it to him. They knew he was too young to understand, and even if he had not been, they would have been reluctant to tell him something so private. He found comfort in determining that one day he would return. As he was leaving, carrying a tattered piece of old stair carpet, he announced to the old house, 'I will come back.' A faint rustling in the outside eaves sounded as if the old house had replied. 'Please do, for I shall miss you.'

Word spread through the village, and another family of gardeners moved into the main part of the house; Robertsons from across the river. They worked in the gardens of the big houses, and like Hugh Weir and his family, they tended their own plots also. The house welcomed them in.

Sarah Robertson had grown up on a remote island, and had not learned English until she was fifteen. She thought in Gaelic, she dreamed in Gaelic, and spoke to the animals and the birds in Gaelic. In the tiny home she had known as a child, the family shared the space with cattle, sheep and the family pig. In the severity of the Scottish winter, on the wind-tossed islands bordering the Atlantic, why would you be so cruel as to put these creatures outside?

Although she moved to the mainland, learned English and got married, the sense of being just one part of the natural world never left her. No pigs, cattle and sheep; but hedgehogs, squirrels and rabbits found their way to her door. And now here she was in a house surrounded by trees providing homes to numerous birds, many of them new to her. She loved to listen to them call to each other. Every spring she was excited to hear the first sound of the cuckoo.

When her children were small, they simply shared the space with the animal kingdom. Children more or less the same size as dogs and cats have to learn to accommodate their four-legged companions on the communal space of the floor. Territorial battles are fought out, with unspoken truces as to who belongs where.

'When you are tiny, you are the same size as the animals, and so you learn to respect their space. It is only us big ones who think we have a right to dominate,' was her view.

One day her eight-year-old, Douglas, came home with a tiny crow, only semi-conscious. One wing was broken.

'I had to bring it in,' he explained, 'or a cat would have got it.'

A box was found, an old blanket was torn into strips, and some leaves to provide a smell that would be familiar, made a safe haven for the injured bird. Douglas' little fingers gently opened the bird's mouth, and into it Sarah dripped a tiny amount of milk. The bird rallied. Within days, it managed some oats soaked in milk. Then some mashed meat.

Each day it was carefully lifted onto the table, so that its box was cleaned. By this time it had a name; 'Feudail,' Gaelic for 'found'.

Once it was clear the bird was going to survive, Sarah's husband Neil made a tiny splint to attach to the broken wing. He had been unwilling to undertake this delicate operation when the bird was so weak; the shock of the pain might have killed it, but now it was on the mend, a splint had to be fixed to help the wing heal. In the garden where he worked, Neil had spent days catching crows to feel the shape of their skeletons. He was sure he knew how to set the wing, and so the operation began.

Feudail was very loud in its reaction; it was in pain. But it was not strong enough to move, and of course, it could not fly with one wing. Neil had heard that in the medicine cabinet in the house of the garden where he worked, there was something people took to reduce pain. He asked one of the house servants about it, and she had brought him two drops on a tiny plate. He carried it home. If it killed the bird, at least he had done his best. They all had.

That bird screeched as its wing was set. Time for a little milk laced with the stuff from the big house. The bird was suddenly silent, but it was breathing. Next day, Feudail was much calmer. Slowly it had strength to stand, and then was lifted onto the table to take staggering steps.

Weeks passed, and Feudail was strutting its way round surfaces at table level. It began to flex its wings, and the family decided this was the moment to take off the splint. Would the wing just collapse? It did not. It was an odd shape, but it could move as a wing.

The bird was transferred to an outhouse where it could safely re-learn to fly. Eventually one morning when Douglas opened the door to see the invalid, out it flew. Off Feudail went. Douglas watched, his joy tinged with sadness.

Now and again, for a long time thereafter, a crow full grown with a twisted wing would come and sit on the windowsill.

Feudail knew where home was.

To Beth by far the most interesting people living in the house around that time were two old ladies, Margaret and Ruth Cook. They were one year apart in age, born about ten miles away in a remote farmhouse. All their lives they had lived in this sheltered part of the world. Of all the older people who lived in the house, they were the only ones who had been born into the community.

Their years spanned almost exactly those of Queen Victoria.

They had been born to Alexander Cook and his wife, Helen, in January and December 1820. Alexander was a dairyman working on one of the local farms. These little girls and their brother James grew up in a tiny cottage. Beth and her mother had visited the ruins of the little cottage once, carefully climbing the hill where the family had been so surefooted.

The footprint of the house was quite clear. Two rooms, each with a window, and then the byre. As farmhands went, Alexander Cook was doing well. Two rooms and two windows was more than most people had. Like all farm cottages, the kitchen contained the recess bed for the parents, as well as the fire where all the cooking was done, and the table around which the family gathered. The adjoining room had multiple uses: the parlour for visitors, for even in so remote a place people did visit one another; the schoolroom when there was time for lessons once all the work on the land had been completed; and a bedroom with truckle beds pulled through from underneath the parents' bed.

Inside was a tight fit, but outside there were fields and hills and a long shoreline, all places of excitement and discovery. To little children the horizon was miles away, and the sky even further. The rich strong colours of spring gave way to the blues of early summer, and then came the pink flowers of high summer, and in the autumn the russets. The building they lived in stood solid as the world changed around them. How rich they were compared with people in overcrowded city tenements!

Their lives were dependent on the weather. All agricultural workers lived one bad summer from starvation. If the crops failed, they starved. If the crops failed, and the landowners displayed none of the Christian compassion they professed, the workers were evicted. Alexander Cook was a dairyman, a job which was more secure than that of most agricultural workers. Animals had to be tended, and were not as susceptible to the weather as were the crops. Nothing, however, was secure. Adults lived with this constant fear, and in time the innocence of the children became steadily tainted by their growing awareness. The fields, the hills and the shoreline became places to be watched over. Understanding and forecasting the weather became a vital skill. Acting on it to protect the animals and the land was essential to survival.

To generations of Scots, security came from education. If a man could read and write, he could work where he was not weather dependent. The cost was high, and so only boys had this opportunity. It made economic sense. Boys would grow to be men, who worked in offices. Girls became women who learned their household roles from their mothers. What would be the point of educating girls? It would not provide them with work. Their work was to run the home. But for boys, education was a lifeline, and many struggling families paid for a tutor rather than put meat on the table.

The Cook family was one of them. So in this small household, James learned to read, while Margaret and Ruth trained to become wives and mothers. They learned milking from a very early age, when they were still small enough to get under the cow. They learned how to make butter and cheese. They learned how to read a stream (a 'burn' in Scots) to find the deepest, coldest part in which to store food. There was a trick to this, as not only had the corner pool of water to be deep and cold, it also had to be protected from sudden surges which would sweep the stores away. They learned to sew and mend. They learned to spin and knit. They learned which plants were medicinal, and which were dangerous. They learned how to use the natural plants for food. They learned to cultivate kitchen gardens. Their lives were in preparation in this land that was theirs. Who owned it? The owner whose name was on the document, or those who lived its rhythms?

In time, James went to the city and became a clerk in the office of a merchant. He was clever and rose quickly. He became the family safety net; this he knew was his duty. He had no more choice than did his sisters. To begin with he enjoyed city life as it was so different. The anonymity was strange to him, but not unpleasant. As time went on, he found himself drawn more to the sons, like himself, who had been educated to go to the city. Arriving in the city from different parts of Scotland, they found they had a collective understanding of childhood. As they came to know one another better, they could together find expression of what they had separately and silently become aware of, but which they had individually crushed down. Their economic security came at a bitter price – isolation from their homes, and who they knew themselves to be.

Alexander and Helen moved to a larger farm by the time the girls were twenty. News took a long time to reach the village, but in time it did arrive. Margaret and Ruth were fascinated by the young queen. She was their age, and so to them they were on parallel paths. They heard of the coronation and the wedding of Queen Victoria to Prince Albert. Rather shocked they were that she proposed to him rather than what they expected would happen for them, but perhaps that was just London ways. They never did understand the correct explanation, that as a queen she was higher up the scale than he, and so he could not propose to her.

Time rolled on, and the Queen produced children one after another, nine in total. Then Prince Albert died young, and Victoria retreated into a forty-year grief. She isolated herself at her two retreats, one in the Highlands and one on the Isle of Wight. As queen and empress, she commanded the world to come to her. She was bitterly lonely in her grief. In time stories spread that she had developed a friendship, firstly with one of her Scottish tenants, and then with an Indian servant. The Misses Cook were scandalised.

'How could the Queen do such a thing?' they declared. 'We do not believe this.' But as the decades rolled on, and no one had proposed to Margaret and Ruth, might they deep down have wished for a John Brown or an Abdul Karim?

The Misses Cook were by no means alone in their community. They had their parents, and after they died, they had each other as constant companions. Their brother came home when it was possible. Everyone knew them, so neither were they were isolated.

They were, however, isolated from the norms of their world. The Queen had set the pattern. Wife and mother was how it should be. They were neither, so were outside society's expectations.

For Beth, living all the changes in the second half of the twentieth century, she only had a tenuous memory of what that must have meant. As a little girl in the fifties, she knew what was expected for her. It was in all the fairy tales she read. Only her grandfather had spoken of an alternative possible way. By the time she was old enough to want to choose a path, there was a choice. She knew she was the lucky generation. But imagine if she had not had that choice, and the life she had been prepared for had never come. Beth shuddered at the loneliness and disorientation of such a loss. For how long did the Misses Cook go on hoping? Did they speak of it to each other? Or did they bear the disappointment of failed expectation in silence?

Beth had often wondered why they had not married. Careful analysis of the records for their early years indicated there were few young men to marry, and fewer still who could provide them with any form of economic security. The building boom which brought many young men to the area did not begin until they were well into their thirties, by which time they were regarded as too old. They were the unlucky generation.

They were, however, the contemporaries of widowers. Hugh Weir was their age, but when he remarried, he married someone of childbearing years. No matter how you looked at it, time had cheated them.

Add to that they were inseparable, so whoever married one, married two. Beth smiled, thinking the answer would have been two brothers, but in no amount of searching the censuses could such a solution be found. The Misses Cook were dependent, first on their father, and then on their brother.

By the 1850s, as the building boom began, their parents were dead, and supported by their brother, they rented a small house in the heart of the village. They watched the shops being built. They saw the daily activities at the pier. They eked out their small income from their brother by using the skills their mother had taught them. They baked for the builders, and they sewed for the new occupants of the big houses.

As the boom rolled on, Margaret and Ruth took regular strolls to watch progress. No two houses looked the same, and it was fascinating to watch as each took on its own shape.

They came to know Mrs Morrison, the fish woman. She caught the fish and trundled it round the village in a barrow, passing the Misses Cook as she did so. The Misses Cook always made sure that they were accidentally at their window, or in their garden, when it was time for Mrs Morrison to pass. That way they could hear all the gossip.

The village had always been law-abiding and quiet, and the downside of the building was that 'less reputable' people began to arrive looking for work. Indeed one day, when one of the residents hit his wife with a poker because she did not have his breakfast ready, Mrs Morrison could not get the story out fast enough.

'You should have seen the blood! That Robina ran for help to Mrs Reid, you know the baker's wife you work for.' Ruth and Margaret bristled at that comment, but they were not annoyed enough to turn away.

Mrs Morrison went on, 'They were both drunk. Eight o'clock in the morning and they were both drunk. What has the world come to? The polis had to come. That Mr Turner told her to take tobacco leaf to stop the bleeding. Never miss a trick to sell his goods. I hear the wound is two inches long and half an inch round. The neighbours say this happens all the time.'

Margaret Cook asked tentatively, 'Who did this?'

The answer made her shrink into silence. She had seen John Henderson when she was out looking at the new houses going up. He had smiled at her. Her heart had fluttered. He was her age she gauged, but she knew nothing of him. Who was this Robina?

'That is his good-for-nothing wife,' was the answer. Margaret shrunk back further. In the world she had grown up in, she knew everyone. Her community was changing, and she clung to the solidity of her past. In her daily life she tried to adapt to this new world, but inside her, uncertainty grew and hope faded.

During the 1860s, Ruth and Margaret had moved around a number of houses in the village. As the merchants built ever larger houses, smaller houses were harder to come by. Their brother built a grand house, and they lived for a while in a section of it. Behind it there was a cave in the cliff face which rose sharply from ground level.

In this cave lived an old man. He was older than the Misses Cook, but they had known him all their lives. He had been a shepherd when their father was a dairyman. When he had grown too old to work, he lost his home on the farm, and the only place he could find to live was the cave. By the time James Cook was building, Andrew Williamson was well set up in his primitive home. The sisters resisted all attempts by their brother to remove him. He too had known old Andrew, but his years of working in the city had wrought changes in him. His sisters had to remind him, gently and then forcefully, of where his duty to the old man lay. And thus it was; he had not yet grown too far from his early values. A grand house was built. Two sisters lived in it dependent on their brother, and behind the house an old man dependent on the two sisters. James Cook did not choose to tell his visitors of this arrangement. To the sisters there was nothing unusual about it. It is what you did, woven together in a small community. People were not alone and isolated. They were part of an integrated whole.

In time, Ruth and Margaret found this no longer to be what their brother believed. He sold the house and gave them a small annuity to live on, but he no more provided, or indeed arranged, accommodation for them. Nor did he visit them.

Margaret and Ruth became nomads. This was a very lonely time. They were not alone. They had each other. They were not isolated. The village was becoming very busy. But they were dislocated from the world in which they lived. Their world no longer made sense, and in that they felt themselves to share the loneliness of the Queen.

~

In the village, the 1870s were exciting years. A school was being built. Ruth and Margaret regularly walked past to see it grow. One day, they noticed Mary Weir standing looking at it.

'Hussy!' Ruth said. 'She is setting her eye at any one of the builders.'

'No,' replied Margaret. 'That is Hugh Weir's daughter. She is no hussy.'

And then they heard.

'What are you thinking about?'

'I want to learn to read. I hope my little brother will be able to teach me.'

'I can teach you if you wish.'

'Can you read? How did you learn?'

'The minister, where I lived before I came here, taught me. I am learning my trade as a joiner, but I also wanted to read. I want to understand ideas. Robert Burns was a gardener's son, and his father insisted he learned to read. I am a gardener's son, and my father wanted this for me too. I think reading should also be for girls. Would you like me to teach you?'

'Yes, very much, but I must ask my father.'

'Peter, will you get back here and get on with the job?'

'Let me know what your father says.'

As Mary walked away, she was smiling. 'Good morning Miss Cook, Miss Cook,' speaking to each of them in turn.

'Good morning, Mary.'

As they walked on – swallowing the disappointment, always just beneath the surface, that they would never experience what they had just seen – the sisters wondered if Mary Weir and Peter McIntosh had even noticed them watching.

They watched the love of the young couple grow, and they stood outside the church when the time came. A wedding is an event in a village. It may not be grand. But it is fun. The bride in her homemade dress, and her handsome groom stood on the steps of the church. They glowed. No one seeing this could wish them ill. The whole community made their way to Hugh Weir's house to toast the young couple. Children ran in the garden. All the adults contributed to the feast. Someone produced a set of bagpipes, and the dancing began.

Ruth and Margaret tapped their feet, and decided they were not too old to dance, although they knew next day their bones would think otherwise. Singing began. Most of the singing was in English, but there were a few like old Andrew who could sing in the Gaelic, spoken by the community in the early part of the nineteenth century.

At one point having been whirled off her feet, recovering on the grass, Margaret thought to herself, 'This is a lovely house. One day I will live here.' Startled, she realised the words unbidden had been 'will,' not, 'would like to'. Certainly she would like to, but it was more than that. She had a certainty that one day she would live here. 'Not yet,' she thought, 'but one day the time will be right.' Her transient life from cottage to cottage in the village would be over. This place would be her home. Here she could not be lonely. This house had drawn her in.

After that when she and Ruth walked to the home they had lived in as children, she suggested walking the route in a different way. They went to where they had begun life, and then walked to where they had lived in their twenties, and finally in their sixties past the house where one day Margaret knew she would live. It was a walk that marked stages in their lives. One day they stopped, and looked over the wall. As they watched a family at play Ruth said, 'You know, Margaret, one day I would like to live in that house.'

And so it was decided. They would watch and wait.

When the school was completed, they liked to walk past there also. How they would have loved to go to school. Laughter, friends. And how they longed to have been able to read.

The first 'maister' was an Irishman, John Robertson, and he was in charge of the school for nearly thirty years. His wife taught sewing in the school, and the sisters, being very good seamstresses, helped out also. Their payment was learning to read. What joy that brought them! When they had offered to help with the very elegant stitching, which would give the girls employment in the big houses, they had no thought of payment. They had knowledge which would be useful. They had no daughters to pass the knowledge on to, so why not the girls of the village? Mrs Robertson was very keen to take their help, but was embarrassed that payment was not possible.

'Oh no,' said Margaret, 'we do not want money.'

'But we do want to read,' whispered Ruth, amazed at her own audacity.

John Robertson smiled. He was delighted to take on two pupils who would give him no trouble. And so the lessons began after the children had gone home.

In these years, Miss Margaret and Miss Ruth found themselves at the heart of the community. All the children knew them, and so when they walked along the road, they were not just the two old sisters. They told the children stories of when they were young. They taught the children what they had learned of the land. They borrowed books, and they read to each other, and then to other old people in the village.

When it became too dark to read, the old people told stories of their childhood.

'You should write this down,' said old Andrew. 'Now you can read, does that not mean you can write? That way people in the future will know what it was like here in the past.'

Ruth and Margaret were astonished. How could they possibly do that? And then the idea took hold and, 'How could they possibly do that?' became, 'Why not?'

Once the idea had taken hold, they explained their idea to the headmaster and asked if they could buy paper. Next time they arrived to teach the girls sewing, he had two brown exercise books and two pencils each.

Home they went with this new adventure, and on the long summer evenings they sat outside to write their stories, working at an old wooden table which had just appeared one morning, but which they were sure they had seen in the school.

At the back of the book they added their medicinal recipes; the uses of garlic, fennel and assorted roots. 'We should leave this knowledge also,' Margaret had suggested.

'And we'll write our cake recipes too,' added Ruth, 'just for fun.'

Then a new minister came to the village. He had come as a holidaymaker when he was young, and this was where he wished to preach. When he arrived in the village there was no manse, but over time, the community decided there had to be a manse. The cost amounted to £3,000. Much of this was donations by the summer visitors, but a significant amount was raised by the community in a three-day bazaar. The sisters were in great demand. Their sewing was exquisite. Their baking a favourite.

Occasionally their thoughts wandered to the Queen, alone and isolated in her castles. How lonely a life she had compared with theirs. She did not have village children running up to her for a cake or a story. She did not have ladies alighting from their carriages at her door asking for a sleeve to be repaired, or a piece of delicate detail to be added to a hat. Slowly the sisters came to know that while they had not followed the expected path, they had found their place.

The minister published his sermons. His fame grew, and people came to the village, just to hear him preach. In the winter the population was about four hundred; in summer it could be two thousand. One day the Queen wrote to him, commanding him to come and preach to her. Margaret and Ruth Cook were most annoyed. 'If she wants to hear our minister, let her come here,' they said.

What a day that would have been if Queen Victoria had come. Ruth and Margaret imagined her coming into the pier on one of the steamers. They had even picked out where they would stand to see her. But no, she did not come. The minister had to go to her. To their amazement, they were not as disappointed as they would have expected to be.

'Do you think we have become sorry for her? Stuck away with no friends,' Ruth ventured. Was it treason to say this? How could they feel sorry for her? She was a queen, an empress, a wife (and now a widow, like many women they knew, but who were not hiding away), and a mother. They were two old ladies whom no one had wanted to marry. They had no children. But they had found a peace with their lives now. They had passed through a time of feeling abandoned by the world, and had now made a place for themselves in the world around them.

Beth knew the nature of that pain. The passing of the years had lessened, but not deadened it. Caught unawares, it could still scald. She too had felt as the sisters had done. She had married, but that had ended in pain. She had no children. She lived at a time when it was easier to carve out a life, but that had not lessened her sense of being out of step with society. Her friends had children, and often she had found herself out of the conversation. She had nothing to contribute. These had been hard years, and yet she had found a way, through her work, and in the life she had outside her work. It was strange to her to think that she had the shared experience of two old ladies who had eventually come to live in this house. Her life and theirs had been so different. Yet that absence from their lives bound them into the same sense of having missed out, of having failed somehow. She wished she had known about the two sisters when she was going through her own loneliness of loss. All three women had in time found a way; women who shaped their worlds to find their peace.

On top of a kitchen unit sat an ancient jug. It had belonged to Beth's grandmother, and over the years had served in the collecting of brambles from the hedgerows, and occasionally as a vase. Beth recalled her grandmother telling her that it had once been used to convey ice cream from the village shop, when there was spare money for a treat.

On the jug, marking her sixtieth year on the throne, was a portrait of Queen Victoria. A husband and nine children and yet she looked thoroughly miserable! There she sat, eyes downcast, side on to the artist as if barely tolerating his presence, a picture of loneliness.

On a whim, Beth went outside to cut green shoots from the early spring branches. She filled the jug with water, and put the early shoots into it. Sunlight filtered through the window, picking up the shades of green, and, as the sun moved into the room, the shoots glistened.

The old queen had chosen to be portrayed as lonely and unhappy. From her reading, Beth knew this was how she had shaped her widowhood, either by choice, or at least partially as a consequence of the insular nature of her position.

Despite all their disadvantages, the Misses Cook had found a way through the disappointments in their lives.

And of herself? Beth knew she was a work in progress.

Chapter Five

The eighties had slid into the nineties, and, as they did so, Ruth and Margaret seemed no nearer to living in the house they had chosen to be their last home. As each year passed the amount of time left to them diminished, it seemed, at an ever greater rate.

One spring day, as they were out for their walk, they saw an old man shuffling towards them. Their eyesight for the close work of sewing was good, but seeing into the distance was long gone. Hugh Weir stopped beside them.

'Good morning, Hugh. How are you? And how is Sheena now?'

'She's not so good since her fall. But Mary is only four hooses away, and keeps her eye on us at least three times a day. Actually, I am on my way to see you two.'

Up on the hill these three old people caught the attention of a young shepherd. What do they have to say to each other? 'The good old days,' no doubt. How old are their days, he wondered. The Battle of Waterloo? Thinking back on his schooldays, he remembered the date of that momentous event. That would make the group on the road about eighty. A bit before their time perhaps, so he thought maybe they were talking about the glorious Charge of the Light Brigade in the place with the funny name. Crimea, was it? Or maybe they were just moaning about the young people who had come to the village and changed their world. Maybe it was their aches and pains. He was always fascinated by how old people talked about their ailments. He supposed once they had exhausted talking about the past, they had nothing else to talk about. How awful to be that old! He shuddered and strode on to attend to the sheep. Into the spring cold sunshine, the lambs would come. New year. New life.

Of course he knew who the three on the road were, and he was always respectful of them when he met them. But what did he know of who they really were? Can such knowledge ever cross decades, or is living a very long life itself an act of isolation?

Hugh continued, 'Peter tells me that the downstairs hoose is going to be let. Now is your chance. A bit of excitement in our old age can set us all sprightly again. It's never too late.'

Margaret and Ruth stood dumbfounded. Was the house about to have a space for them? Could this really be true?

'Are you sure, Hughie?'

'Aye I'm sure. I was on my way to tell you. Since the day my daughter got wed you have aye been telling me you want that hoose, so I wanted you to know before someone else gets it. Right glad I am that I met you. I don't know if I would have made it to where you are living at the moment. I might have had to go home and send one of the bairns to tell you. So Margaret, Ruth, go and tell that wife of old man Leitch you want the hoose.'

Just in time remembering to say thanks to this man they had known almost all their lives, Margaret and Ruth turned and raced off back the way they had come. The unseen watcher on the hill thought, 'Now that is odd.' What on earth had he said that sent these sisters moving at a speed the young shepherd did not think them capable of? He watched Hugh Weir watch them go, but he was not close enough to see the look of delight on the old man's face. 'Hughie,' she had called him. No one had called him that in many, many years. They had beamed at him, their wrinkled faces transformed at the news he had given them. He just hoped that old besom would not turn them away.

No dignity spared, they hurtled along the road, hanging on to their hats, holding up their skirts to keep the hems out of the mud.

'No time to stop and talk,' they called out to everyone they met as they hurried on. By evening the whole village knew the Misses Cook had been in a very great hurry today. Speculation as to the reason was the gossip of the day. Most likely bowel problems was the judgement; no one got close to the truth.

They reached the house of the old besom herself. Latch up, down the path, deep breath. They rang the bell and waited. They heard movement inside, and then the door opened. There was old Mrs Leitch.

Without polite preamble Ruth blurted out, 'Can we have the downstairs house please?'

Now, Mrs Leitch could be mean when it suited her. She looked at these two people she normally viewed from a distance. After their brother had removed their respectability by selling his house, they were no longer in Mrs Leitch's circle of acknowledgement. But something stopped her from saying what came first to mind. She saw in them the poverty she would have known, had her life gone differently, and she also saw in them an excitement she had not known for years.

'We've wanted to live there near on twenty years,' Margaret said. 'Your husband made such a beautiful house. Hugh Weir says it will soon be available for renting. Can we please have it?'

Mrs Leitch looked them up and down. She saw the mended dresses, the threadbare hats, and the look in their eyes. Against her will, but from a habit of years of overseeing accounts, she heard herself say, 'Can you afford it?'

They stood stock still. The bluntness of the transaction had not featured in their dreams.

'I don't know,' came a very small voice from one of them. Mrs Leitch never did find out which one. Perhaps they themselves barely knew. Their excitement was eclipsed. They were two old ladies, whose dreams had been dashed again.

'What are you paying where you are at the moment?' Mrs Leitch heard herself say. She had a reputation for being, as she would say, very prudent. The shopkeepers would call her just plain mean.

The Misses Cook answered as one.

'Heavens, how can people be so poor? How do they live?' Mrs Leitch thought.

She looked at them, and said gently and with no hint of pity, 'So much? The rent for my house is less than that.' She told them the figure and followed it with, 'It's yours if you want it. But don't be telling anyone what I am charging you, or I will put it up, or you out.'

The Misses Cook stood dumbfounded for the second time in an hour.

'Are you sure?' said Ruth.

'Yes,' said Janet Leitch. 'I am sure. I lived in that house once myself, you know. I didn't only live in the main part of the house. I lived in the downstairs part too, for a short time, many years ago. When you are settled in, and it has the feel of a home, I would like to sit by its fireside again. We might take tea. Just make sure you love that house as I once did.'

Off they went up the path and through the gate. They both had to lean against the wall, so weak they were with all that had happened. In the space of a morning they had got the word from Hughie, almost burst into a run, thought their hope would not come to pass, and were offered the house for a rent they could manage, even when the time came when they could no longer sew.

Eventually they set off, and as they passed the house they looked over the wall. This would be theirs soon. They could see themselves in the years ahead in the garden. Just before they got home, they met the son of one of their neighbours.

'Do you know Mr Hugh Weir?' Margaret asked the little boy.

'The old man along past the school?'

'Yes,' Ruth continued. 'Will you run and tell him that the Misses Cook have been successful? We have had a wonderful day and would like to give you this to share our happiness.' She produced a sixpence. The little boy stared in amazement. He had never seen such a fortune. 'Now go and bring back his message, and the sixpence will be yours.'

Off he sped. The Misses Cook went inside.

'Do you think we should celebrate, Margaret? We have that bottle of Madeira James left behind.'

Like children embarking on a forbidden jaunt they opened the wine, poured a glass each and sat, each in her own thoughts of the adventure ahead.

In no time at all, the little runner was back.

'Mr Weir said he wants to be invited to have a cup of tea with you once you are settled.' The child had said it over and over again, as he ran along the road, just in case he forgot the exact words.

'Thank you,' Ruth said and gave him the sixpence with the instruction to spend every bit of it on whatever he pleased.

The world went to sleep smiling that night.

Chapter Six

Time crawled to the date they would move in. With every dawn they feared something unforeseen would occur, that would mean they would never reach their new home. With every drawing of the curtains they were one day closer.

At last the time came, and three young men of the village came to help them move. When they reached their new door they were almost afraid to open it, lest at this final hurdle their dream would shatter. But no. The little downstairs house was just as they remembered it from when they had 'accidentally' trespassed in to see it on the day of Mary's wedding. Servants' housing was seldom locked, even when not in use.

The coal cellar was on the left as they went in the door, and round a corner was the kitchen. The old sink was underneath the one in the house above, where Beth now lived; both sinks fed into the same original drain. Opposite it, and immediately underneath the one above, was the fire where the cooking took place. The recess was also a vertical mirror image of its upstairs neighbour. The only difference with the upstairs house was in the little cupboard under the stairs. In the downstairs house the cupboard was not under a staircase, so it was full height, and, as if just waiting for them, it was lined with shelves ideal for storing their preserves.

Next came the sitting room. Not as grand as the one above, it did not have a bay window, but was still a goodly sized room. There was space in this house; each room was the size of the room above it, and as Mr Leitch had wanted a grand house, so the servants' quarters underneath had acquired generous rooms. The supporting walls, rather than philanthropic ideals, created space. Beside the fire was a deeply shelved cupboard ideal for the sewing materials. They would be kept warm by the fire; the constant battle against the impact of dampness on the Misses Cooks' thread, needles and cloth was over.

Above the mantelpiece they planned to hang a portrait of Queen Victoria. Painted in the early years of her reign, she was smiling.

Lastly the bedroom with its lovely sea view.

'Where do you want the beds put?' came a voice from the doorway.

'Over here,' said Margaret.

'No, here,' said Ruth. The bickering of childhood. They were both determined to have the view.

'Make up your mind as we bring the rest in.'

For an hour or more their helpers configured and reconfigured the room till eventually one of them said, 'Try it out, and we will come back when you have made up your mind.'

And try it out they did. From only one bed was the view possible. The sisters solved this by changing the occupant of the bed every Monday. When the sheets were changed on washday, so the sisters swapped beds. It was a good arrangement, and one Mrs Morrison relished relaying to the whole village as she went around with her barrow and her fish.

'Who's got the view this week?' they would be asked. They laughed heartily when they first heard this kindly question, not in the least abashed by their sleeping arrangements being the talk of the village. Such a question would not be asked of a stranger.

The garden leading down to the river was the view from the bed. Oh how they loved that view and that garden! It was a very big garden, much of it under food cultivation. The little downstairs house had a section of its own.

Within the week, Hugh Weir was making his slow way down the path to their door.

'I've come to take tea,' he declared. It was clear this was not his sole motive to visit. He was itching to feel again the richness of the soil in this garden. Without waiting to be asked, he advised – or did he tell? – them what to plant.

'No time to waste. We're already in March.' His grandsons were dispatched to dig. He supervised. And always the kettle was boiling, and the cakes were ready.

Margaret and Ruth loved the wild flowers they had known as children. They debated how they would approach Hughie with this. They could remember the time when they would not have dared speak up, but not now.

They broached the subject over a piece of gingerbread.

'We wonder if we can have some flowers also, over here against the wall. Is that possible do you think?' Ruth felt very brave in daring to even ask such a question.

Pause.

'Aye, I suppose so.'

A second pause.

'Where would we get them?' continued Margaret.

'Leave that tae me. I don't hold wi' flowers myself, but if you want to waste good growing ground on them, I suppose at oor age you can. Naething like a tattie and an onion coming up. No' bonny, I grant you that, but you canna eat flowers.'

'Oh yes you can,' came the reply, 'if you know the remedies and recipes from our grandparents' time. That was long before you became a gardener,' Ruth hastily added, to avoid ruffling of feathers.

'I was a vegetable gardener, and aye I did the fancy stuff too, but that was not for eating. Do you no' remember that before I came here my faither was a gardener at thon castle? They had no need to grow anything to eat, nae tatties, nae onions, and certainly nae old flowers and plants. But yes my granny did talk about what was safe to eat from the hedgerows. Och I was a wee boy mind, and I didnae listen any more than did your brother.'

And so another thread was woven into the lives of the three of them. He taught them how to grow vegetables and the 'fancy stuff', and they taught him of the plants eaten by the poor from mediaeval times.

A rosebush was planted against a wall. They never asked him where he got it, but its blooms did look remarkably like the ones growing at the new manse. Primroses, bluebells, primula arrived next. One morning Ruth looked out of the window (it was her turn) and there they were. Two Weirs planting a bush just about to burst into bloom. To the surprise of everyone, possibly including the old gardening expert, the hydrangea survived its sudden relocation. Ruth and Margaret watched in delight as the pink and blue heads reached to the sun. The potatoes and onions were lifted in September, and by late autumn, the daffodil bulbs were finding their way in to snuggle down for the winter.

No matter the weather, the constant change outside the window was a source of fascination. On windy days the sisters watched the white-capped waves, on wet days they watched the pattern of the clouds, and as the nights shortened, they watched the stars. They lived their childhood once more.

One day Janet Leitch came to see them. When they saw her on their doorstep, their world froze. What Janet Leitch saw was not a welcoming smile, but raw fear. Had she come to evict them?

'Is it not time for me to have that cup of tea?' she said. Smiling.

'Yes, yes come in, Mrs Leitch. We have a cake almost ready.' Terror clawed at Margaret's voice.

'Can I just look round first? I have memories here.'

Off she went into her own world. Margaret and Ruth made the tea and waited for the cake. Twenty minutes went by. The cake was ready. But Mrs Leitch sat on in a still silence. The sisters went into the garden, each in lonely silence waiting. Eventually they heard a voice.

'Thank you. Please come in out of that wind, and let me try your cake.'

Back into the house they went, watching every gesture of their visitor in whose gift their tenancy lay. The tension fractured.

'Are you here to put us out?' Ruth's voice was barely a whisper.

Mrs Leitch was as shocked at this panic-stricken question, as they had been at her appearing on the doorstep.

'No. No. No. No. Why would you think that?'

They had no answer beyond a lifetime of disappointments. Mrs Leitch was no fool. She saw what they could not say. And so the afternoon passed in conversation and silence and tea and cake, until the shadows began to lengthen. The room was becoming cold.

'Can I put the fire on?' their guest asked.

'Oh no, that is for us to do,' said Ruth, leaping up.

'Please,' said Mrs Leitch. 'I want to remember that too.'

And so the Misses Cook sat and watched their landlady and visitor build a fire. To their surprise, she was good at it. She must have learned a long time ago, before she had property and servants. They watched her curl the paper and count the sticks, laying them crisscross as a bed for the logs, which had been toasted at the side of the fire the night before. Once the match was struck, and the fire had caught, on went the little pieces of coal tucked into corners to keep the blaze going.

As the fire caught, the room darkened and the paraffin lamps were lit. And still the three of them sat on, listening to the sounds of the flames, watching the colours as they danced through orange and red and blue and green.

At last Mrs Leitch got up to go. She was going back to a large house, in which a servant had lit the fire and turned down her bed. But since the death of her husband, and her son in the city running the hatters' business, she was now alone. The sisters had never envied her. They feared her, and the power she had over them. But tonight they felt sympathy for her. She was alone, and she was lonely.

'We shall see you home,' Margaret said. The three of them donned their coats, and up the path they went. Soon they were at her door.

'Thank you,' she said. The Misses Cook smiled as Ruth handed her a little parcel of cake.

Chapter Seven

In the late 1890s, the village was agog at the prospect of a new enterprise. There was only one hall big enough for community events. It belonged to one of the churches, the minister of which was opposed to it being used for anything except what he agreed with. Within the village were the young men who had come to build in the 1860s and 70s, now with their own businesses and houses. They would build a hall.

Their first meeting took place in the recently built very grand hotel. A plan was drawn up. They had the skills between them to build, but they did not have the finance. Some of the owners of the big houses gave donations. Not all. Many of the owners of the big houses simply came on holiday, and saw no reason to contribute to the wellbeing of the village in the winter when they were not there.

Undeterred, the year-round residents decided on another three-day bazaar. They had months to prepare what they would sell. The community certainly had its share of entrepreneurs who came up with some very unusual money-making activities. A nail-driving competition was open to all except those who drove nails into wood for a living. The nails had to be driven in straight and hold fast. It was won by Miss Coats, heiress to the biggest thread-making company in the world. The Misses Cook were the judges of a second competition, hat trimming – to be done by men. That caused a great deal of laughter. After they had awarded the prize to the winner, the Misses Cook offered to take all the hats home, make them wearable, and return them to their owners. For this they enlisted the help of Janet Leitch – after all, she was the widow of a hatter and had an eye for a good design. For months afterwards, the three of them saw the hats they had resuscitated on the heads of both the wealthy ladies, and their servants.

A third event at the bazaar was a washing competition for men. Zinc baths and wooden tubs were carried to the field where the bazaar was taking place. Numerous hot water vessels were brought. A little piece of soap each, a scrubbing board. The washing saved up for days, dirty from the mud of the fields, was allocated, two items per tub. The women stood back and watched. The result – a great deal of money raised, and a great deal of very wet, still dirty clothes, which, rather than carry home and start again, the women washed, while the men stood and watched just how it should be done.

The land on which the hall would stand was negotiated with the owner. A constitution was written establishing that the hall belonged to the people of the village. The building began. By 1902, the hall was up and ready for use. The day of its official opening was marked by events both inside and outside it. It was a hall for the future, and so many of the events centred on the children; races, tug o' war, boxing. A poem was even written about this community venture. The village people were very proud of what was indeed their hall.

It quickly became the focal point of the village. Dances took place despite the wrath of the minister. Lectures were arranged: 'A Trip to Africa'; an impersonation of Charles Dickens' characters;

and the magic of a cinematograph show, comparing the life of a child brought up in the village with that of a child in the city.

Ruth and Margaret attended everything possible for them. There was no street lighting, so they could not go to the hall on a winter evening. When word of this reached Mrs Leitch, if she herself was not going, she sent her coach to convey the sisters, in return for some essential sewing. For the sisters, travelling in the coach was the most wonderful thrill of all.

In the third section of the house lived the coach, the horses and the coachman. The sisters knew Walter well. He often helped them with their coal and logs, and then would find on his doorstep a little package of shortbread. Sometimes he came into their house, seated himself by the fire, and listened as in turn the sisters read the newspaper aloud.

But when he drove them in the coach, he dressed as smartly as he did when conveying his employers. He may have been talking to the sisters in the garden in the afternoon, but very formally, down the path at the appointed hour, he would come to take them to the hall. He knocked on their door and waited.

'Good evening. The coach is ready. Who is coming first?'

Up the path one of them would go, Walter carrying a lamp, leading the way. He settled the first sister in the coach, and then went back for the other.

'Wrap up well in the rugs on the seats, and off we go now.'

They were going less than a mile, but it still had to be done just right.

'Isn't this wonderful? Who would believe we would ever travel in a coach? We are just like the Queen now.'

When they reached the village hall, the coachman helped them out one at a time.

'When shall I come back?' he asked, knowing full well the answer.

They smiled as they replied, 'About nine o'clock, Walter, please.'

They were not at all like the Queen. She neither smiled, nor said please. And as for addressing her coachman by name, that was entirely unheard of.

There was always someone waiting to escort them into the hall. They made their way in, talking to friends and neighbours as they moved towards the seats kept for them at the front. They were too tiny to see from anywhere but the front row. They listened intently to every speaker. Stories of faraway places and new inventions were coming right into their village. They felt themselves to be at the helm of a new world.

As the century was drawing to a close, events from thousands of miles away crept into the village. The Queen and Empress ruled one quarter of the world land surface. Part of this enormous empire was South Africa, a place the Misses Cook had heard of from the minister. He often spoke of missionaries who had gone to that distant land to convert the native people. The Misses Cook followed what was happening in the weekly local newspaper, which carried not only the story of the bazaar to build the hall, but also world news. Some kind of arrangement seemed to have been made, whereby the Dutch and the British each had an area. No mention was made of what had happened to the people who had been there from the beginning of time. Perhaps they just stayed put and worked for the Dutch or the British. Did not that happen on farms here? The people who worked on the farms had different owners as the land was bought and sold.

But then things seemed to go wrong. Gold was found in the Dutch area, and the British government ignored the agreement, in order to acquire the gold. The Misses Cook secretly sympathised with the Boers, knowing that if someone found gold amidst their potatoes and onions, their roses and primroses, they would not want it taken from them. They too had an agreement – their rent and their tenancy, and if they found gold it was theirs to do with as they wished. The Misses Cook decided this must be the actions of the Government. The Queen would never do such a thing. Had they not told her?

All this was far away, but it came right to their door one morning when the postman called.

'I am going off to fight the Dutch Boers in South Africa,' he announced. 'I fancy the adventure. Too quiet for me here. I want to ride a horse, and fight like the Light Brigade.'

Margaret and Ruth did not quite know what to say. John Golden was a kindly young man, born and brought up in the village. With the development of the community, a post office had been set up. The mail came by steamer and was delivered twice a day. He always called on them, although they got very few letters. He liked to look in to see them, and often was rewarded by carrying away a piece of cake.

Shortly after his departure, from the garden the sisters watched the Royal Navy ships going down the river. They were carrying the soldiers who would go into battle when they reached the bottom of the world, four weeks or so ahead. How their world had changed! Never did Margaret and Ruth ever think they would know someone who would go so far away. Even their brother who worked for a company in Glasgow, which made a great deal of money across the ocean, had never left this island on which they lived. They themselves had only once boarded one of the steamers, thinking they might venture to the city, but during the journey they thought better of getting off, and just came home again. On their way they had passed the shipyards on the river. What a noise there was with all the hammering! How can anyone live with that? Huge numbers of people were going about their daily business. Margaret and Ruth knew they would be entirely lost in that world only an hour from their quiet home. These shipyards built the ships that went all over the world, one of them carrying John Golden on his adventure.

How fast the world had changed during the lives of the two sisters. As the twentieth century dawned, the changes speeded up. Beth thought of all the places she had travelled to on her adventures. Only seventy years after the Boer War, she herself had begun to see the world. In 1900 ordinary people only went abroad with the navy or the army, or they were emigrating with no expectation of coming back. By the time Beth was in her twenties she could work, and go abroad on holiday, and come back to her job. As a teacher she had had long holidays, and thus had been able to travel extensively. Europe and then Asia, Africa, America; they had all been within her reach. Without any doubt her travels had influenced her, and contributed to shaping her world view. She felt a flash of sadness for the generations before her who had not had this opportunity, and wondered if, because it had not been possible, they had had no desire to explore. But even as this idea crossed her mind, she knew this was not true. Scotland had sent explorers all over the world, and each exploration must have begun with the idea and the desire to learn and expand.

The Misses Cook had heard this in John Golden.

In time, John Golden came home. But his was not the face of a hero who had had a great adventure. At a reception held in the hall, during which he was given a gold watch and chain by the people of the village, he told a story very different from what they had all read in the newspaper.

The public at home had not been told the truth. The British Army commanders had bungled over and over again.

'The Boers knew they could not defeat the British in a pitched battle,' he told people, 'so they fought it differently. Luring us into traps, and then picking us off. The commanders had no idea what to do. They should have known. After all, that is what the Americans did to us over a hundred years ago.

'The commanders would not listen at first when we told them we cannot wear our red coats. We were too easily seen by the enemy. Eventually they did listen, but not before many of us died in that faraway land. On one occasion nine hundred of us went to the slaughter, and nigh four hundred fell, all through a London drawing-room general's mistake, who took good care he did not come to the front himself.

'Only one general knew what to do. A Scotsman like ourselves. He did what the clans have done for centuries when pursued by the Red Coats. They used the land. Some of the high command did not even know how to read a map.'

As Margaret and Ruth lay in their beds that night, they wondered if John Golden had been lonely. He had cut himself off from his home to go for an adventure, which did not turn out as he had expected. What did that feel like, they wondered?

Next time he called on them, they asked. They had planned easy questions first.

'What does South Africa look like?' began Ruth.

'Are the colours like here?' continued her sister. 'Are the plants the same?'

'Slow down, ladies. Do I smell baking? Often when I was out in the country, the veldt they call it, hearing the sounds of animals I did not know, I could hear the sounds of home. Next I would see home, the greenness and the trees. South Africa is beautiful, but it is different. It is brown and orange, not green, and there is no river to watch. Yes it sometimes felt lonely when I thought of home, but of course no one would admit that. The loneliest moments came when I remembered the smells of home, new mown grass and the leaves after rain.'

'Did you smell our cakes out there?' ventured Ruth.

'Oh yes I surely did. And when I did, I felt not so far away.'

He told them of army life. He was never alone. There was seldom silence. No one moved away from the protection of the group. The Boers were waiting for a stray soldier who wanted a moment of isolation. But as the sun dipped over the horizon, there was a loneliness that was almost tangible, as one after another of these men longed for home.

'Do you wish you had not gone?' asked Margaret.

There was a pause, and then he gave the answer that in their hearts both wanted to hear.

'No, I am glad I went. I learned a great deal about myself through the people I met. I learned what matters to me, things I had never thought about. It is great to go away. And it is even better to come home again.'

It was not possible for the Misses Cook to go away, they both knew that, but they had found this same adventure through their reading.

After he had left, Margaret said, 'Ruth, I was thinking that maybe one day it will be possible for young women to go away and have an adventure, see new things and come home again. Would that not be wonderful?'

'Oh it would. Maybe it will happen. After all, we never thought we would be able to read.' They shivered with excitement at such a possibility.

Where would they have gone? They sat in silence, grinning with the imagined adventures they were keeping private. The old walls listened, as they absorbed the silent dreaming of these two old ladies.

It puzzled them that the Queen, who had the opportunity to go anywhere, went nowhere. What did she spend her time doing? She did not sew or make preserves or cakes, so what did she do? What did she think about? Did she wonder about people like themselves, or were they subjects not people? And did she dream? Despite all the years of learning everything they possibly could about Queen Victoria, they knew they did not know who she was at all.

The newspaper they read from cover to cover each week reported on the Queen. Gradually the news shifted to her deteriorating health. They stopped talking about her at that point; it was just too close.

On January 22nd 1901, Queen Victoria died. The news reached the village very soon after. Almost no one had been alive before her birth. Few could remember a time when she was not on the throne. An age had ended.

The funeral took place. The coronation of her son Edward followed. In every town in the land, and in many throughout the empire, there were huge celebrations. But not for Margaret and Ruth Cook. They had walked side by side with the Queen throughout their lives, and as her life ended, they knew theirs too were drawing to a close. They did not go out so often. They baked less. They could no longer sew. Their visitors became fewer. Hugh Weir could no longer manage the walk along the road.

The Robertsons upstairs helped them. The family who lived next door in the little cottage which Mr Leitch had overshadowed also came to check on them two or three times a day. They were not alone.

Ruth Cook died on January 15th 1908 in the bed looking to the river. She had been bedridden for seven years. It is as if she had given up when the old queen died. Margaret had kept going, looking after her as best she could.

Beth felt the coldness of loneliness when she thought of how those years might have been. Had their conversation and companionship of almost ninety years evaporated along with Ruth's will to live? Had Ruth become confused and retreated into her past? And if that was true, had it been a comfort for them both to escape into a life they had shared? Or had Margaret become more and more lonely as she lived day by day caring for her failing sister? Did she feel she was the lone standing stone of her family?

Ruth's funeral took place in the village church, and she was laid to rest in the nearby cemetery. Margaret went home, but without the purpose of her life, she retreated into herself. The neighbours watched the steady decline. They built her fire, they cooked for her, they read to her. As the days lengthened, Margaret's life drew to a close. She began to fade away, as if she was just disappearing.

On April 8th she contracted pneumonia. It was unthinkable that she would die alone. She had watched over her sister, and now the neighbours watched over her. They simply took turns on the other bed. It was young Jeanie from next door who was there, as she slipped into unconsciousness. Banging the ceiling with a broom, she alerted the Robertsons upstairs. And so Margaret passed away. She was no more alone than had been her sister. In death she was part of the community she had lived among in life.

The nineteenth century did not end on December 31st 1899. For many, it ended with the death of Queen Victoria. In this house it ended with the passing of the Victorian sisters, Margaret and Ruth Cook.

Chapter Eight

Beth was stiff. She had sat on her grandfather's bench for hours. The spring sunshine was not generous with its warmth. Clear blue sky and bright sun rid the gloom of winter, but it would be many weeks before it was a pleasure to sit outside into the evening. The daffodils would need to take their leave, the bluebells come and go. Only by the time the pink flowers came through would sitting on the bench till after dusk be comfortable.

She stood up to go inside, and as she did so something caught her eye. It seemed to be a whisk of maroon velvet. She looked carefully. No, there was no velvet there. Yet she was sure she had seen it on the path. And then a glimpse of a grey cap at the section of the garden where the vegetables had grown. Next a little boy sitting on a branch of the laurel tree. What was going on? She had never held with a belief in ghosts, and yet!

After her mother had died something very strange had happened. One morning trying to force down some breakfast at the kitchen table, fearful of the misery in the empty hours ahead, she had gradually felt a very strong sense that her family were with her, as 'presences' was how she described it. They were there smiling, encouraging her to keep going through the grief. She had tried to shake this off as absurd, not rational, but she could not deny she had sensed it. As she had looked up, instead of the empty room, her mother, young again, was standing at the door, her hand on the doorknob; her aunt, never a hair out of place, with a dishtowel over one shoulder at the sink; her father as an old man in his chair at the table, cigarette in hand, and through the window she could see her grandfather on his bench, her granny standing near him on the path, holding the dog by the lead. All exactly as they had been in life. For a moment, just a moment, her torment evaporated, and in the instant she felt this tiny glimmer, they disappeared. She pleaded with them to come back, not to leave her like this, but they were gone. It only happened once. Could they have come back to help her? Or had it come from some place deep inside her? Amidst this strange comfort, she was confused that her brother was not in the group watching over her. The more she thought of this, the more she became sure of the impossibility of what she knew had taken place. Her brother could not be with them. He was alive, drowning in his own grief.

Beth never understood how this had happened in these few minutes that morning. But she knew that it had happened. It could not be denied. Something beyond the science of rational thought had indeed occurred, at a moment when she was hovering on the edge. She seldom spoke of it. To talk of it would have somehow made it a story, and it was too precious for that. In time she knew she did not need to understand how it had happened. What mattered was what she took from it. During their lives, those who had gone before her had also known grief. They knew she would one day feel whole again, as they had done. They had thrown her a thread of hope to grasp. Over the months, late in the evening, she would sit in the armchair in the kitchen and talk to them asking for advice. Not all at once. It depended on what she needed to ask.

Over the following years, she gathered them all together to tell them what she had been doing and where she had been. They were never presences as they had been that morning, but when she was telling them her adventures, large and small, she was sure they were listening.

When she did this, she felt they had never left. Her rational mind disputed this. People die, and then they are gone. But to Beth this no longer fitted. As the flowers die each year, they bloom again the following. Can we leave an imprint of ourselves on a place that reappears when needed, or do we carry the imprint of our loved ones inside us, and turn to it unconsciously when in despair?

Easing movement into her limbs, Beth still sat on the bench thinking. And, if this was possible, could it extend beyond her family to the ancestors of the house, those who had lived here before her parents and grandparents, and who had left their imprint on their home? Was it possible, she wondered, that the earlier residents of the house had become so real to her that she could see a whisk of Margaret Cook's maroon dress, and Hugh Weir's grey cap? Up there in the tree, one of Peter and Mary's children? She did not know, she did not need to know, but she was warmed by the comfort this gave her, so she sat on in the fading light; growing cold, watching and waiting.

In the slow fading of the light, there came the slightest of sounds, gathering strength with each moment that passed. Through the old wooden gate came the Misses Cook in their tight-bodiced Victorian dresses and little leather boots picking their way over the gravel. Their bonnets had flashes of ribbon. Margaret liked red, Ruth blue. Down the path they walked, chattering as they went. They stopped level with Beth to watch Jack Weir, Hugh's son, digging the potato patch.

'Good crop this year,' he said. 'I'm sure of it.'

'I'm hiding,' came a voice from the tree.

'I can't see you. Where are you?' Their eyesight had long gone.

'Up here.'

'I can see you now.' It was not true, but it is amazing how the loss of one faculty improves another. They turned and pointed to where the voice had come from.

The little boy came down from the tree to walk with the old ladies. He knew they liked to go along the edges of the garden. It was on a slope, and so they had to be careful they did not slip. Little Peter gave them directions where to step to avoid the uneven patches. Down to the bottom they went, along a path and back up the other side. Trees fringed the garden but not so high as to block the view to the river beyond. Three sides of a rectangle they walked.

One of the loveliest features of the garden was the stone wall separating it from the next property. It was about twenty metres long, and at its highest point three metres tall, declining in height with the slope of the garden. It was grey whinstone, each slab cut to fit its neighbouring slabs. Over the last few decades cement had been used to fill up the holes caused by weathering – although it had been originally built without cement. Not only did the stones fit, there was the added skill that the whole structure had to be balanced and counterbalanced so that it did not slide down the hill. The elegance of the wall was in its engineering as well as its aesthetic. As Beth admired the work of the architect, so too she admired the work of the stonemason. Did the threesome walking round the garden admire the wall? Beth was sure at least two of them did. Given that the Misses Cook were about forty years old when the house was built, it is likely they knew who the stonemason was. Beth watched them touch the stone and exchange a word private between them. The stonemason had touched it. The Misses Cook had touched it. She would touch it too. An imprint across one hundred and fifty years. Perhaps. Certainly the stonemason must have been proud of his work. She imagined the admiration of the Misses Cook for the wall, or, she wondered, was it for the stonemason himself, a long lost dream of romance? She herself had always admired that wall, and could understand how such an artist would be a very attractive man.

At every turn of the garden stroll, they stopped to look at the house. Seen from different angles, it changed character. Looking up at it from the bottom of the garden, it was huge. The stone had been painted white, with the windows edged in blue. The grey blue of the slates was at times the grey blue of the sky, and at other times the river. The windows looked east, west and south. The north-facing wall had no windows, but carried all the chimneys. 'That was clever building,' thought Beth. 'The north-facing wall does not get the sun so it was heated by the fires.' Nineteenth-century insulation was the coal fire. With modern central heating many chimneys had been blocked off, and this had brought a new problem. Dampness had damaged chimneys, which then began to crumble. Central heating heats the air, not the walls. Beth had kept three of the chimneys open, and the house stood strong.

The light was fading. The shadows had fled, and Beth went inside. Had this really happened, or had she imagined it? She had watched two old ladies and a little boy bound together by a great deal of affection. She knew they had taken their stroll of the garden for her benefit. Perhaps those who had lived here before her had not completely gone; perhaps they had left part of their very selves to reappear when needed; the house held worlds from which she could draw wisdom. With time she might understand, but would she listen? She knew she had a tendency to being stubborn. The question was not so much 'Would she listen?' as 'Could she listen?'

And while she waited, the house would protect her.

She made her evening meal and carried it to the parlour. Light came by the flick of a switch, but instead she lit lamps positioned round the room where their paraffin predecessors may once have sat. Four separate flicks of a switch, one in each corner, cast shadows that transformed the room from its daytime appearance. The lily of the valley became three-dimensional. Its leaves, picked up on the cornice, surged with energy. They did not lie flush against the ceiling but were individual, just like a real plant. They had not been made from one cast. Each section was visually linked to the one on each side of it to create a whole border of lilies ready to burst into bloom. Here again was an unknown craftsman, another person whose skill, nay his art, left his imprint on the house.

Beyond this room was the room where Beth had slept as a little girl, as a teenager, and as an adult. Now it was her library and her study. Books from floor to ceiling. New shelving had been built alongside the bookcase her grandfather had made her, which still housed *Alice in Wonderland* and *Fairy Tales* by the Brothers Grimm. She had taken reading for granted; it came with going to school. But as she looked at the shelves groaning under novels, drama, poetry, biographies, history, travel, she paused to wonder about life without them. It was unimaginable. Had the books made her who she was? Or had she sought them out because of an innate pleasure in the act of reading? Which had come first? What was indisputable was how reading had widened and enriched her life, exactly as it had for Mary and Hugh Weir and the Misses Cook.

Looking round the room she recalled that the computer now sat where her bed had been, and when she worked at her desk she could look out of the window and see, from the room above, the view the Misses Cook had bickered over. Often when she sat there she barely noticed the view, so intent was she on her work. But tonight she stood and looked. The house was silent in a silence of comfort.

Sometimes this room was not at all silent. It faced the river, and in winter when the doors were locked, and darkness fell by four o'clock, the wind howled. There was little to protect the house from the gales which swept up the river from the Atlantic. Winds of seventy mph were not uncommon. Usually they were accompanied by horizontal rain. The river boiled in anger. The windows creaked with the strain, but the old house did not give in.

Tonight all was still. The river was glass, lit only by the moon.

Hours had passed since Beth had wakened that morning. She was tired now, which puzzled her as all she had done was get up, breakfast and sit on her grandfather's bench. She had been tired when she had wakened. Misery makes you tired. She had spent so much of the day thinking of unhappiness experienced by the ancestors of the house – no doubt that had added to her tiredness.

But it was undeniable that she had also experienced the excitement and the joy of many of the events in the lives of the people who had gone before her. She had drawn new pleasure from features which made the house beautiful, features she normally only glanced at.

Every person she had thought about had sat in this house, had walked in this garden. They had laughed. They had cried, and it seemed to her that somehow they had come back to remind her that the house, now wrapping itself round her, had seen unhappiness before. These old walls, which withstood the winter storms and protected those living inside, would protect her against this storm she was facing. The windows creaked and howled but they did not break. The storm always passed.

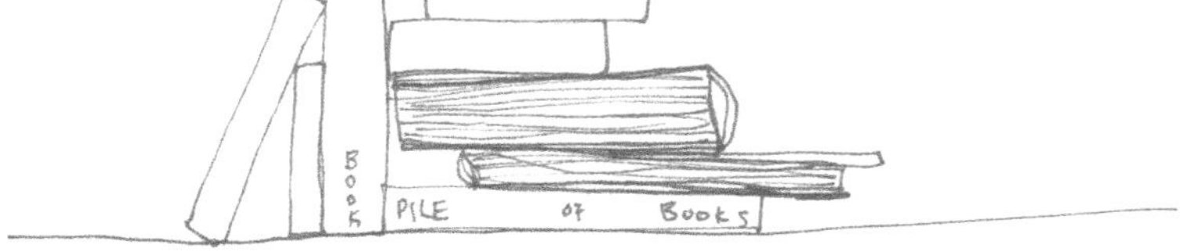

Chapter Nine

The Misses Cook lay alongside their parents. The long nineteenth century was over. By 1908, Edward the Caresser had been on the throne for seven years. His coronation had been a vast and lavish event, forcibly celebrated across the quarter of the globe which made up the British Empire.

The gilded age of the Pax Britannica screeched ever louder. 'On our Empire the sun will never set. Britannia rules, and will always rule, the waves.' Beneath the facade of imperialism, people in every corner watched.

The empire had been fraying at the edges for decades. By 1908, it was being rent apart at its centre. Canada had partially separated. India had rebelled. In South Africa Britain's invincibility, based on nothing but self praise, had been shredded. Incapable of seeing what was happening, the King, his acolytes and his mistresses threw ever larger parties, while the clamour of resentment growled below.

On the River Clyde, the shipyards produced one fifth of the world's shipbuilding. The cacophony of hammering increased. Demands for increased wages and safety equipment were brutally put down. Ireland, where King Henry II had established England's first colony more than seven hundred years earlier, rebelled against rule from London. Women demanded the vote, chaining themselves to railings in order to be classed as persons. The suffragettes on hunger strike in British prisons, the rebels incarcerated and tortured in Ireland, and the Indians massacred on peaceful protests were bound together by the same ideal – the human right of self-determination.

To this, few listened.

The King's cousin in Berlin, Kaiser Wilhelm II, envied Bertie, the family nickname for King Edward VII. Germany had only recently become a united nation, after centuries of existence as individual little states. Bavaria, Saxony, Thuringia linked with other small states to become Deutschland. Becoming one nation was not enough. Its leaders wanted an empire comparable with that of Britain.

To build an empire, it is necessary to have a navy to carry both soldiers and the machines of destruction to the places identified on the map destined for conquer. The people, who for centuries had inhabited these lands, were irrelevant. They would be destroyed. These newly acquired territories would belong to the conqueror.

The shipyards of northern Germany began to mass-produce battleships. Britain became uneasy. A series of crises occurred in which both nations said plenty, and did little. With each occurrence the tension mounted. It is no more possible for nations to hurl insults, and then continue as if this had never happened, than it is for people.

In the village where the Weirs and the Cooks, the Robertsons and the Leitches lived, change was also underway. When Hugh Weir had died in 1904, he was recorded in the local newspaper as one of the oldest residents in the community. Mary and Peter lived in a grand house along the road. Their children, now parents themselves, were part of the group of citizens running the village.

The minister, who had drawn so many to hear his sermons, had long been followed by a different minister, who by 1908 had been in the village for over twenty years.

There were fewer grand new houses being built. The rich now went abroad, and their holiday homes in Scotland had become less of an attraction. Nevertheless the Bowling and Tennis Club continued to be widely used in the summer by the visitors, the Curling Club by the year-round residents in the winter. The nine-hole golf course was used by both groups. In the hall, dances and lectures continued to take place on a very regular basis. There the Choral Union practised and performed.

Behind the hall on a hill sat a very grand hotel, for twenty years the finest on the river. It was a playground for the wealthy who preferred gracious living in a hotel to the responsibility of a large holiday home. It was also a source of employment for the locals year-round. In 1904, a hot June day had resulted in the sun shining on a glass dome, igniting wooden beading underneath. Despite being close to the river, there was a lack of water to extinguish the fire, for the simple and tragic reason that the hoses were not long enough to stretch from the shore on to the hill. Most of the villagers worked to save what could be saved. They enjoyed the fame of the hotel, and economically many depended on it. Clothing was spread onto the ground to break the fall of furniture thrown, or lowered, from the windows. Salvaged items were carried across the road to the hall. The heat had been so intense that it had melted gold jewellery in the safe, leaving only the stones visible.

There was no loss of life, but for those for whom the hotel was their livelihood, it was catastrophic. In time the hotel was rebuilt, and was once again bustling with visitors. The village reputation of being the place to holiday had been restored. What was not so easy to restore was the sense of security that the workforce had briefly experienced. They had discovered their lives to be as fragile as those of their tenant farmer ancestors.

In the white house with the blue-edged windows, there were changes too. In 1909, Neil Robertson and his family had moved away. He had been offered work as head gardener at a castle in the east of Scotland.

Janet Leitch's son, Alan, with his wife and their daughter, were living in the main part of the house. The coach house still held the horses and the coach, but there was no one living in the coachman's house above. Mr Leitch had to drive the coach himself. The family fortunes had become straitened. They had not moved with the changes in style demanded by London high fashion, and to keep the hatters' business afloat, the family had to rent out the larger of their two houses, the one along the road from which Janet Leitch had come to visit the Misses Cook.

Underneath, where the Misses Cook had lived, were Francis and Martha McLean, and their son David. They had lived in the community all their lives, but had found themselves homeless, when the house they lived in was sold. The little house was rather too little for them, but it was accommodation until somewhere more suitable came along.

David loved it. The world just seemed to open its arms to him every time he stepped out of the door. The tied house where he had come from had been hard against a cliff face, and consequently was both dark and damp. This new house was to him palatial. It looked to the light.

In the early winter of his first year of moving in, he became fascinated with the sunrise. He watched the sun rise over the hills on the other side of the river, and then followed it, as every day it came over the horizon slightly further south. After midwinter he observed it returning on its journey north. By the summer he had asked the headmaster and the minister about this. They lent him books, they lent him a compass. He worked out his landmarks, and by the following winter he was ready.

Each morning from the autumn solstice he made his way up

the hill to a specific point where landmarks were easily identifiable. On to a carefully drawn diagram of the hills over which the sun rose, he marked exactly where it did so. He then took a compass bearing. And home he would go. There this raw data was carefully transcribed on to a master diagram, each location, time and date noted. By the spring solstice he could clearly follow the journey of the sun.

He continued for six more months, even although in high summer this necessitated being on the hill by 4am. In the following winter he repeated the whole exercise to check for any variation. He also added a second chart which involved exactly the same measuring, but from the seat in the garden. He wanted to know what difference there may have been at a lower altitude.

David was a farm boy, and an astronomer in the making.

In the little cottage, whose view had been obscured by the original design, was an old lady with her son and daughter. Johnnie was an apprentice plumber, learning his trade to become a master plumber in the village, responsible for its drains and its sewage. This latter was a matter of permanent concern. Only the main part of the house had interior toilet facilities. When Mr Leitch Senior had built his holiday home, an inside flush toilet was a symbol of wealth. It was installed close to the kitchen, so that it could drain into the same location as the water from the sink. It had never been relocated. The other houses had outside dry toilets, which were emptied when they became a nuisance to the nose.

Throughout the decades when the house had been rented, the flush toilet was a source of constant curiosity to the village children. All they wanted to do was pull the chain and watch the water flow. One of them was particularly fascinated by the gurgling sound of the drain. On the handle of the toilet pull chain were the words 'W. MacNab, Master Plumber'. They all knew him, and when they met him on the road constantly assailed him with questions. 'How does it work? Why does it not overflow? How does the water get into the metal box?'

Beth's parents had added a bathroom upstairs, but had retained the original WC complete with its ancient pull chain. The dry toilets, however, had undergone conversion in her lifetime. As houses acquired modern bathrooms, the outhouses had become sheds.

On the hill behind the house sat two farmhouses roughly a mile apart. Both families had sons, who had left school as soon as they could at the age of thirteen. These boys Hector and Graham were firm friends. The third of this threesome was David McLean. Throughout their childhood these boys roamed the hills, trapping foxes and rabbits, gathering berries and chestnuts. In the summer sometimes they would climb to the top of the hill and lie in the sunshine watching the clouds. A game had developed when they were young – guessing the shape of the clouds, which over the years had taken on a slightly more lurid tone!

As time went on, they talked of the futures they dreamed of. This was a new world, and it would be theirs. They were not going to live out their entire lives in this small place. The more openly they talked, the more their dreams always ended with them coming back one day. They knew they would go, but it was unthinkable that they would not come back. This was where they belonged.

As farm boys, they were rooted in the land. They could not remember a time when their lives were not controlled by the seasons. In spring they were always present, watching, at the birth of the lambs and the cattle. No matter how often they saw it, they were awed by the mystery of birth. They watched every baby sheep emerging from its mother amidst blood and mucus, staggering onto its legs, knowing towards where to grope. Every ewe knew what to do. They did not need to be told. They were programmed.

Watching the cattle being born was to the children an even more astonishing feat. The babies were bigger. How did these legs get organised as they needed to be? These boys knew only too well that sometimes that did not happen, and the whole family would be awakened by terrible screaming. Out their fathers and older brothers would go to help a struggling cow. Success was always celebrated. Failure led to distress. It was not just the financial implications of success and failure. Farmers cared for their animals, and losing an animal carried with it not only loss, but a sense that somehow they had made a mistake; they had failed to learn what their fathers had taught them.

From the top of the hill the threesome could stand in one spot, and by the simple act of turning in a complete circle, they could see a different world. Beyond the top of the hill was moorland, green in the spring, purple in the autumn, and, when drenched with the winter rains, a dangerous peat bog. To right and left stretched the long back of the hill range, on which they stood.

In the distance in one direction the river turned a corner, and in the other it flowed out ever widening to the ocean. Strictly speaking it was not a river, but the estuary of a river. A tiny trickle at its source, it grew deeper and wider as it passed through Glasgow. On it went until it became an estuary (a 'firth' in Scots). No one ever referred to it as an estuary; it was the River Clyde, or the Firth of Clyde. Houses stretched along its banks on both sides, until they gave way to the sharp peaks of the Arran mountain range drawn along the western horizon.

In front of them the land swept down to the river, the farms and houses of their village hidden by the curves of the land. On the tops beside them were the sheep. Out of their eyeline, they knew that closer down to the farmhouses were the cattle, and in front of their homes grew the crops; oats to feed both the family and the hens living round their doors, and in the fields hay for the animals through the winter. The family horse, essential for pulling the wooden plough, dozed in the sun. The threshing machine, awaiting its season of the year, sat in the byre. It was a scene replicated all over the country. A way of life understood by, and understood only by, the whole farming world. It had changed little over the centuries. A community of land and time, bound by knowledge.

In spring the land was ploughed in preparation for the seed potatoes, the onions, the carrots, the corn, the oats and the hay. As the tatties raised their shoots above the ground, the earth was banked up into raised rows. This had been the earliest job for the children on the farm. As tiny people, they could raise the rows with only minimal bending!

In summer the crops were watched over, the dread of unexpected severe rain never far from mind. Farmers were meteorologists by necessity. The hay was cut, and a second crop sown. The sheep were clipped, first those without lambs, and then those with. The wool was washed, combed out and spun. The girls learned to knit, the finished items either worn by the family, or sold. Wild strawberries and raspberries were gathered for preserves to see the families through the winter. Nothing was wasted.

Autumn saw the crops being gathered in – tattie howking, it was called – and the land being made ready for its long winter sleep.

Throughout it all, the farmers watched over their animals – meat, milk, butter, cheese, wool – the animals were the livelihood of the farmers. On them the humans depended.

In summer, in the hills checking on the sheep, the boys lazed away hours listening to the birdsong. Thrushes were such shy birds they did not come near the houses, but up there in the hills they had plenty to sing for themselves. Closer to home, in the byres round the farmhouses, blue tits had set up home, using leftover pieces of wool shorn from the sheep, and on occasion scraps of excess hair clipped from one of the farm dogs.

'Do you think birds dream as we do?' asked David.

'Maybe. Don't know,' was the considered reply. This set the three of them off on a metaphysical conversation about the expectations of the animal kingdom.

'Are we better off because we can dream? We can do what the farmers who lived here before us could not do. We can go away. They could not.'

'Did they want to?'

That was a conundrum. Was it better to have no dreams, to be tied to a life from which there was no deviation, or was the choice, which their generation was just beginning to have, in itself a complication?

'Aye they could go. They could join the army. Do you no' mind the postman who went to be a soldier before we were at the school?'

'And he came back again. He hated it. Said the generals were useless. People did not like him for saying that, my father told me. The minister even preached against him, suggesting he should be arrested for saying such things.'

'Is that why he left the village?'

The boys fell silent. Could the people they knew do such a cruel thing?

'Do you think there is going to be a war? It says so in the paper.'

'Maybe, but it will no' affect us.'

The three of them sat alone with their own thoughts, each wondering what the future might bring, until Hector, who could stand the strained silence no more, stood up and announced, 'Come on. Race you to the bottom!'

And off they ran – young men running into an uncertain and exciting future.

A century later, the view had not changed. It was such a beautiful day that Beth decided to take herself up the hill to where the farm lads had been. Television aerials, satellite dishes and cars were not visible from up there.

'What brings you up here?' came a voice she knew to say hello to.

'I came up here years ago, and just wondered how it had changed. It is such a lovely day for a walk.' She was wary of telling the truth, that she had been imagining it as it had been a century before. 'It's beautiful.'

He sat down beside her, his dog stretching out in the sun. 'Stone Age people must have seen this too. Then thousands of years later the Battle of Largs, 1263. What a ringside view of that struggle. People here would certainly have heard it. It is only four miles. The sensible ones must have been terrified of what might happen next. You can almost see the Viking dragon ships coming up the river.'

'Yes,' she said. 'It's hard in a place like this to not see the past.'

'Why would anyone not want to see it?'

'Plenty don't.'

'We can't avoid it without losing part of who we are. We learn from it.'

'Yes, I believe we do.'

They sat in comfortable companionship, and then walked down the hill together. At the road, they parted to go in different directions.

'I hope we meet again soon,' he said.

Beth smiled and nodded. Calling to his dog, he walked off along the road, whistling as he went. Beth watched him, listening as the tune steadily receded.

Chapter Ten

More changes came in 1911. The Leitchs' fortunes improved and the family moved back into Springbrae, their big house along the road. No longer young, but still very strong, Hugh Weir's son Jack was the head gardener where his father had worked before him. Knowing that in time he would pass this job on to his son, he had been looking to rent a house with a garden, where he could grow his own vegetables long into old age. There were a number available, to all of which he found objections, because he knew which one he wanted. When the owners were actually living in it, that did not seem likely, but when he heard they were leaving, it might just be possible. With trepidation strange to him, he approached Mr Leitch. 'I have come to ask you if, when you move out, I can rent this house. As you know, I lived here as a child, and I want to come back.'

Into the silence he added, 'To me it is home.'

Although Mr Leitch had known Jack Weir all his life, he realised he did not know him at all. He knew nothing of how this man thought. He was astonished that someone could feel this way about a house he did not own. Belonging was determined by ownership, and that was that. He named a price for the rent. It was higher than Jack Weir expected, but if he could sell some of his produce from the garden, it would be possible now that the government was talking about pensions.

'Thank you,' he said politely. 'Yes I can pay that.'

Arrangements were made, and Jack Weir went home to tell his wife what he had done. It was not his way to do things without discussing them with her, but he had felt such a compulsion to live in the house of his childhood that he had feared speaking to her.

'You have done what?' she said. 'Without talking with me. Do I not matter?' Catherine Weir was hurt, not angry. She liked the house. He had spoken of it so often that she knew what it meant to him, but she was stung that, after years of marriage, he had done something in which she was not an equal. That is what she had loved in him from the beginning. He had always treated her as someone with an opinion to be listened to. They had not always agreed, but they had always discussed. And now he had not trusted her with something so deeply felt.

Of course they would move. The house itself was not a dilemma for her. They would have more room. She too had always found it attractive. They would have space to grow vegetables, and perhaps flowers. But the security of her life was fractured. The bond she had believed in had somehow been breached. She was adrift in a marriage, which had in a moment changed. She was alone.

She turned away.

'I did not know how to say it to you.'

'You have been telling me for as long as we have known each other. Words when we were young. Now when we pass the house, and look over the wall, I know how much you have always wanted to live there. I knew it perhaps even more than you knew it. It is in your eyes, and in your smile, and in your quiet each time we walk on.'

He knew what he had done. He had often stood silent when he heard friends talk of how they spoke to their wives. Standing in the kitchen of their tied cottage, he wondered if he was really just like them. How could he have done this? How would their life together ever be the same again? The joy, which they should have been sharing, he had ruined. He was never more lonely.

In his marriage this was a feeling he had not known. They seemed to have belonged together from the first time they had met. Catherine Ross she was then.

She had come from the north of Scotland not long after the death of Queen Victoria. From a remote community, she was restless for adventure. As a child at school she had seen pictures of Edinburgh with its castle high on a rock. She simply decided she wanted to go to Edinburgh. It was easy to find work as a domestic servant in the capital, and she saw this as a stepping stone to whatever adventure came next.

The form it took was the family she worked for in Edinburgh coming to the village on holiday, and she, as one of the servants, came too. This did not please her. She had not left her quiet Highland home to work in another quiet part of the country. In Edinburgh she looked forward to her half day off a week when she could explore the city. Anonymous in the crowds, this was new to her. She walked the closes and wynds of the Old Town, and saved a halfpenny per week to have enough money in six months to pay the entrance fee for the castle. That had been a wonderful afternoon. She walked where the kings and queens of history had lived. She saw the ancient cannon cracked from use. But in truth what she loved most of all was the view from a height. From the castle walls she could see the whole city stretching to the river, and beyond that the county of Fife. At home in Caithness it was so flat, the sky was almost a perfect bowl, and while that had its own beauty, she discovered that she rather liked height. 'One day I will live on a hill that stretches down to water,' she decided.

When she arrived in the village, the house the family owned was not on a hill. It was along the shoreline yards from the river. It was a lovely building, but did not hold for her the interest held by the one she saw on the hill, the one facing the wrong way. When it came to her half day off, off she went. At the gate she could see the garden and the unusual shape of the house. High above one of the windows was the face of a lion. It had been cast in iron, as if put there to guard the building.

'Lovely place, isn't it?'

She turned. 'Yes it is.'

'I was born here,' Jack Weir told her. 'I lived here as a child, and one day I want to come back.'

'Where do you live now?'

He told her which house he was in now, down on the front road. He told her he was a gardener, and she told him where she came from, and of the Edinburgh family she worked for.

'There are fewer of these families come now,' he said. 'But there is still work for us.'

She watched him looking at the house and saw in his eyes a longing, a depth which she had never seen in another person. Over that summer they spent her half days off together. They walked in the hills. Always at the end of their walks, they hung over that garden wall.

The summer drew to a close, and she went with her employers back to Edinburgh. Before they parted they agreed to write to each other. Through the long winter the letters flew back and forth, and they came to know each other through their views on the events they wrote about. As an invisible servant she saw a great deal of family relationships, and she wrote of how little respect she often saw, and how wrong she thought this was. He wrote of a future in which he hoped there would be more fairness, where men and women would make decisions together. She described the misery of the poverty she saw on her walks through the city, and how she had come to value the world in which she had grown up. On her half days off, she walked further to explore the outer limits of the city. Often on the hard surfaces of the pavements, she found herself thinking of the long summer evenings walking in the hills. He wrote of the land settling in for the winter, and on one occasion of the lion with its mane covered in snow.

By the following summer, she was very excited to set off with the family again. She had been home to see her parents, and although she very much enjoyed her visit, she knew she would not return there permanently. Without admitting it even to herself, she knew where she wanted to go.

She was afraid that over the winter she had dressed him in clothes that were not his, but as soon as they tramped the hills again, through their winter of letters they knew they had grown together. By the end of the summer when she was due to go back to Edinburgh, it was agreed. In that autumn she arranged to take him to visit her parents, and while they had hoped she would come back to live in Caithness, they were happy with their future son-in-law.

Jack Weir and Catherine Ross were married very quietly in Edinburgh, and after the wedding they went to the castle. They both knew they would be unlikely to be in the city again, so this was an opportunity for him to see it; a house on a hill with a river beyond.

They came back to the village and settled in a house on the shoreline. Their first children were born there. They were happy, their most precious moments when they could find time and space alone to talk with the sincerity of the treasured letters neither would part with.

And now at the moment when his dreams had been realised, he had broken the trust he had known with Catherine from the beginning. He knew that what he had done had been thoughtless, but he could not understand why she was unable to overcome this single lapse in consideration. She did not punish him. She did not speak of it. She just withdrew, confused, trying to make sense of why she was reacting as she was.

As the weeks passed, and the time came for them to move, the silence between them grew. They wanted to speak and mend the fracture, but neither of them knew how.

The village saw the change in Jack Weir. They could not understand it. He had talked so often of what he would plant in the vegetable plot, where his father had grown. What on earth had happened?

Even close friends could not ask, as that would have overstepped a line they could not cross. And the silence continued to grow.

At much the same time, the McLeans moved out into a larger house further along the road. David had been very unwilling to go. He was determined to keep a close eye on the house and find a way back. Unaware of the turmoil in Jack Weir's life, David approached him one day on the road.

'Mr Weir, I wonder if, after you have moved, I could come to work with you in the garden? I don't want paid. I just love that house and don't want to move away. I have to, but I hope you will let me come now and again. Please.'

What could Jack Weir say? He felt he was looking at his younger self.

'Anytime you like, David, just you come.'

When Jack, Catherine and their family moved in, the house seemed delighted Jack had kept his promise and had come home. And then when David arrived, well was that not proof of just how much it was loved!

Into the downstairs house came a little family from Glasgow. They did not live there permanently, but like so many visitors they came on holiday. However, they were different from regular summer visitors. They were not rich. They were like the other tenants of the house, struggling to not slip into poverty. The tenant who took it over, John Elliot Connell, desperately wanted his family to have access to fresh air and freedom, not possible in the teeming Glasgow tenements. To that end he worked as a sheet metal worker, and also had a second job as a pianist in a dance band, in order to pay for the house in the country.

He had been born in Liverpool in 1887. His grandparents had come from Ireland to Liverpool via Glasgow. The name Connolly determined not only the owner's nationality, but also religion. Glasgow was not an easy place for Irish Catholics. Liverpool was worse. Shipping companies competed for orders, and when an order was agreed, the workforce had to move. In order to work for many of the shipbuilders on both the Clyde and the Mersey, a workman had to be both Scottish and Protestant. The Connollys had left Glasgow in the 1860s as Irish Catholics, and arrived in Liverpool as Scottish Protestants, calling themselves Connell.

John Connolly, who had been born in Glasgow, grew up in Liverpool as John Connell. In 1885 he married Jane Ferguson, herself the daughter of a Scottish blacksmith, who had gone south following the work. They had three children, two of whom died in infancy, and were laid to rest in paupers' graves.

And then Jane disappeared. She just disappeared. John did not turn to his family. He did not turn to her family. He, with his remaining child, John Elliot Connell, went back to Glasgow, where he lodged with his cousin, who looked after the little boy to enable John Connell, formerly Connolly, to work. Jane Ferguson/Connell was never spoken of again. As the years passed she did not recede, but grew ever larger in her son's mind. Why had she left him? Where had she gone? Would he ever know?

In these years as the orders were won by the shipbuilding companies, John Connell and his son, John Elliot Connell, became nomadic. Glasgow, Liverpool, Barrow-in-Furness, wherever the ships were being built. By the time he was twenty-two, John Elliot

Connell had re-settled in Glasgow, and completed his apprenticeship as a sheet metal worker. Leaving his family behind, he took lodgings in the Partick area of the city, and then he married his landlady's daughter, Maggie.

Margaret MacKechnie, always known as Maggie, had been born into a mining family on the outskirts of Glasgow. Her ancestors had come from the Highlands half a century before, migrants in search of work. The next generation became metal workers, transforming raw iron into the steel that was required to build railways, trains, ships. They moved into the city, deliberately renting a house with an extra room, in order to take in a lodger. That rent was vital, in case work disappeared.

John Elliot Connell and Margaret MacKechnie married in June 1911. Their first son, yet another John and thereafter know as Wee John, was born the following April. Before their marriage, Maggie had worked in a bookshop in Glasgow. One of the regular customers was the Leitch family, whose hatters' business was in the same street. When Maggie was leaving to get married, a conversation took place which would change the lives of the new family.

'And where will you be living?' said Mrs Leitch.

'With my parents to begin with, and then we will move when we can, but we will need to be here in the city.'

'I do not live in Glasgow all year. I have two houses at the coast, one I live in, and the other I rent. I know I am very lucky.'

Maggie smiled. What could she say? Politely she asked about the house, and then listened with growing intensity.

'If there was ever a time it was empty, and we could afford it, would you allow my husband and I to rent from you?' she heard herself ask. 'I would like to stay in a place, which is quiet and has trees, if only for a few nights. My grandmother has described the hills and the rivers of the Highlands, and I wish very much that one day I might see them.'

Mrs Leitch stared in astonishment. Was this slip of a girl getting above herself now she had found herself a husband? A quick glance at the sincerity in the eyes of the young woman, and listening carefully to her words, dispatched that selfish thought. She was ashamed. Mrs Leitch could see that was not the situation at all. This young woman just wanted fresh air and quiet away from the city, and to expand her horizon if only for, as she said, a few nights. Possibly they would be the only few nights in her life. Mrs Leitch shuddered at the thought of being cut off from the quiet of the village.

'Yes, possibly. You have our address in your records. You can write to me when you can afford to think about it,' she said, not unkindly.

The following year, John and Maggie did just that. But they did not write. They pushed the pram with the newborn baby to the address that Maggie had kept. It was a house in a grand tenement. They rang the bell. A servant answered.

'Can we speak to Mr or Mrs Leitch please?'

'Who shall I say is calling?'

'Maggie MacKechnie, now Connell.'

She disappeared. Mrs Leitch came to the door.

'Well, I did not expect this, but I am no less pleased to see you.' The pleasantries could wait. 'Are you here for the house?'

'Yes, if we can afford it.'

They were invited in. This itself was strange. People with wealth did not invite into their homes a former shop girl and her husband. The conversation flowed across the tea and the scones. Mrs Leitch told them all about the village and the house, and named her rent. She clearly loved the place, and they could sense she felt cut off when she was not there.

In Maggie's family, stories had been handed down from her Highland grandfather. She had heard of the sense of space people had in the countryside, of the changing sea and landscape, of a community bound together by belonging to a place. John's life as an industrial nomad had been lonely. He yearned to have a place where he could belong, where he could take his family away from the noise and stench of the city. As they listened, they were drawn into the place she described and the stories of the people she told them about.

They were honest. They could not afford it at that time, but they said that if John could get work as a musician, they would be able to afford the rent in the future. They asked if they might come back when they had the income to make it possible.

And thus it came about. Dance halls were growing in the city. John could earn a good sum on top of his wages as a metal worker. By the following year it was possible.

And so, without ever seeing the little downstairs house, where the Misses Cook had lived, John and Maggie, with their one-year-old son Wee John, took on the yearly responsibility of a house they could only visit on holidays. But this was not only for a few nights. This was the beginning of a very long, and very, very happy tenancy.

Beth's grandparents had found their home.

Chapter Eleven

On August 4th 1914, Britain declared war on Germany, and by so doing, the last piece of the jigsaw fell into place that would lead many nations of the world into a bloodbath.

Germany could put 4 million men into the field, France 3 million, Russia 5 million. Britain 100,000! As an island, Britain relied on the Royal Navy. The British army was in fact considerably larger than 100,000 men, but it was scattered all over the world protecting the British Empire. Only 100,000 men could be called up immediately.

It was clear that many more men were needed, and so the call went out for volunteers. From walls, pillar boxes and the sides of buses all over the country, Lord Kitchener, the British Secretary of State for War declared, 'Your Country Needs *YOU*'.

And the nation responded! It caught the imagination of young men in their hundreds of thousands. They would go abroad, meet the local lassies, have an adventure, come back heroes.

The village was no exception.

For the threesome of Graham, Hector and David, this was the opportunity, cast by chance, for which they had been waiting.

The summer of 1914 was hot. During July these three young men went about their farm work, and in the evenings met up with friends in the village, people with whom they had gone through school, played football, run races, competed in tug o' war, swum in the river, roamed the hills; people they had known all their lives. They were yet too young to have best girls, but their evening walks always took them to where the girls met. The conversation focused on each other. Not for them to discuss what was happening elsewhere in the world. Their world was of themselves, chess pieces on a board of their own making, moving around each other into 'arrangements'. Who would walk out with whom? That was much more vital.

In late June, an archduke had been shot in a far-off land. This would not touch their world. Hector was far more concerned with the affections of Graham's sister. But, as if caught in the path of a gigantic plough, the horse of which had bolted unstoppable out of control, day by day the events in that far-off land closed in on them. Germany marched into Belgium. Britain threatened to defend Belgium if Germany did not retreat. Germany moved steadily onwards. It had begun so slowly, and then with increasing speed in the last days of July, such that it was difficult to keep abreast of events. But by 11pm on August 4th, Britain was at war. The news had barely reached their remote community, when it was followed by the call for volunteers.

Which of them suggested they enlist, none of them could remember. It was a silent agreement born of their short lifetime together. They were pals, had always been pals, for as long as they could remember. They would go together.

They were not the first to enlist from the village. Two of their friends wanted that glory. But on the day when they set off to join up, they walked the five miles to the recruiting station. Pretending to be nineteen, they talked of the adventure that lay ahead. Not for a minute did they have doubts. They would say they were doing it for King and Country, or for 'gallant little Belgium,' bullied by its powerful eastern neighbour. But in truth they knew they were doing it for themselves. They were no different from the young of the generations before them; they wanted adventure. Those who signed up first lost no time in decrying those not yet enlisted, and no one wanted to be branded a coward. Besides they all knew it would be over by Christmas, and no one wanted to miss the fun.

The recruiting station was in the Burgh Hall of the neighbouring town. The hall had been built forty years earlier, to provide a space for community activities, just like the village hall. It was very grand with its turret, its crowsteps and its carved stonework. It was a hall making a statement about how the town saw itself. There was no question but that this would be the recruiting station.

By the time the farm lads reached it, the hall was ablaze with flags and banners. A brass band added to the carnival atmosphere. 'Tipperary,' 'Land of Hope and Glory,' were roared alongside the Boer War tune everyone knew, 'Dolly Gray'.

> Goodbye Dolly I must leave you though I'm very
>   sad to go,
> Something tells me I am needed at the front to
>   fight the foe.
> See the soldier boys are marching and I can no
>   longer stay,
> Hark! I hear the bugles calling, 'Goodbye Dolly
>   Gray!'

The priority was clear. Duty, not loved ones.

Men, women and children were outside cheering the young volunteers going in one door as civilians and emerging from the other as soldiers. 'Taking the King's Shilling' was a cause for celebration, and the pubs were full.

Standing apart from this, watching, was Sergeant Hugh Currie of the Argyll and Sutherland Highlanders. He was forty-three years of age. Twenty years earlier, he had enlisted. As a young man he had left the village where he had grown up, and gone 'to be a soldier'. What he saw as he watched was his younger self.

Six years into his service, he had been sent to South Africa, and, like the former village postman John Golden, had seen disaster result from incompetence. Generals, he had learned, were trained to fight wars which had already taken place. Thus they were trained in strategy of what was already known. They were not trained to deal with ingenuity on the part of the enemy. Indeed, British arrogance did not permit there to be ingenuity afforded to the other side.

Hugh Currie had seen this, and when he came home, he left the army. His father had been a gardener, and from his earliest days he had learned plants. Sickened by what he had lived through in South Africa, he sought work in the gentleness of tending and growing, and shortly after his return had found work in this quiet community. He did not speak of his army experiences. He watched what happened when John Golden spoke his mind, and he knew what not to say. He had urged John Golden to keep silent, but to no avail. They had spent many long summer evenings walking together in the hills. To begin with, people assumed they were reminiscing on the glories of the Boer War; in fact they were trying to work out how the most powerful military force in the world had been almost brought down by untrained, under-equipped farmers.

They knew it was not their fault. The Scottish soldiers lived up to their reputation for courage. The only conclusion they could come to was failure of the high command to develop successful strategy. They talked of their sadness at the loss of their army friends, of their loneliness so far from home, and of the army life they had imagined, so very different from the one they had lived. Together they could temporarily emerge from the isolation of individual experience into shared understanding. For them there was impending tragedy if nothing was learned. Nothing had changed. In 1914 war was still spoken of as glorious, not, as they knew, obscene.

Once John Golden had left the village, Hugh Currie did not speak of the South African war again. He married in 1908, and settled down to civilian life. Despite his misgivings, he joined the Territorial Army. It boosted the family income. As a former soldier, he trained men in weaponry and drilling. He also used the campaigns in Africa to teach men map reading, how to look at a situation from the point of view of the enemy, and to plan accordingly.

'In this situation what would you do?' he often asked, after outlining a location on the veldt, every detail of which was engraved in his memory. He relished with hidden satisfaction their solutions to real military mistakes, which he had survived.

As a territorial soldier at the outbreak of war, he had no choice. He once again was going to war, but this time with a heavy heart. Standing outside the recruiting station, he was out of step with the scene surrounding him. He looked at the poster of Lord Kitchener, and recalled the disastrous strategic errors in South Africa:

'Your Country Needs *YOU*'.

'It does not need you, Kitchener!' he thought bitterly.

Graham, Hector and David were too young to go into the pub in the village – everyone knew their age, but in the town, as enlisted soldiers, they were heroes. Carried on anonymous shoulders, into a tavern they went. One drink was as far as the generosity of the crowd went. They themselves had no money, and before long, they began the walk home.

Two miles on, the euphoria and the alcohol were wearing off. They became quiet, but it was not the quiet of the years on the hillside. An awkwardness had crept in. Each silently began to have doubts, but could not speak. Each of them had been repelled by what they had seen at the enlisting station. All that excitement and encouragement from people who were not going to risk their lives. Going to war should be more serious, more dignified. In silence they walked on.

When they reached the burn at the end of their road, without a word they climbed the hill to a cleft in the rock with a very deep pool. For a decade or more they had swum there on hot summer days. Sunk in their own thoughts, they took off their clothes and leapt in. Always this had been the scene of whooping and laughter. They swam, they jumped off the branches of overhanging trees, they scrambled on the rocks. But today silence. They knew that whatever the future held, they had done something which would mark them permanently.

They climbed out of the water, dried themselves on their clothes and walked down the hill.

They parted at the road to go home and tell their parents what they had done.

'I've joined the army.'

'I'm going to France.'

'I'm going to be a soldier.'

Three homes, almost simultaneously, stopped.

At the farm, Hector's father smiled. 'I'm proud of you, son. You show them what we're made of.' His mother turned away.

'Mother.'

Silence.

'She'll come round,' his father said.

His brothers shrieked with excitement.

'Can we come with you?'

'Don't be daft. It would be far too dangerous for you.' The words spoken without thought. As his mother turned to look at him, he knew he had wounded her beyond healing.

In the farmhouse along the road, Graham's parents raged.

'You're too young. Whose idea was that? Which of your daft pals?'

'I will go right now and stop this,' came from his father. 'What do you think you were doing?'

'I'm old enough. I can make up my own mind. I am old enough to fight for my country.'

'We'll see about that.'

In David's house there was silence. His mother had lost her older brother in South Africa. When he had joined the army she had thought he looked wonderful in his army uniform, but when word came that he had been killed, that memory burned. Buried so far away, she could not visit his grave. Part of her did not really believe he had gone. One day he would come home.

And now it was her son.

David's father was a keen reader. From an early age, he had enjoyed books. It was the ideas they contained which drew him. He read whatever he could, and over the years had developed his own code for living. The words from the pulpit were not for him. He sought explanations and analysis, not belief. His first encounter with the perception of war was in reading *War and Peace*. Narrated by men embroiled in the carnage, war sat very differently from its description by armchair soldiers. Political philosophy found its way to his house, and over time he became firm in his opposition to war. Surely the human race could do better? He had followed with increasing anxiety the international events as they hurtled forward in the heat of July. He had dreaded the outcome. And then it came. And now this. He had no words. The deafening minutes ticked by, marking what remained of the life of his son.

In silence, he left the house. David and his mother were bereft of words. She followed her husband to the gate. David watched them both from the window. His father turned right at the end of the path. His mother turned left.

After the sun had gone down, they came home, one after the other. No one spoke. In the morning no one spoke. By evening the conversation turned only on the work of the day. A second night of loneliness wrapped around the three figures in that house.

When Hugh Currie went home, his wife was waiting for him. She knew he had to go. After John Golden had left the village, sometimes she watched her husband sitting in his isolation. He could sit in the same chair in very different moods, sometimes telling funny stories to their two young sons. But there were times when he sat in his chair, and something about his stillness told her he was remembering. She once had asked him why he dwelt in these painful memories, and his answer, long in coming, was that he could not stop them. They were written inside him, and from time to time demanded they be listened to.

That night, he sat in his chair. He was not only remembering; he was thinking. He wondered if he should go and speak to the parents of all the young men who had enlisted to go. In the end he rejected this idea as it would do no good. It was already too late. He could not stop the inevitable. Nor could he give comfort to these parents. He knew very well that a number of the generals, who had bungled in South Africa, were the very same generals who would bungle again. The only competent commander in South Africa was already dead.

On the following Sunday, he saw all three families at Church. He could not speak to them. Nor could he listen as the minister praised their sons. He just watched the misery, fury and fear in five of them. Hector's father alone enjoyed the moment.

The silence in David's house remained. None of them knew how to break it. On Sunday evening, David left the house. He did not seek out Graham and Hector. Instead he went back to the house of his childhood.

During the previous three years, he had taken Jack Weir at his word that he could come any time. On clear mornings he regularly checked the sunrise. He often worked alongside the Weir family in the garden. From time to time he was given some carrots or potatoes to take home, but this was not why he went. He just liked being there. He would look up at the house of his earliest memories, and dream that one day he might come back. The house he now lived in was a fine house. It was bigger, but it was not the place he thought of as home. It was merely temporary; in time he would go away, and then come back, and this is where he would live.

For the first time, he approached it with heavy heart. He made his way in the gate, but there was no one around. Realising the time, he supposed the family were at the evening service. If so, he could sit in the garden and think without interruption. There sat the old wooden seat, which seemed to have been resident in that spot forever, judging by the state of it. It had been carved out of a tree trunk. He sank on to it. What had he done that had caused such pain? He loved his parents, and was too young to grasp what he had done to them. He knew his father disagreed with war, but could he not see this was different? He knew his uncle had been killed in South Africa, but that was far away. It would not happen to him, so what had he done that was so wrong?

He could not undo his enlistment. He also knew that if he could, he would not do so. His parents had to see he had made a choice that was his to make. For the first time in his life, he dreaded being in the same room as them. He just wanted the weeks of waiting to be over, so he could leave behind the weight of guilt crushing him. He wished he had someone he could speak to. He went over in his mind all the possible people he might turn to, but there was no one to whom he could describe just what had happened in his family.

The gate opened, and in came Johnnie the apprentice plumber from next door.

'I saw you walking along. I hear you have joined up along with your two pals and some of the lads from the other end of the village. I'll enlist tomorrow. It is impossible not to. I don't want to go, but what else can we do? What would folk say?' His shoulders sagged.

He was a few years older than David, so while they knew each other, the gap in their ages kept them apart. And yet here they were, sitting in this empty garden, aware that a life and death decision had been made, and it was one over which they had no choice. Volunteering was not volunteering when pressure is brought to bear. Their age isolated them from those who shrilled, 'Fight!'

'My parents won't speak to me. I don't know what to do. I didn't tell them before I went to join up.'

Johnnie said nothing so David went on, 'Have you told your mother?'

'Yes. She said nothing. My sister thinks it exciting. She does not understand.'

'History does repeat itself,' thought David. Is this not what his mother had said she felt when her brother joined the army? How had his grandparents reacted? He realised he did not know.

They sat in silence as the evening closed in. David looked at the house, and wondered if the walls of the house had ever before looked upon such unhappiness.

He got up and went back along the road.

Chapter Twelve

On August 3rd 1914, tragedy struck the Connell family. Outside war hysteria was rampant, inside was the private grief of the death of a child.

The little family had first come to the house in the summer of 1912; John, Maggie and their little son Wee John, then three months old. They came as often as they could through that autumn and winter, and for two full weeks the following summer. Friendships developed with the Weirs in the upstairs part of the house, and also with the Patons in the little cottage over the wall. Often the men sat out in the garden smoking their pipes, discussing what was happening in the world. Only John Connell knew the city, and the others were as interested in what he told them of life there, as he was in their life here. He was a member of a trade union, and spent long hours striving for workers' rights. The full-time residents of the house and cottage were not part of any such organisation, but were just as concerned about their rights. Their lives, on the surface so very different, were bound by the same conflicts of employment.

The women shared ideas too, and not only on household

matters. Very quickly Catherine Weir and Maggie realised they were both of the same thinking. They were desperate to be classed as people with legal rights, one of which was to vote. There was no opportunity to pursue this in the small village, but Maggie talked of her campaigning in the city.

'It begins with conversation,' she would say, 'and when enough people agree, you can do something. Even talking about it to others is important. It makes people think of what they might not otherwise have thought about.'

John Connell had also come to know David McLean. He had seen him working alongside Jack Weir in the garden and assumed him to be a relative. When he found that not to be the case, but that David simply came to the house because he felt it to be his home, John Connell felt a sharp stab of envy. Belonging to a place, and wanting to belong to it, were aspects of life he had never known.

One very early morning he saw David on the garden seat with a sheet of paper. He went to investigate, and David began to explain to him his charting and checking of the sun. For all the uncertainty of John Connell's background, what was certain was that he had sought education and knowledge. A basic education was followed by hours in the libraries, established with the money of the philanthropist Andrew Carnegie, himself from a struggling Scottish background. Lending libraries, free to working people, changed lives. Free education since 1872 was one thing; access to learning was quite another. John Connell and David McLean had the same thirst for knowledge, not only to better their situations, but also for its own intrinsic value.

When the little family came in 1914, there were five of them. In October of 1913 Maggie had had twins, two little girls. They were named after the two mothers: Jean (a version of Jane) Ferguson, John Elliot Connell's missing mother; and Williamina Gemmell, after Maggie's mother, her name before her marriage.

They arrived in mid July, when the crisis far away still seemed remote. By this time, Wee John was a toddler and spent many hours of that hot summer at eye level with the flowers. There were neither flowers, nor playground, where they lived in Glasgow, and in this garden of greens and pinks and browns he had found a world beyond dreams. It was a constant battle on the part of his parents to prevent him putting the flowers into his mouth. It seemed to him the natural thing to do with something so lovely. He just wanted to eat them. He also loved watching the insects. At eighteen inches high, he was very close to them. Ladybirds were in abundance, and he yelled out whenever he saw one. When the yelling started, his parents thought there was something wrong, but quickly realised he wanted to show them his find – the spotted insects he touched so gently. Bees he also liked, but abruptly learned not to touch them. Instead, he sat watching them going about their pollen work amidst the blooms.

He was walking freely by then, and off he would totter on the sloping garden until he fell over, not on to hard ground but rather the softness of the grass. He joined in when the potatoes were being raked, his little fingers doubling as a rake. Jack Weir stood him against the potato shoots as they grew, to see if they, or he, grew faster. He liked when he was bigger than the potatoes, but was very annoyed as they outstripped him. How could they grow faster than him?

During this time his sisters lay side by side in their cots. Wordlesssly, his expression made it evident what he thought. The spotted 'beasties', as he called them, could at least walk.

The family often went to the beach, where Wee John and his father poked about in rockpools. Crabs and shellfish aplenty. He loved the colour of the rocks, some pink, some black – all different shapes. When the tide was out, he was at his happiest rolling in the sand. His father would sometimes take him into the water paddling. It was very cold, but he loved the feel of the movement of the water against his legs. His father was a strong swimmer, and sometimes Wee John would sit with his mother and sisters to watch his father moving, seemingly effortlessly, through the water.

At night he would cuddle up to his father who sang to him. He did not yet know words, but he liked the tunes, and would beat along with them with his little fists on the sides of the chair in which they sat together.

The holiday drew to a close. At the end of July they went back to Glasgow. John went back to work.

The twins had begun teething. Jean was a quiet child, and negotiated this new stage in life with ease. Not so her sister. For her it was a struggle. One tooth came through, but with a great deal of pain. When the second one began to come, it was worse. Her crying became screaming. Maggie tried every remedy advised by her mother, neighbours, friends. Nothing was helping. Visiting a doctor meant reducing the food on the table, but it had to be. He had nothing to offer but hope that the tooth would break through, and ease the pain. John and Maggie took turns trying to comfort the child, while the other tried to calm Wee John and Jean, both bewildered by the constant screaming.

By the evening of August 1st, the baby's temperature was rising, but not worryingly so. Next morning it was higher. No thermometer was needed to indicate what everyone could see. The child had a fever. In desperation they went back to the doctor. He was a kindly man with many years of experience. He had seen this progression from teething distress to high fever many times. He was powerless. There simply was no medicine in existence to fight it. As gently as he could, he prepared them for the almost inevitable.

Aching with pain, John took his daughter home. By then her siblings had been sent to their grandmother across the road. The screaming continued. The fever raged. The parents constantly wiped her down with cool water in an attempt to lower her temperature, desperately hoping that the fever would break. Just after midnight, she began to shake uncontrollably. The screaming stopped, as she slipped into unconsciousness. In a hideous quietening the little body convulsed again and again, until the fits slowed down, and then stopped. The life of this little girl had ended.

John and Maggie sat holding their dead child as the heat of the fever, and then the warmth of her body, turned cold. And so they sat all night.

In the morning, John attended to what needed to be done. Maggie went to see her other children.

On the 5th of August, as the flags waved and the crowds cheered, John and Maggie Connell buried their daughter. They were alone in their grief, isolated from each other, and from the world around them.

Chapter Thirteen

The time between the date of enlistment and the call-up was one of disconnection. Nothing was as it had been; nothing familiar was beyond tomorrow. Hector's father boasted. Graham's parents raged. David's parents and Hector's mother drew into themselves. The easy family patterns they had all known were already destroyed by gunfire.

The village community tore apart. When the war was over, people theorised that the division which emerged in communities was between those who had gone and those who had not, those who had lost loved ones and those who had not. But the split was deeper and had begun much earlier, originating with Kitchener; those who supported his guilt-ridden demand, and those who did not. The real divide was between those for whom the call to war was clothed in patriotism, and those for whom it wore a shroud.

On the night before they were due to leave, David went back to the house he loved. Jack Weir looked out of the window and saw him sitting on the old wooden garden seat. He turned to his wife, and the wordless understanding of parents passed between them, 'Thank God ours are too young.'

Johnnie, the plumber from the cottage over the wall, soon appeared. These two young men sat in jagged silence. Isolated together, they wondered if they would ever sit in this garden again. The river ran so peacefully. The trees were shedding their leaves, the russets and the golden scattered across the grass. It was impossible to believe that where they were going could exist in a world of such quiet.

In the morning, David left at 5am. He just could not face the parting. He picked up his bag and left, never looking back. His parents had heard him moving around. Lying stiff and apart in their bed, they realised what he was doing, but they did not know how to reach him. What could they say? They could not risk an argument. They could not plead with him. They could not say they were proud. Their son leaving home to go to war, in silence, was less terrible than him leaving in anger. As soon as the door latch fell they hurried to the window, hoping he would turn round, hoping they could smile and wave and wish him well, but the empty weeks of no words had gone too deep. He walked on wrapped in misery. They stood trapped at the window in despair.

He met his two pals at the steamer which would take them to Glasgow. The brass band was indulging in a grotesque orgy of celebration. 'Rule Britannia,' 'Land of Hope and Glory,' 'Dolly Gray,' 'Tipperary'. Flags, cheering, wishing the young men well – no one saw it as other than a great big adventure.

Except Hugh Currie. He looked at the threesome, and when their eyes met, he saw that they were not caught in this wild excitement. He wondered why not. He had been when he was their age. But, he reflected bitterly, when he had joined the army there had been no one saying anything to counter what was preached in every classroom, every music hall, every parish; 'King and Country' meant glory, adventure, success. Britain had not fought a continental war in eighty years. A skirmish here, a skirmish there, but that was all. Nothing to worry about.

After South Africa, British failures hidden behind lucky escapes were not so easy to conceal. Men had come back with the truth. What Hugh Currie saw in the forced smiles of David, Graham and Hector was uncertainty. They did not view the future quite as he had. Doubts, albeit not many, had been sown by disillusioned men like John Golden.

Graham's sister, Isobel, was there to see her brother off, but in truth she seemed more interested in wishing Hector well. She liked the idea that she had a young man brave enough to go to war. The night before, they had met, and, in the hush, both knew that when he came home they would step out together. He held her hand, and gently kissed her. They promised to write. Neither of them considered there would be any other future.

As the steamer pulled away, the threesome looked back at the land they knew so well. It always surprised them how different it looked from the water. The houses were so tiny, a strip along the coastline. Even the big houses were dwarfed by the hill behind. They could see the sheep happily munching the grass near the tops. Two small figures were just visible on their way up the hill, two of the girls at the farm. Such a change, even only a few weeks earlier, would have been unimaginable.

The steamer went to Glasgow passing the shipyards on the way. No longer building liners, they were building warships. The hammering had taken a violent turn.

In Glasgow they were herded on to a train to go south. The train was full of thousands of young men from all over Scotland, setting out for training at an army camp in a place called Bedford. No one had yet located it on a map. Many of the young men were from Argyll, some were Gaelic speaking. Others came from further north and belonged to a different regiment, the Seaforths. They spoke a strange language which they called Doric. The Glasgow lads were there with their language too, in some cases impenetrable to all but themselves. It suddenly occurred to David, that, although they were all going to the same place, they had all come from very different places with very different lives. Their paths would never have crossed until the assassination in that far-off land had brought them together. They were a community forged by chance.

Almost on cue to reinforce this, singing began. Young men were accustomed to singing. They sang in church. They sang as they walked to work in the cities. They sang in the hills and on the fishing boats. And so, on the train, they sang. The songs they knew were soon increased by songs which were only now becoming familiar. It was not surprising 'Mademoiselle from Armentières' was not known at home. It was coarse. Not wanting to be left out of the group, David joined in singing words he did not like.

Carlisle, Preston, Crewe. This was new land to everyone on that train. They looked out on cities half hidden in smoke. The land was flat with little distance between the towns. Not somewhere David would want to live. He thought of the garden he loved, but the pain was too sharp.

Graham listened to the conversation at his end of the carriage. Many of his new-found friends had also signed up without their parents' knowledge. He heard in their stories what he too had done. Some of the furious parents had gone to demand that their sons' enlistment was cancelled, but that was not to be. The arguments which had raged in his farmhouse were no different from those in the cities and the fishing cottages. His new-found community was bound together by the belief that they were right and their parents were wrong. They would prove who was right.

Hector sat silent. For the first time he began to have serious doubts. Would he ever see Isobel again? When they had been standing at the station, he had heard the words, 'I'm proud of you, son. You show them what we're made of.' The words rang hollow, and then they stung. Hearing his father's words from someone else, they were empty. They had been spoken by a mother while the boy's father had turned away. He looked at the little group of three, and what he saw tore at him. Before he had left that morning, his father had talked on and on. Pride, loyalty, country, king, even the deceased queen and empress was doing her bit. His mother had made his breakfast and then handed him a bundle of oatcakes she had baked. He loved her oatcakes, and as she held them out to him, in her eyes he read they were her final gift.

Somewhere beyond Crewe, he unfastened his pack and took out the bundle. He opened it and removed one, carefully wrapping the rest away. He looked at it and saw not just an oatcake, but her hands making it. He had watched her do this hundreds of times. He remembered being told to go and play when she was baking, and he, at table height, had been trying to get some of the mixture. A little older and in charge of the griddle suspended above the fire, his little fingers would snatch up the broken off bits. Always when he went up the hills to search for a lost sheep in winter, she made up a little bundle wrapped in cloth for him to take. He touched the oatcake and felt her hands. Desolate, he tasted her baking.

Johnnie-from-over-the-wall was a few carriages away with his own age group, many of whom were apprentices in different trades. This was a holiday till Christmas when they would return to their jobs. He found two other plumbers, and they happily exchanged their knowledge. It interested them how differently things were done, and only slowly did they all realise this was connected to the land through which they laid their pipes. Living in a small community, it had not occurred to any of them that other communities were built on different rock formations.

Once they arrived at Bedford, they marched to barracks. David found himself in a room with a whole group of young men. He had no brothers, so had never shared a room. Graham and Hector came from overcrowded farmhouses. To them this was just a variation of home.

The training began. Many youngsters from the cities were underfed and underweight, and so the building of stamina was a priority. Races were run and the threesome excelled. The sergeant was a bully, and each time David, Graham or Hector exceeded his expectations he demanded more. He wanted them to fail. He needed to ridicule them.

'Would Hugh Currie do this? He is a sergeant,' Hector said.

'I don't think so,' was the reply.

They hated the sergeant. They wanted to humiliate and destroy him, just as he did them. In their short lives, they had never felt this of anyone. Sometimes they discussed how they would go about doing this. They knew their thoughts would not become actions, but there were times when they were so angry that was almost possible. In the release and pleasure they found in talking about it, their brutalising had begun.

Hugh Currie, however, was not there to turn to. He had gone straight to France, where he encountered what he had experienced before. The British army fell back in disarray, until by the autumn of 1914, they were entrenched. The losses were enormous, but the little community in Argyll was untouched. No one had yet been killed. Christmas had come and gone.

1915 saw little change. The training at Bedford continued with long route marches through the English countryside. As farm boys, they itched to examine the soil. At the end of every hour of marching they were permitted a five-minute rest, and while others stretched out wherever they could, the farm lads in the battalion were drawn to looking closely at the land. Here it looked and felt so different. One of their number from slightly further north had a hazy idea of why.

'It's the limestone under the earth that makes it so different. We don't have that.'

'What do we have?'

'Volcanic rock.'

Joining the army had turned into a geology lesson!

In France the regular army lived in trenches of mud, under daily shelling and in constant fear. Nothing in South Africa had prepared them for this.

In April of 1915, gas was used for the first time. Hugh Currie was one of its victims. He was barely able to breathe, and by the end of 1915 he had been sent home. For him the war was finished, but by no means was it over. Anxious parents trod their way to his door to ask of their sons. One look at him stopped their questions. They saw the face of war.

The little family from Glasgow came for their summer holiday. They knew many families in the city whose sons had been lost, and coupled with their own loss, their holiday was not the happy time it had been previously. The nation was gripped in a vice of frightened waiting. Wee John by then was taller than the potatoes and demanding adventures in the hills. His father took him on long walks, but the length of the walk had to be balanced against how long he would manage until he got so tired he had to be carried.

Father and son gathered berries and plants on the hillside to take home to Maggie who was experimenting with the recipes neatly written in an old exercise book she had found in a cupboard.

Jean, meanwhile, sat beside the flowers. She just stroked them or picked them, matching up colours and dressing her dolly in flower outfits.

At the end of 1915, the threesome came home. They were granted four days to see their families before they went to France. They had looked forward to this; it was all they had talked of for weeks, but as the time grew nearer they were unsure. Graham dreaded another row. Hector wanted to see Isobel, but was wary about his parents. He could not purge the scene at the station from his memory. David knew he was now more at one with the views of his parents, but had no idea how to say this.

In the end they nearly did not go. Johnnie-from-over-the-wall insisted. He was going. His mother had told him he had to come home for a few days – there were drains needing fixed. He refused to lie for his village chums. So they set off, filled with anxiety of what lay ahead. First the train then the steamer and their families waiting for them at the pier. Very quickly it was clear everyone was being very careful. No one wanted a quarrel, so no one spoke freely, each isolated in unsaid words. Never had they known such loneliness.

Nothing changed over their days at home. As Hector and Isobel sat on the hillside, she tried to talk to him of their future. He clammed up. In her hurt, she wondered if, while he had been away, he had met a girl he liked more than her. Doubt scraped at her heart, but she was too afraid to ask. Awkwardness grew between them, and they began to sit further apart.

Her brother Graham reassured her that that had not happened. But what he could not explain to her was what he could not express even to himself; that gradually the young recruits had stopped talking of their futures. They had, one by one, lost the assumed certainty of their dreams, the years ahead no longer a given. The tentacles of death had already begun their destruction.

David could not talk to his parents about the confusion of his dual thinking. He still believed in his duty, and thus believed in the rightness of his enlisting, but he had come to see that the flag waving and enthusiasm masked a grim reality. He was afraid, but this he could not say. No more could his parents, so great was their fear. All three sat in their cottage kitchen, their self-imposed silence swirling around them.

On the night before they were to leave, David was drawn to the house he loved, but this time he did not go in the gate. He did not want to take his aching misery into this place of comfort. He stood and looked over the wall. The house stood unchanging, solid, comforting. He loved its shapes. At one point he thought he saw a movement of crimson velvet and a grey cap. He looked closely, but there was no one there. In the evening light the house seemed to be smiling to him. He would come back.

In the morning, the young soldiers said their goodbyes and walked to the steamer. No brass bands now. The death toll had ended that. They recalled how they had stood looking at their coastline, but this time they turned their back on it. They knew where they had to go.

Chapter Fourteen

Carlisle, Preston, Crewe, London, the Channel ports and onto the ferry. As the coast of France drew closer, the Highland lads were becoming excited. They had left their homes for an adventure, and in the safety of the ferry crossing to France were managing to crush down just what that adventure might entail. Before enlisting they wanted to go abroad and meet the local lasses. Today they would not think of coming back heroes. To be a hero there had to be killing, and today was not the day to think of that.

They had a few hours to pass in Calais awaiting the train which would take them to the Somme area of France. Falling in with new-found friends, they made for the nearest *estaminet*, the French word they'd learned for the pub. In Bedford they had learned to drink whisky. At first they had been wary of English pubs, but to their surprise found they had been made welcome. One man had put it succinctly, 'We like the Scots from the countryside, but not them from the city.' They wondered if they would be so well received in Calais. Had not Scotland and France once been allies?

The wine was horrible. The coffee was the next experiment. It was worse. Perhaps the *estaminets* were not for them, after all.

Once on the train across France, the singing swelled to a crescendo. David wondered what the French peasants working in the fields made of this noisy machine, filled with men singing songs they did not know, snaking its way across their land. He joined in the singing, but was more interested in looking out of the windows at how the fields were laid out, what was growing, what machines were in use.

The hours passed slowly. The singing dried up, and in the distance they could hear a rumble, which grew louder with every turn of the wheels.

'That is an odd sort of thunder, French thunder,' wondered Hector aloud. It did not roll as normal thunder does. Rather it was staccato.

'It's the guns,' muttered Graham. No one had spoken of how loud guns would be. He longed for the silence in the hills of his innocence.

Hours later, they reached their destination. Moonlight bathed the land in silver. As they marched to where they would make camp, they could see the farmland spreading out in all directions. Machine guns and artillery had replaced crops, but could not deny the essential beauty of this high plateau.

Nothing prepared them for the noise or the smell. Farm boys had encountered rotting deer left to bloat through the winter. They had smelled dogs, not cleanly shot by farmers protecting their sheep – injured dogs that had crawled away to die. Weeks later they would be found. Farm life breeds strong nostrils. But the stench of decay of men and horses was new, and it was visceral.

They reached their allocated spot, a ravine near the two small communities of Beaumont and Hamel. It was a typical village at the heart of a farming world, not so very different from home. The houses were different, but the community nestled round a small village was no different. What had happened to the people whose homes and farms and lives this belonged to? Where had they gone? It occurred to many of these farm lads that the French farm boys living here would have spent the summer of 1914 just like them, working on the land and seeking out the local girls in the evenings. Where were they now? Where were the girls? David tried to imagine what it would be like if the nations of the world, with thousands of men and their weapons, had turned up in his village. He would have joined up, as the boys here must have done, to defend their land. But for him it was very different from his French counterparts. His land had not been invaded. He knew where his parents were. They were at home working the land, but where were the parents of the French lads who had joined up?

Displacement from his family and place of origin instilled in him a loneliness greater than anything David could imagine. He looked at the white walls of an abandoned French farmhouse, and longed for the house he loved at home.

The volunteers who had signed up in 1914 had been trained and brought to the Somme area to break through the German lines. During these two years, the Germans had dug deep underground bunkers and strong fortifications to defend the high ground. The Pals battalions, as the groups of friends who had enlisted together were called, had been brought here to do what the regular army had failed to do.

Day after day the twisted rage of the guns made preparation for the assault.

The men waited and they waited. They wrote home. Time was heavy. Each morning David watched the sunrise, but that only served to remind him of what he had left behind. In the trenches did it matter where the sun rose? What mattered was that each sunrise might be his last. The tension grew. Few spoke, each alone in his own thoughts.

It was for this that they had come.

On the evening of June 30th, the men were told by the British generals all would be well. The Germans in the trenches facing them had been destroyed, and there would be not even a rat left alive. It would be easy. Some of the men seized upon this assurance, believing that by the next day they would be writing home as heroes.

The night dragged. The men waited. At 7.20 on the morning of July 1st, a massive explosion destroyed one of the enemy fortifications. Ten minutes later the whistle blew, and the men climbed out of their newly dug trenches. The Germans, hidden underground below their own shattered trenches, came out of their deep bunkers and watched as the British soldiers, massed into a line, walked towards them. Once again the High Command had bungled. They had had no idea that the enemy had been underground.

The young soldiers made their way onto the field. Over the guns they could hear the screaming of the dying, some of them only yards from where they had begun their attack, never having fired a shot.

When eventually their turn came David, Graham and Hector moved as they had done in their poaching youth, almost telepathically, instinctively, every sinew straining to avoid the guns as they had evaded the gamekeeper. Gradually they lost sight of each other, each isolated in his own instinct for survival, as the inferno raged on.

'What the hell happened?' when they found each other again.

'Not a rat left alive?'

They had grown up in a world of deference to those older and of higher rank. It was a deference laced with trust. But here they saw starkly that their seniors did not know better. They could not be trusted. They made judgements born of inexperience and arrogance.

'This is what John Golden said happened in South Africa.

Once I asked Hugh Currie, and he only half answered, but I could tell he thought those in charge were out of their depth. They could not imagine the enemy could develop something they themselves had not thought of. And now, for the most part, it is those same generals who are here.'

For four and a half months, the battle raged. Men sent against machine guns fed by a never-ending supply of bullets. The bodies lay unburied, turning black, yellow, red.

In November a new strategy had been devised. Instead of sending men weighed down with heavy packs walking into the enemy in broad daylight, how about sending the fastest, carrying very little, under darkness?

The runners were brought in to do this. In the early hours of November 13th, David, Graham and Hector tore across the hill, dealt with the enemy in the first trench with knives, and then ran on to make the breakthrough expected four months earlier. The Battle of the Somme was over.

They had survived. They wrote home, but they did not tell the truth.

During that long summer Jack Weir and his family grew their vegetables, and watched as the postman delivered the telegrams. It was the habit in the village that when a death occurred everyone visited the grieving family. This was different. The parents of those who had not been killed could not visit the parents of those who had been. The village divided. Those broken by grief grouped together in an ever growing number, while the others stayed apart. Graham, Hector and David's parents often came to Jack Weir's garden as, without sons in arms, their sons had become his too. The mother and sister of Johnnie-from-over-the-wall were also part of this group. Secretly as they watched the agony of friends and neighbours, they were riven with a tortured guilt they could not bear to harbour, that their sons were still alive when so many others were not, overwhelming and unexpressed relief that this was so, and terror of what tomorrow would bring.

An unquiet quiet descended on this once happy place.

When John, Maggie and the children arrived that summer, they kept to themselves. Wee John particularly whooped and yelled in excitement whenever he got here, but the joyous noise of childhood, it too, had been killed by the guns. And so the family kept a distance from the community they had come to love. They walked high on the hills where no one could hear them. The conversation between the women was muted also. It was hard to think of a better world to strive towards with so many people overwhelmed by grief.

The insane noise of the summer of 1916 in France was echoed by whispered shreds at home.

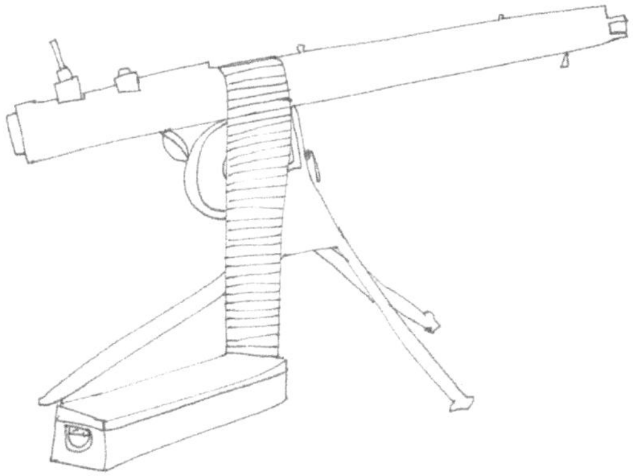

Chapter Fifteen

Knit one. Purl one. Knit one. Purl one.

Knitting black wool by the light of a paraffin lamp was not easy. Catherine Weir clacked her needles next to the fire, logs spitting as the coal nestled round them. She was keeping the home fires burning.

With no sons at the front, Mrs Weir knitted. Scarves, socks, jerseys – she sat outside all summer in the evening light, knitting. Now as the winter crept in, she continued. If she stopped, just because it was becoming difficult to see the stitches in the shadowed room, she felt guilty. The village lads were facing heaven knows what. What were sore eyes?

She knitted for 'her' four boys, David, Graham, Hector and Johnnie-from-over-the-wall. As she completed each item, she took it to the parents who sent it off. Struggling to see the stitches, she made mistakes she had not made before. Trying to fix them in order that the knitting was perfect often made it worse. She reached a compromise; she would leave a little mistake in each so that every item was unique. She took it further by knitting into each scarf the initials of who it was going to. To do that she had to knit in the late morning when the winter sun was at its highest. She knitted in hope, and she knitted in fear.

The rift between her and Jack took a long time to heal. One evening Jack had come home with the news of another village death in France.

'Why can't they just talk to each other? Why can't they find a solution? This is self-destruction.'

'How do people talk when they don't know the words?' whispered Catherine. Both husband and wife stared at one another. What of their silence? What of their life together? How could they breach that wall?

Some days later Catherine came home to find her husband on the garden bench. He was reading a letter, his shoulders heaving as he did so. She moved closer and listened.

Why don't they understand each other? Why don't they talk?

She heard the words in the letters she had written to him years before expressing her views on the household in Edinburgh where she had worked. When she had sent these words to him, she believed that their life together would be different. They would always talk as they had written. And yet she had let a wall divide them and she did not know why. She knew she carried as much responsibility for that wall as he had by arranging the house without talking to her first. But she did not know how to reach over it.

She sat beside him on the bench. She took the letter from him and folded it neatly.

Barely above a whisper, 'I wanted to believe you meant what you said in your letters, but when you did what you did I was afraid.'

Isolated, frightened, reaching to each other they measured every word.

'Can we again be the people who wrote these letters do you think? Can we go back to those days?'

'I heard as I came through the gate what you could not say to me. I heard your truth. Do you understand mine?'

Timidly he took her hand. In their eyes was their future. It would take time. It would take talking; talking without recrimination. On the garden bench a new layer in their relationship was laid down.

The winter of 1916 was cruel. The village was no longer immune. Hugh Currie, sent home barely able to breathe, had not survived. He was buried in the local cemetery, and to that grave came the families of those who had died in Belgium or France, and lay there unvisited. Only the fatally injured were buried at home.

And as if in a different world, village life went on. The carriage hirer, Mr McDirarmid, suffered a freak accident to one of his horses. It was tethered to a carriage and suddenly bolted down the pier. When it reached the edge it stopped, but the carriage somersaulted over the animal's head, dragging it backwards into the water. The horse drowned. The carriage was brought back up, repaired and sent back into service. The price of the four-mile journey to the nearest town increased.

The last resident of the community who could remember the days before the coming of the big houses, died at the age of ninety eight. He had never once left the peninsula. A new doctor came to the village. Debates raged about raising the school leaving age to fourteen. A weird occurrence in the sky appeared in the early spring; a meteor, a comet, an omen? People old and young discovered chewing gum brought from across the Atlantic.

In France, the men dug in to withstand the cold and await the next move. This did not, of course, mean they were safe. Shelling went on day and night. The threesome were still together, and each of them wrote home once a week. They wrote on different days, so that the families could read all the letters and piece together a week's stories. There was a great deal of laughter at the story of Hector going into an *estaminet*. A bit of banter had led to the tables being pushed back against the wall, and him teaching an eightsome reel. A piper had been sent for. The reel grew in numbers, and soon had spilled into the street. Never had a quiet French street seen such a ceilidh. Wine, dancing, singing, bagpipes, laughter five miles from the slaughter.

Farm lads could not stop themselves from touching the soil. This earth was good earth. Crops would grow well here. Not a place for sheep, the grass would be too lush. It was rolling land, easy to plough, seemingly limitless. Above it, the sky was almost a complete hemisphere of blue. Of this, too, they wrote home.

By April of 1917 the next move was ready. Near Arras a breakthrough was planned. The Germans had a particularly strong defence there, as it comprised high ground and a chemical works essential to the war machine. Flanked by the Canadians, the Highland Division comprising, among other regiments, the Argyll and Sutherland Highlanders and the Seaforth Highlanders from the northeast of Scotland, took their places in the line. Johnnie-from-over-the-wall wondered if his fellow plumbers from the train to Bedford were there, but dismissed the thought. They were probably long gone. Lined up for the second wave were two battalions of the Argyll regiment and one of the Seaforths. In front, in the first wave of the attack, were the Royal Scots, the Gordons and two more battalions of Seaforths. Pipers and kilts. If the breakthrough was made, no doubting which nation had done it.

Hector, Graham, David and Johnnie-from-over-the-wall were in the line. Was it harder to be in the first wave or the second? In the first wave you faced the enemy, still hoping they might not be there. In the second, you had heard that they were.

Waiting to go, the lads stood silent, each aware that this time their luck might run out. Before each attack, regret seeped through David. He wanted to go back to those days of 1914 to do it differently. He may still have enlisted, but he would have tried to mend the family fracture before he left. Graham had long given up wanting to be a hero. He just wanted to go home. Hector, too, had lost all taste for the adventure for which he had come. Johnnie-from-over-the-wall thought of his sister, and how proud she was of him. Could she ever understand?

The whistle blew at 7am and the first wave moved forward. Thirty minutes later, the second wave advanced. Into the hail of bullets they ran. They fought their way past the line seized by the first wave, and on they went to their objective which they also took, to enable the third line of enemy defence to be taken the following day.

At nightfall, David waited for his pals. They did not come.

'You there, give a hand, and get out there to help bring in the injured.' A task they all dreaded, but tonight he went without rancour. He found Hector first. A clean bullet hole in his head; at least it had been immediate. He laid him out as in a burial and kneeled beside him, numb.

'Get on with it. Nothing you can do for him.'

It felt inevitable. About a hundred yards off was Graham, almost sliced in two. Machine guns can do this with seemingly mathematical precision. With his innards still spilling out, he was harder to arrange in a dignified way. The best David could do was close his pal's eyes.

Mechanically he carried out his orders. He knew that once he was finished, if he sought permission to go out into no man's land again to bring in two of the dead, he would be refused. Two soldiers fewer. The grim arithmetic demanded he be kept alive. And so, without a word to anyone, he went back to them, Hector first. He lifted him onto his shoulders and carried the dead man back. If challenged, he would say he had been alive when he lifted him. No one challenged him, and he brought Hector behind the line. He went again. Graham was much more difficult, but somehow he managed. He found a spade and began to dig with the speed that only farm lads can do. In silence he buried his pals.

His winter of loneliness began.

He wrote home, but he did not tell. His parents read his letter without immediately realising there was something missing. They were always so keen to hear of him that they sometimes skimmed over the bits about the other two. When they read his letter again, they knew. They retreated into isolation. Until the telegrams arrived, they could not speak.

Graham and Hector's parents separately watched each day for the postman, but he did not come. No letter, but also no telegram. To fend off their terror, they reassured one another that the letters must have gone missing. Days passed, with each set of parents afraid to go to the others, David's most of all because they knew.

When the blinds in the two houses were drawn down, four more parents swelled the group of anguish.

In the July of that summer, the Connells had come to the house again. Once again, the village was not as it had been. The little house, the hills and the shore were cloaked in silent collective grief.

Amidst this seemingly endless march to destruction, children grew up unaffected by the distress in the adult world. The joy of Wee John running in the garden was infectious. It momentarily lifted Mrs Weir out of the loss of 'her' boys. Jean, now almost four, made flower necklaces for anyone who came her way. And in a cot slept a little girl of two months. Named after her dead sister Williamina Gemmell Connell, Beth's mother had been born and brought to this house which she was to know for the next ninety-four years.

Chapter Sixteen

The war was over, and by the winter of 1918 the survivors were coming home, not all at once, but randomly piecemeal. David was in no hurry. Going home without his pals was terrifying. When his turn came, he was frozen with fear. Train, steamer, train, steamer and he was home. His parents met him and quietly they walked up the road.

Later, 'I'll need to go and see them.' There was no need to say who.

His mother's gentle words were razors. 'They may not want to see you. It has been very hard.'

He nodded.

He made his way to the first farm. Up the path he went, every footstep heavy. One of the blinds was still drawn down. He knocked on the door. It was opened. He stood in silence.

'Who is it?' came from the back of the house.

'David.'

Silence. And then Hector's mother came. She had aged. Her body stooped, her face hardened.

'What do you want? Why are you here?' Just a hint of emphasis on the second 'you'.

'I came to see you. I carried him in, and I buried him.' He was not looking for gratitude, just something of their shared years.

Marble, she stood frozen.

'Just go,' said Hector's father. 'Don't come back.'

David wanted to hurl, 'Proud of him now are you?' But he didn't.

He walked away. He had the second farm to visit. Crushed by what had just happened, he had to get this over with. Up the second path he went. He knocked. This time both parents opened the door. They had seen him coming.

'Will you come in and tell us? Please.'

This was in many ways more difficult. He explained what had happened, but when it came to him finding Graham, he did not tell the truth. He could not utter the obscenity of their son's death. In time silence crept in to the still room, and then muffled sobbing. It was time to go.

The village picked up again. Returning soldiers went back to work. The grief in some houses slowly lifted, but in others it grew in unspoken secrecy. David went back to working on the land. In the evening, he tramped the hills alone. No matter where he went, his pals were there, happy and laughing as they had once been, but he could not join in. He tried meeting the girls of the village, but that too was strained. Isobel resented him just because he had survived. At one point she accused him of cowardice. He had been hiding. That is why he survived, and her Hector had not. He was so stung he almost blurted out the truth, but he did not, not in defence of himself, nor out of compassion for them, but out of loyalty to his pals. He would not use them, nor would he describe the indescribable.

Slowly it came to him that he could no longer live in the village. The idea just rose from somewhere deep, one day when tending a sick sheep in the hills. He had brought it comfort, and for the first time in so long, felt he had done something of worth. The guilt of coming home and taking up his life as if nothing had happened was overwhelming. He worked, and he sat at home, isolated with knowledge, and lonely with guilt.

Johnnie-from-over-the-wall had also survived. On winter nights secluded by darkness they sat in Jack Weir's garden. Sometimes they talked, and sometimes they did not. Johnnie-from-over-the-wall adapted better. He went back to his business and avoided talking about the war. 'I'm here to fix the drains,' was his rallying cry, and thus he re-entered the village community. David, working alone on the land, had no such bridge.

One night as he sat in Jack Weir's garden, he sensed the old walls speak to him. 'You can go back.' He had read that cemeteries were being laid out on the Western Front, and workers from Britain were being employed to do this. Many of the old soldiers who, like David, found that they could not fit into life at home had gone back to Belgium and France. They were with people who understood. Burying their pals eased the guilt of surviving.

He said nothing to his parents to begin with, but the idea grew inside him. When he did speak of it, he was surprised at how they took it. They had watched his suffering over the months, and although they did not want him to go, they knew that he could not continue as he was. They wanted him to stay, but they knew he had to go. He wanted to be happy staying, but knew he never would. His dream of going away to have an adventure, and then in time coming home to the house he had always thought of as home – that too had been destroyed by the guns.

He waited until the War Memorial was unveiled. A number of families in the village decided on a simple Celtic cross with names on three sides of its base. It was set in a sloping garden facing the village hall, where on the day of its opening, David and his two pals had raced as children. Along one side of the garden ran a low wall with a decorative iron fence, creating a distinct and sacred place.

The day of the unveiling in January 1921 was ferocious. The rain hammered, and a fierce wind tore up the river. The dedication service took place inside the hall, and then the villagers walked to the memorial for its unveiling.

Soon after this David left, promising to come back. He went to France, and settled into his new life. He managed to get posted to the area where he had buried his pals. One grave was still in existence, but the other had been destroyed. Hector's name would go on the Wall of the Missing.

In time, David married a young French widow whose husband had been killed. Before her marriage she had lived on a farm with her parents, and she had come back with them to reclaim their land. Many of the cemeteries were laid out in the French fields, and in one of them they met. His French was weak. Her English non-existent, but what bound them was shared understanding of grief and loss. Slowly they built a life together.

David regularly came back to visit his parents. He urged them to come to him. They went once, but only once. The war had separated them. For so many it never really ended.

After his parents died, he no longer had the pull to return, but he never forgot.

Once when Beth was a little girl, she saw someone she had never seen before sitting on her grandfather's garden seat.

'There's an old man on your seat, Grandpa.'

'Oh!' He looked. 'Oh,' he said again.

He joined David on the bench. What passed between them Beth never knew, but the house heard every word. He had lived with the horror locked inside him until his wife died, and in his grief, had touched the burden of that earlier unspoken loss he had carried silently for four decades. He had come back because he knew that in this garden, and only in this garden, could he finally tell the story of what had happened on that terrible day.

Beth watched the two men, her grandpa and a stranger, on the garden seat, and even as a child, she knew that whatever was being said was very important. The stranger talked and her grandpa listened, only occasionally speaking. As the afternoon wore on, these two old men sat quietly smoking their pipes. When David left, he lifted a small stone from the path, and slipped it into his pocket.

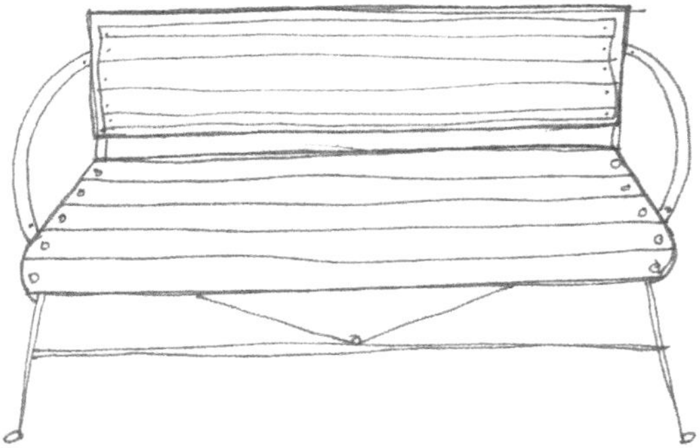

Chapter Seventeen

Beth had first gone to the Western Front when she was researching her family tree. In preparation she had read in depth on the battles which had taken place in the locations she was setting out to visit, and had become very familiar with the black-and-white images of destruction which appeared in book after book.

Nothing prepared her for the reality of what she saw. The Somme area of France was simply beautiful. Gentle rolling farmland, lush greenery, crops swaying in the breeze amidst a comfortable quiet everywhere she looked. It was a delightful place through which to walk and cycle. This once tortured land had reclaimed its very self.

Her second shock was the cemeteries. No photograph conveys their peace. She could sit in any one of them for hours, and feel its calm.

From her reading she knew that a decision had been made not to bring the dead home. The reasons were twofold; one was logistical, and the other, that rows of coffins would have done nothing to encourage the war effort. Neither the dead themselves, nor their families, featured in the decision.

The reaction at home had been outrage. To calm the situation, and also in order to not repatriate the bodies, the solution was, as far as possible, to identify where each man was buried. Cataloguing of the makeshift graves fell to a small team, determined to be able to give at least some degree of comfort to the thousands upon thousands of distraught families.

When the war was over, cemeteries were laid out to a design reflecting the order and beauty of an English country garden. The headstones are identical; there is no difference between the grave of a career officer and that of a conscripted teenager. Each cemetery had to be configured such that the line of headstones would follow the contours of the land, and centre on the War Stone and the Cross of Sacrifice. On each stone are the name, age and regiment of the dead soldier, and on most of them there is a cross. On many of the stones there is no name; this man, so badly damaged that he was beyond identification, is Known unto God.

The cemeteries are beautifully maintained. Originally laid out by men who had survived the war and could not settle at home, their descendants have carried on in the family job which still passes, even now a century later, father to son.

The third shock for Beth was the Memorials to the Missing. Men Known unto God were still human remains. The Missing, however, were the group who had just ceased to be. Of them there was nothing left; not a hair, not a nail, not a fragment of bone – nothing. These men could not have graves; there was nothing to bury. All that remained were their names, and so memorials were built to the Missing. The names of these men are engraved on monuments, or on walls framing the cemeteries. Touching a name is akin to touching a gravestone. This man once lived and loved and experienced human touch. His name on the wall was, and continues to be, as significant to his family as is a headstone.

In the early summer of 1914, the French people living in this area had no idea what was about to overwhelm them. They went about their business in this lovely part of the world, with the same regularity as their ancestors had done for centuries. Six months later their rich farmlands were ripped asunder, transformed into a world no longer of crops, but of trenches and hastily constructed graves. Four years of agony had begun.

When the war was over, and the farmers returned to their shattered land, they found the dead. The British and the French agreed that these graves would become permanent. Scattered across the landscape, bodies which had lain unburied for months or years also had to be interred, and for them new cemeteries were designed. All the war graves were given to Britain 'in perpetuity'.

Sitting in a cemetery in France one day, Beth's thoughts turned to other places of tragedy she had visited in her own country. They hold no sense of peace. Glencoe and Culloden are still tortured. In neither is there a glimmer of comfort. Here it was different.

She wondered if it was the beauty of the land itself which made the difference, but no, Glencoe has its own stately grandeur. She imagined this area without the cemeteries and shuddered. If the dead had been put into mass graves, as they had been in previous centuries, the land around her would be cold and lonely. The Somme is a place of comfort, not in spite of the cemeteries, but because of them.

These men had been buried together. From all over the world they had come, men of different skin colour, different languages and different religions. They were men with very different stories, and when they talked of home, they saw in their mind's eye different images of what that word meant. Despite these differences, they were also a community bound by their experience even before they came to fight. They had all once known the innocence of childhood. They had all known sunrise and the hope of a new day. They had all dreamed of their futures.

They lay here a community of the dead, bound together by the obscenity of what they had known together in this land. At home Hugh Currie was buried in the local cemetery, alone. He was not with his pals. He was not with anyone who understood. Here they were buried surrounded by land which gradually became agricultural again. People came back here to live and work the fields. On a daily basis, the farmers saw the graves. The cemeteries were the silent witness to what had happened. Here the men were not forgotten. They became part of the lives of the people who came back.

When Beth found Graham's grave, she kneeled on the grass, and touched the name on the stone. He had come from her village, had attended the school she herself had gone to. She paused, not sure what to do next, and then, as if it was the most natural thing in the world, she sat down, made herself comfortable and told him the village news for the last hundred years, with specific details of who had lived in his house after his parents had left. She had brought a plant from his garden, and dug it in beside his grave. The twin threads of belonging to home and belonging with the men he had fought alongside is what gave the cemetery solace.

She sought out Hector on the Wall of the Missing, and after telling him the village news, she described to him Graham's gravestone. It was not easy to tell them of David's life after the war, but it had to be done, and to each of them she described David as an old man, sitting on the garden seat they had all known.

And if one sat long enough in the cemeteries, the voices of the dead could be heard. What did they say? Did they regret? Did they warn? Did they teach? Were they pleased people had not forgotten them, and for a hundred years had come, trying to make sense of the senseless waste?

These young men had gone so full of optimism, and here they lay. In the cemeteries she could not banish their emotional journey: had they travelled from elation to regret? Carried along by the national mood, not experienced enough to think through the consequences of their choices, or had there been words said in anger or stubbornness with the consequent pain they had inflicted on those they loved – did they regret?

She thought of choices she had made in her own life which had withered into regret. Snatches of her own voice, stubborn and determined, shocked her. Did I really do that? Did I really say that? How could I have been so stupid and so cruel? She pushed the remembrances down. She would think of them another day. Instead she turned to philosophy – that was much easier: how on earth do we as humans know if we are making choices for the right reasons? Would the soldiers, pushed to their limits, have any clearer understanding of this?

When she came home, she missed the cemeteries.

Time had moved on. And now years later, in this strange world of her isolation, she missed their sense of community even more. On the hill one afternoon, knowing that this is where David, Graham and Hector had walked, she met her new-found friend with his dog, and was momentarily surprised at how pleased she was to see him.

'How have you been?' he asked.

'Fine,' she replied and then with no preamble asked, 'What do you think of the theory that a place has meaning only through the eyes of the beholder? Or might it be as it is, because of those who have previously lived in it?'

He appeared not in the least surprised by the abruptness of such a question. 'Have you ever gone to look at a house you might be thinking to live in, and everything in it is exactly what you want, and yet you can't get away fast enough? Or conversely have you been in a house which is completely wrong marked against your list of essentials, but you feel its warmth and kindness?'

'Yes,' she replied.

'That can only be if places hold their stories. Why do you ask?'

She explained her hours of thinking about the Western Front.

'I think the cemeteries add to the beauty of the land, partly through their own loveliness, and partly through the stories of every man who lies there. If this is true, a place develops an identity at least in part by those who have passed through it, and in the case of these men, who also never left it.'

'Yes,' he said, 'and it is true of a house also.'

The conversation rolled on, and much later Beth sat alone in her garden. She thought of her family far away. She thought of her friends, some in the village, some in the city where she had worked, and others scattered all over the world. Each belonged to a community she was part of, her family by birth and upbringing, her professional friends by values which had informed their working lives, friends by their shared interests.

Sitting on the old bench in the garden at home, she knew she was part of another community; those who had lived in this house, who had carried it with them wherever they went, and had left part of themselves here.

What would they say if she could organise a picnic for them all? Which part of the house or the garden would they seek out? She chuckled at how they might argue over who was getting the seat. Who would climb the apple tree with its branches spreading over the wall? Who would offer thoughts on the potatoes growing in their rows, and the tomatoes on their canes in the greenhouse? Would a strange man she did not know turn out to be the architect checking on his building?

The old house would draw together its family, many of them strangers to each other, and as Beth found her place amidst the merrymakers, her loneliness continued to slip away.

Chapter Eighteen

By the 1920s, the old house had stood for nearly sixty years. It had not aged. No wrinkles on the walls, its window trim and the wooden roofline varied with the years, sometimes brown and sometimes green. The walls were always white. Because it faced south rather than east unlike the other houses in the village, it was very distinct when looked at from the river. High on the hill, it stood proud. The fields stretched upwards behind it, and over the wall, beside the little cottage with no view, an orchard grew. Its trees had matured by then, and the branches closest to the wall knew no legal bounds as they reached south to the sun. The plums and the apples quickly disappeared.

Inside the houses, there had been few changes. None at all in the smaller houses, but in the main house, even before the war, Mr Leitch had brought in one huge change. Electricity. That was the future. Once he had moved out, and Jack and Catherine had moved in, Jack Weir was the first gardener in the village to have this new invention. At first they did not use it. Catherine in particular was afraid it might cause a fire, and so when she was knitting she did so outside, or by the paraffin lamp. In time, however, they had come to like the ease of the flick of the switch. Their eldest daughter regularly invited her friends to see the magic light. Her brothers took it for granted.

They had settled into the house with their young children, the rift between them gradually scarring over.

The house too was happy. It rather liked its occupants. Jack Weir with Catherine upstairs and John Connell and Maggie downstairs. Little did it know it was settling into a quarter-century tenancy upstairs, and a half century downstairs. But that indeed was what happened.

To the little house underneath, the Connells came as often as they could. Wee John found a friend in Neil Weir, only two years older. These two were inseparable, and through Neil, Wee John came to know many of the other boys in the village. They took him into the hills where he learned the gentle act of poaching. They trapped rabbits. They climbed trees. Sometimes they asked him about his life in Glasgow, but no matter how he described it, he knew it was narrow compared with what they had.

The village had a boys' football team by the early 1920s, and in summer, matches were arranged of locals versus visitors. Wee John was in a category all his own. Sometimes he was counted a visitor, and sometimes a local. He rather liked that. He often went to the farm with Neil and helped with the milk delivery. After the cows were milked, the liquid was loaded into huge cans, and then onto a horse-drawn cart. The roads had not been sealed, and they could be muddy and stony. Manoeuvring the horse and cart down a steep rocky lane was not easy. The horse could stumble, the cart overturn, and the milk be lost. The weight of the cart could thrust the animal forward until it lost its grip on the ground. Small children were enrolled into the operation, counterweighting against any false step on the part of the horse. Wee John would come home with a jug of cream, unheard of in the city.

One of the boys had access to a small rowing boat, and out they would go with strict instructions not to go beyond a specific marker in the bay. They did not need to go far. The adventure was the boat itself. The rocking motion, when they were stationary in order to fish, was gentle, and when they pulled hard on the oars, they were riding the Atlantic.

Sometimes they fished from the pier, and sometimes they jumped off it into the churning wash from the steamers. This attracted a huge number of spectators, both on the steamers and on the land. Near the pier was a shop owned by an Italian gentleman who sold ice cream. That was a rare treat. The boys would carry shopping, or run messages, to acquire a halfpenny here, a penny there for this scarce dreamed of feast.

When the days were short, Wee John's favourite time to visit was Hallowe'en. If the wind was coming up the river, it was always a wild night. The trees growled as they were forced beyond their comfort limits. Stories were told of wild boys from thousands of years ago rising from the land to join the world of the spirits on that dark night. The boys of the village, disguised as the wild boys of the past, roamed from house to house singing and dancing.

For all the sophistication and modernity of electricity, people were rooted in this land, part of the community of all those who had gone before them. There is something special about belonging in a small community. It is not always harmony. People argue, and in extreme cases may not speak to their neighbours for months or even years. But they always belong. It has nothing to do with rich and poor, born there or not. All over the world, in every small community, membership is exclusive to the people who love it, and for whom it is home, no matter whether they live there permanently or not.

While her brother roamed the village with his new-found friends, Jean, by the time she was eight, had formed what became a lifelong friendship with a girl along the road. Marion Crawford's father was a friend of Jack Weir, and one day she came to the house with her father. She and Jean took an immediate interest in one another, an interest based on fabric. Maggie's sister, Annie, made clothes for her niece Jean. Annie had always been good at sewing and knitting. She could stand at the window of any one of Glasgow's exclusive shops, work out, and then memorise a pattern. Very occasionally she would take notes. She bought old clothes from the rag-and-bone man, washed them, cut them up and designed dresses. She ripped out old jerseys and then mixed the colours and patterns into new configurations and designs. Jean was the eager recipient of this. She always wore unusual and beautifully designed homemade dresses and skirts. Getting dirty was anathema.

Marion's mother shared this talent, and so Marion was always turned out in very pretty clothes. She, unlike the rest of the village girls who seemed not to care how muddy they got, liked her nice clothes. These two little girls had found a kindred spirit. In Glasgow, Jean strove to keep her clothes uncrushed and clean. In this Highland community, Marion did likewise. No one else in either community could understand them. To both of them, white lace gloves were the most desired item imaginable. They were too young for this to derive from a desire for social standing. They just liked pretty things. Jean had made flower dresses for her dollies from when she was very little, and her own dresses took on the same attraction of rich colours.

The village was a very safe place, and so these little girls graduated from supervision in the garden to walking beyond the gate, but they only chose to do so when the lanes were not too muddy. Just to be on the safe side of remaining spotless, off they would go in heavy shoes, each carrying a little bag with their special shoes – sandals whitened with Blanco, a cross between bleach and white paint. When they reached where they had decided to sit and chat, the heavy shoes came off and on went the sandals. Eight-year-old little ladies became nine-year-old little ladies. By age ten, they had reached the epitome of pleasure; Annie had made them white lace gloves at Christmas.

By the time they were twelve they had learned to sew and knit extremely well, and spent hours designing their own clothes. Jean sometimes accompanied her aunt to look in the shop windows of Glasgow, and then sent her findings by letter to Marion. On each of Jean's visits, there was a long backlog agenda to work through in looking at styles, designs and colours. By then they had realised that different dress styles worked better with different hairstyles. They both had long hair, painfully corkscrewed into tight ringlets every night. In tandem with knitting and sewing, they worked on hair creations never seen anywhere else.

One day Marion announced, 'Wouldn't it be great to earn a living designing clothes and hairstyles?'

'Oh it would, but when we go to work, we will have to sew what we are told to sew.'

'Do you think, someday, girls will be able to invent like we do?' Marion continued, determined there would be a different future.

'Maybe, but not girls like us.' Jean was a realist.

Marion was not so sure. The world was changing in so many ways (after all, soon women would be able to vote).

The third child in the Connell family was Williamina, always called Mina. By 1921, she was just four and content to run around the garden. One day she went exploring. At the bottom of the garden, she had spied a path. Where did that go, she wondered. When no one was looking, she toddled off. Down the side of the wall, along the bottom, and instead of turning back on the third side of the rectangle, she set off on what to her was a magic path to a magic wood. The trees were overhanging on both sides. In July they were in full leaf, so she was quickly invisible. The path went straight for about 150 yards, and then there was a turn followed by a downward slope. She peered round the corner, but found no wicked witch's house. She went round the corner, and on down the path. Another turn! A tentative peer round it, and again the coast was clear. Still no wicked witch! On she went. Ahead of her was a gate, but to reach it she had to climb over an obstacle she had never seen before. A pipe ran vertically down a slope to the level where she was walking. This sewage pipe had been buried beneath the ground, but with erosion caused by the winter rain, it had come to the surface. To four-year-old Mina, it was one of life's great mysteries. She surveyed the situation and worked out that if she climbed up the slope down which it came, she could scramble over it, slide back down on the other side of the pipe to the path level, and reach the gate.

'Mina! Where are you?' A frantic voice.

She had to hurry if she was going to see what was beyond the gate. On her little legs, and using her hands to pull her up, she got up the banking, then over the pipe, and slid down the other side.

'Mina! Mina!' Two voices, this time more frantic.

She was not to be deterred. She reached the gate, but it was on a latch which she could not work out. She looked over the wall to a big drop on the other side. She wondered if she could crawl under the gate, and was just working out how to do this, when her father came running down the path, leapt the pipe and seized her.

'What are you doing? Why did you leave the garden?' He sounded so angry. She began to cry. Many years later she knew that voice; the sound of a terrified parent. But to the little girl at the time, her daddy was angry with her.

'I wanted an adventure. You did not tell me not to follow the path,' came the answer with precise logic. Her voice was tiny.

'I suppose I did not. Where were you going to go?' His voice was calmer.

'Just to see what is on the other side of the gate. Does the witch live there?'

He smiled. He had read her the stories. What could he say?

'I'm going to tell your mother I've found you. Stay here and promise not to move. I'll come back and take you through the gate. Count to ten five times, one finger for each time, but mind and count slowly. Do you promise?'

She nodded solemnly, and he ran off up the path. She counted and watched for him coming back. Sure enough just as she got to ten on the fourth finger, back he came.

The gate opened on to a lane. They turned left along the path to stone steps and then walked on down the lane to the shore.

'I know where we are!' she shrieked excitedly.

'Yes, this is a shortcut we can take now you are big enough for us to not need the pram. Let's go back to the gate and go the other way to see where it takes us.'

They went back up the lane to the gate, and then instead of turning on to the garden path and climbing past the pipe, they continued. A long flight of very steep steps came next. They were too deep for her little legs, and she could not reach the rail, but as she was already so mucky she crawled up them on her hands and knees. At the top of the steps the path curved slightly, and they came out on to the road just beyond the garden gate they always used. For the first time she could connect up places.

Jean and Marion were in the garden, having heard the hue and cry. They were relieved Mina had been found, but that did not stop them recoiling in horror from the mucky little girl, beaming with excitement at her adventure.

The muck was washed off, but what could not be washed away was the first sign of both Mina's spirit of adventure, and her ability to devise a strategy when a problem lay in her path.

When the summer ended, and the family went back to Glasgow, she would sit at the window of the top-floor tenement where they lived, and look to the horizon. Their building was higher than the one across the road, so she could see a long way, and in the distance she told everyone she could see her holiday house, her path and her adventure.

Chapter Nineteen

The 1920s were not profitable years for the Leitch family. Hats were no longer quite so fashionable. To offset the decline in hat manufacturing and sales, part of the house was converted. The third section had been the coach house with the coachman's house above it. Mr Leitch decided to dispense with the coach and horses, and convert that section into a very small house which would bring in another rent. Thus the whole building was divided into four sections. Jack Weir and his family were in the main house, with the Connells using the little flat underneath as their holiday home. One of the other two other sections was rented by George Keddie, who had heard all about the house as he worked with John Connell in the same site of sheet metal working in Glasgow. George and Adela Keddie rented the house on a trial basis to see how they would like it. They came on holiday for fifteen years. The fourth tenant was from Glasgow. Mrs Fulton was Mrs Fulton. No first name permitted.

This pattern was occurring all over the village. The big houses were no longer occupied to the same extent by the wealthy merchants from the city. Some of them had been converted into boarding houses, while others had been converted into holiday homes, both large and small. For the Leitch family, who spent most of the year in Glasgow, having one resident full-time was ideal. They had a caretaker keeping an eye on the property.

By this time Johnnie-from-over-the-wall was living with his young bride a mile or so along the road. His mother and sister continued in their tiny cottage, and then it was only his sister. Jeanie was an independently minded woman, determined not to be a burden on her brother, and to that end, she set about earning a living. She became a laundress. There were many sheets to be washed in the boarding houses, so working very hard from Easter till October could see her through the winter. She had neither hot nor running water, so kettles were boiled on the open fire, the zinc bath was filled, and she trampled the sheets. This task had an added difficulty. She had no flat ground, and so she asked Catherine Weir if she could bring her bath to the only piece of flat ground in the whole garden. Outside the Connells' bedroom window, she joined the other women in their respective baths.

'Do you think this piece of grass was built up this way to be flat for this reason?'

'Well, it wasn't for a croquet lawn.'

Maggie, Catherine and Jeanie-from-over-the-wall were soon joined by Adela Keddie. The baths were filled. The skirts hitched up round the knees, and in they got. It was an opportunity to blether. Around the flat piece of ground were bushes, and adjacent to it the long stone wall. Jeanie-from-over-the-wall was convinced.

'Why put the bushes here if not to hang the washing on? And look, the hooks on the wall are ideal for ropes.'

She might well have been right. Perhaps it had been designed that way, or perhaps it had just evolved. Jack Weir could remember from his childhood the Misses Cook hanging the washing on the bushes, but not on the wall. The wall hooks might have come later, or perhaps they had been too high for the tiny old ladies.

Jeanie-from-over-the wall had joined the local Drama Group. In the winter they rehearsed in each other's houses and put on the plays, usually comedies, in the village hall. It turned out she had a real talent for comic timing. She could stand on a stage, listen to the audience and judge the exact moment to deliver a funny line to maximum effect. It was a rare talent, which often eluded people with dramatic training. In her zinc bath she often spoke lines from the plays she had been in, her sheet trampling at odds with both the gestures of her hands and the drawing-room accent of the characters she played. Catherine Weir could testify to the other women, who had not yet seen her perform, just how entertaining she was. In her own way, Jeanie was a woman of the future. She was self-reliant, and she had charisma.

She loved to read cowboy novels. The village hall had a lending library and she devoured the books she borrowed by the light of the paraffin lamp, or if in dire straits, a candle. She had long given up her dream of a husband and family. Her dream now was America, not to live there, but to see the Wild West. Buffalo Bill had come to Glasgow with his travelling circus, but that had been a long time ago, when she was a child. Her reading had led her to want to see that vast space. She also wanted to know how the people there washed sheets in a land which seemed to have so little readily available water.

Jack Weir became an important figure in the village. He was an elder of the Kirk, a trustee of the hall and one of the driving forces in the community to improve the state of the roads. Many a long dark night other movers and shakers made their way to his house as the planning went on. The old walls of the house heard all the arguments and debates.

Catherine sang in the local choir and was one of the leading members of the Horticultural Society. Bringing all her farming knowledge from her childhood and merging it with the considerable local knowledge, she and a number of others in the community were breaking the traditional norms of planting. No more was it just neeps and tatties. Courgettes, onions, cauliflower, sweet potatoes were underway. How they longed for a greenhouse! There were two very large greenhouses in the village, each belonging to a wealthy family. No one in these families knew how to grow. They were not there long enough to learn, nor were they interested. The village gardeners had learned. Regularly they gathered in an evening to discuss tomatoes, grapes, lettuces and greenhouses. They could grow these crops where they worked, but without a greenhouse it was pointless allowing a few seeds to make it into their pockets before setting off home!

The Keddies fitted in well. Every year when the factories of Glasgow stopped for two weeks in July, the Connells and the Keddies travelled by steamer from Glasgow. Their youngest daughter was a seamstress, and when Jean and Marion learned this, the never-ending fabric conversations took on a new dimension.

The men of the house also gathered. The Glasgow two were heavily involved in trade-union politics, a world which, although quite different from that of Jack Weir, shared many of its same concerns. Sometimes these men would walk to the local pub and discuss the issues of the day. Sometimes they did so in the garden.

One night, Mr Leitch joined them. He had been watching for some time from his window in the next house, and he liked the idea of talking to them. On holiday with his wife and daughter, he missed his male friends in the city.

Through the gate and down the path he came.

'May I join you?'

'Your path, your garden,' George Keddie muttered. It did not bode well.

'Just carry on, and I will pick up the thread of the conversation.' They said nothing.

Eventually, John Connell spoke. As a trade-union negotiator, he had learned how to pick words carefully. Looking round the group, he was aware they all had much to lose if they fell foul of their landlord; he knew he was least likely to cause offence. Bold honesty was the best tactic, he decided.

'We were discussing strike action. You may have very different views from us, and you could decide to evict us if that were to become clear, so to be on the safe side, we would like to hear what you think of what happened in the recent strike.'

Mr Leitch was speechless. He could not decide if it was insolence or honesty. Groping for the words which would have come effortlessly in front of his city acquaintances, he stated that if wages went up profits would go down, and that would be bad for business.

Economics clearly needed to be explained in the simplest of terms.

'Suppose the workers are paid more, they can buy more and so the whole economy expands.'

Mr Leitch had not thought of that one. The two trade unionists brought face to face with his line of thinking were shocked at how its perpetrator did not see its thinness. They had heard many times that this was how the wealthy thought, but they had never actually heard it expressed.

The silence was broken by the boys coming home clutching a still wriggling fish.

Mr Leitch excused himself, and set off home leaving the other men to a discussion on the intricacies of gutting.

A few days later, Mr Leitch met John Connell on the road. He said he had been thinking about what had been said that night, and would like to pursue the discussion. John Connell was caught. He did not want to discuss this with his landlord; he knew of evictions in Glasgow because of diverging political views, but could see no way of avoiding it.

And so a strange new relationship grew up, not of tenant and landlord, but of Mr Leitch wanting to learn. It could not have come about in the city, but in this quiet place they both loved and felt they belonged in, these two men from such different worlds began to talk. John Connell lent Mr Leitch reading material, and suggested other texts which he would be able to acquire in Glasgow. They sat in neither garden, in order that there would be no interruptions to the dialogues. Through the summer and on weekends into the autumn, the political education went on as they tramped the hills. They looked an odd pair, their very different social classes defined by their clothing.

Beth could imagine them as they walked, but it occurred to her that while she had seen photographs of her grandfather when he was young, she did not have a face to put to Mr Leitch.

She kept family photographs in the parlour cupboard. It crossed her mind there might be one of Mr Leitch. The oldest albums she dug out first – ancient books of photos all neatly labelled. Maggie's mother was there, the Weirs were there, the Keddies were there, but no sign of Mr Leitch, until she spotted in an unlabelled group a gentleman in cravat and frock coat. It was possible.

Photographs are moments frozen in their time. In the past, they were always posed. People wanted to look good for the magic of the camera. Beth had travelled extensively, and had photos from all over the world, photos which were not posed. She had seen Kathmandu on the news recently, and it did not look at all as it had done when she had seen it. In the 1970s it was just a medium-sized town. Damascus she remembered as a beautiful city; now it was partially in ruins. She thought back to travelling with her American friend Carol and meeting nomads on the move in Afghanistan – it could have been a scene out of the Bible. As she found the book containing the photos of that particular moment in time, she wondered if the children in the picture were still alive, adults roaming the Hindu Kush. If so they would surely remember both her and Carol, if only for their rarity value. Her imprint on them; theirs on her.

In front of her she had photos taken in Asia, a world away, and photos taken in her garden, a different world away, photographs from a century ago. Two men pulling a donkey cart in Iran, a woman with a basket on her head in a street in Lebanon, lives swept away by development and war. What sense would they make of their home towns now?

But if the Leitches, the Weirs and the Cooks came into the garden, they would feel they had never been away. Beth knew they would want to talk to her, this strange woman they did not yet know, sitting on the doorstep they knew so well, welcoming them home.

Chapter Twenty

The thirties was a painful decade. By the end of the twenties, the human scars of the Great War had been hounded into hiding. Those who had not gone to war seemed determined to forget it had ever happened, and those who had gone could not shut it out. Society was fractured.

In 1929 an unparalleled economic crash set in motion a worldwide depression. Of the 'Political Debating Club' at the house, the one most affected was the one with the most money. Nobody was buying hats. John Connell and George Keddie were unaffected by the situation as the demand for sheet metal increased. Jack Weir's employers no longer visited the house where he worked as a gardener, but they were unable to sell it. No one was buying houses any more than they were buying hats. They did not visit, but the building and the garden had to be maintained.

An entrepreneur at heart, Jack Weir turned the flower beds into a kitchen garden. He and his wife with her agricultural background grew what people wanted to eat. The Victorian greenhouse with its elegant fretwork of iron became a factory of vegetables! They supplied to the village at a modest profit.

In Glasgow Mr Leitch was advised by his accountant to increase the rents for the houses, but he was unwilling to do so. He tried to explain to his accountant about his mother having lowered the rent nearly forty years before, to accommodate two old ladies for no other reason than that they wanted to live there. To a man whose life had been defined by figures, this was madness. When Mr Leitch expanded on his thinking that he was renting to people whose political views digressed from his own, and perhaps those of his accountant, men whom he had learned from and whom he respected, his accountant gave up. The rent remained unchanged.

Although three of the men lived most of the year in Glasgow, they never met there. Their houses were only a few miles apart, but the social divide between Mr Leitch and the other two was too great. Only in the garden and in the hills was that divide eroded. In the summers of the 1930s this strange political debating group of four, John Connell, Jack Weir, George Keddie and Mr Leitch gathered night after night in the garden. During the winter Alan Leitch had read extensively, and wanted equally to contribute to the debate and to learn from a position of increased knowledge. He cringed when he remembered what he had said the previous summer.

The four of them brought chairs out on to the flat part of the garden, as that was easier for discussion than three in a row on the seat and one on the grass, and there the arguments raged. With his new-found career as an entrepreneur, Jack Weir found himself challenged. As he was primarily feeding people, rather than just making a profit, that added variation to the debate. If he was doing it to feed people should he be making a profit, or paying himself a wage? Perhaps the profit should belong to the owners of the house as they owned the garden. If he was growing to sell from his own garden, would that have been different? That argument went on for at least three evenings.

The old house listened. In its decades of watching over its

people, this was new. It had heard so many ideas over the years. Each era brought new discussion. Economic theory was the most recent, and then as the decade progressed a new word appeared: fascism. Italy, Spain, Germany came under the grip of dictators. Fascism cannot exist without violence both inside and outside a country. Repressive laws were passed to crush out opposition, and old-style military expansion followed on. Britain was not immune from this growing political movement. In some areas, fascist groups emerged admiring Franco of Spain, Mussolini of Italy and Adolf Hitler in Germany.

At the end of the Great War the concept of a League of Nations had been born, the idea of which was to prevent another such disaster taking place. Although it had not got off to a promising start, its ideals were widely shared. In Britain there was a League of Nations Union supporting these ideals, and here in the village a branch of the union was set up. It met in the village hall all through the winter. Preferring the village meetings to those in Glasgow, Mr Leitch made journeys specially to attend them. Speakers discussed whether or not Germany had been too heavily punished in 1919, how far nations could go to involve themselves in the domestic policies of other nations, what attracted people to fascism. In this quiet village, discussion of these weighty matters attracted large audiences.

All four of the debating group were opposed to fascism, but there was no agreement among them on how to do deal with it. The old house shuddered at the thought of seeing the same pain on the garden seat, if more of its young men had to go to war. The Weir boys were not too young now.

The evening political thinkers were replaced by the morning washerwomen, who thrashed out a possible future now that the suffrage battle had been won. The next fight would be over equal employment rights.

Mrs Fulton stayed apart. A widow from Glasgow, she too came

for holidays. She had been wealthy, but had fallen on harder times when her husband died, after which it emerged that he had made a number of very bad business decisions and there was a significant amount of debt. That was before she learned that he had had a mistress for many years, with whom he had a second family he financed. She was bitter. She was angry. She was humiliated. To remove herself from both the ridicule and the condescending, pitying looks of people she had regarded as friends, she sought out a quiet place where no one knew of her.

Had she taken her fellow occupants of the house just as they were, and without telling them her story, had she met them on the terms which they had determined for themselves, she would have been fine. But no, she lorded it. She was Mrs Fulton. She did not trample sheets. She did not work in the garden, and she most certainly did not discuss politics. She was childless and alone in the world, but rather than accepting friendship offered by those she regarded as her social inferiors, she isolated herself and became more and more lonely. No matter how the other women tried to involve her, they trampled the washing and she watched in her haughty way from a distance.

Of course, the story followed her. It was not long before Mr Leitch heard it in the city, and then it seeped out in the most peculiar way. He had told his wife, and she, feeling sorry for Mrs Fulton, one day knocked on her door to see how she was settling in. Mrs Fulton looked her up and down, at the gardening shoes and the loose strands of hair, and did not realise who she was. Mrs Leitch was told to mind her own business. She was a city lady who did not speak to peasants. Mrs Leitch was dumbfounded, and when she told her husband what had happened, he roared with laughter.

'I'll deal with her,' was all he said.

'Don't evict her. You know that is not right.'

'Oh no I won't do that. I'll teach her.'

And so that night he proposed an extension to the discussion group. The women would be invited to put the case for equality at work. All the women would be invited. He spoke to Mrs Fulton who was delighted to be considered worthy of his company, although of course what could these other people possibly tell her? He and she would put them in their place.

The meeting gathered. Mr and Mrs Leitch were a few minutes late, and then down the path they came. He turned to Mrs Fulton.

'I believe you have met my wife,' he began.

She stared in horror, unable to decide what to do. She could not leave, and she could not contribute. Out of her depth, she was an empty vessel.

When the discussion drew to a close Mrs Leitch produced a cake, and Jeannie-from-over-the-wall, tea. Mr Leitch was relentless.

'Mrs Fulton what business was your husband in? Perhaps our paths in Glasgow have crossed.'

She had to answer.

'Ah.' Pause, as if something was clearing in his mind. 'Ah yes, we never met, but I do know of him. Would you like another piece of cake?'

When her lease was up, she did not renew it.

~

The younger generation of Weirs had passed through the village school and were all working. Because of the reduction of wealthy ladies visiting the village, there was not the same amount of work available for seamstresses. The girls had gone to Glasgow, but came home as often as they could. They missed home, and if truth were told, they wanted to marry back into the village. One of their brothers, however, had decided the city life was for him. He only came home to visit his parents, but neither the house nor the village held him, something his father could not fathom. Neil Weir worked alongside his father, and had no intention of leaving if he could possibly help it.

Wee John had a scientific turn of mind and when he went into employment was fortunate, despite the economic downturn, to be offered an apprenticeship in scientific instrument making. He worked five and a half days per week, and also attended evening classes twice a week. He was determined to do well, and by 1935 he was promoted, but with the drawback that the promotion was to London. He was very unwilling to go, but he knew that if he turned this opportunity down, he would not be offered another. With heavy heart he decided to make his way south, as so many Scots had done before him, determined that one day he would come back.

On his last weekend in Scotland, he came to the house. The old walls saw again the misery it had seen in 1914. Although this was different, this was not war, he was not going to where he might be killed, the loss and sadness of leaving were just the same. He loved this house and this garden. On that weekend, as he walked on the hill with Neil Weir, he wondered who was the lucky one. On the face of it, he was. He had a highly skilled job with a very good future ahead. Neil, on the other hand, was in a less secure job, with an uncertain future in difficult economic times. But he was here. He was in a place where he belonged, not a strange place so far away. Wee John had by then been walking out in Glasgow with a young lady, and the imminent departure for London brought this to a head. They married, and looking backwards over their shoulders, they went to London.

Jean, too, chose her future in the area she enjoyed. She was employed in a ladies' department store. It did not take long before she was able to use her artistic eye to offer suggestions particularly about colour, and then she often found herself sought by clients when they could not reach a decision for themselves – sometimes on style, sometimes on shade. On one occasion she offered a suggestion about a client's hairstyle to set off a dress she was thinking of, and here too she came to be in demand. Her wage was small, but she loved her job, and in time she had developed a reputation which led to unofficially training new staff. She always came to the house with her parents on holiday, and by the time she was twenty she was also visiting it on her own or with friends. She finished work on a Saturday at lunchtime and she could be boiling a kettle on the open fire by 5 o'clock. A long evening in the quiet or in the turmoil of bad weather, it mattered not. She was there and she was happy.

Marion was always glad to see her, particularly when she came with piles of patterns. She had begun to draw her own designs, and when she first laid them in front of Jean she was shy. It was so important to her that she could design, that she had drawn in secret. She had wanted to do this for as long as she could remember, and here she was risking showing her ideas to her closest friend. She knew Jean would be honest, and she also would be kind. Jean had looked at the drawings in silence, and then at her friend. She smiled very slowly, her eyes shining in awe. The drawings were as exciting as anything being sold in the exclusive shops in Glasgow.

Mina did well at school, though university or college education was no more possible for her than it had been for her older siblings. Still, she won a scholarship to a school which would allow her to progress further with her education than might have otherwise been possible. Many of the pupils were from wealthy backgrounds. She and her fellow scholarship recipient Iris were the poor girls, and were certainly made to feel it. They worked hard, did well, and hated school. Through their friendship, and the contempt they were exposed to, their views were formed. For years afterwards Mina and Iris sat in the garden ruminating over their school experience, planning the new world they would build.

After school Mina worked in a small office, and like her

brother, attended evening classes, in her case to learn shorthand and typing. From there she progressed to the head office belonging to the Railway Company. Part of her wage was free train travel, so she used this to maximum effect, going as often as she could to the house. Train followed by a short steamer journey was easy. She often imagined living here permanently, but she could not see how this could come about. She was a skilled typist, and that was not a job for which there was much call in the village. So she visited, and she dreamed, but could not as yet plan.

About two miles from the house was a lighthouse. Its beam was as accurate a timepiece as a clock, and on nights when she could sit outside, she watched it sweep across the river with its own rhythm of movement. It was like a dance. Long short short, the beam like that of every other lighthouse had its own pattern. It could have been set to music. Around the lighthouse came the steamer which would take her back to Glasgow. Stretching out her time for as long as possible, she watched for it coming, and then set off at a pace, priding herself she could reach the pier just as the steamer was berthing.

The old house did not change. Its rooms were just the same. The fires kept the dampness away. The wooden trim had turned grey, not with age but with style. It now matched the long stone wall. The borders bloomed with different flowers across the three growing seasons. Rhododendron bushes lined the path. The vegetables blossomed in the rich soil. Over one winter, the snow lay for four months. The land slept under its blanket. The garden seat disintegrated further. A new wooden gate was installed, and on it the name of the house appeared for the first time, River View. From the house on a clear day, it was possible to see the large rock in the River Clyde known as Ailsa Craig. 'Ailsa' is linked to the Gaelic/Norse word for 'elves', and, as a little girl, Beth loved the idea that the elves on the rock could see her house. In her imagination she embroidered the story that they flew to visit her, and could view their island home from her garden.

High on the building, the lion kept watch over the inhabitants of the house as the decades slid by.

Weeks had passed since that first terrible morning of loneliness and fear. Beth had spent her days going through the research she had done, imagining as she did so the lives of those who had sat in this kitchen and walked in this garden.

Each day she took herself for a walk up onto the hill or down to the village shop. Seldom did she meet someone who did not want to stand and chat, or if they were in a hurry, at least wave a cheery greeting.

'Lovely weather we are having after that grim winter.'

'Aren't the daffodils beautiful this year? It'll be the bluebells soon.'

'How are you managing?'

It occurred to her that only in a small community did this kind of conversation take place. In busier places the first and the second comment might happen, but certainly not the third, the question that required a response.

At home she sat alone, choosing a different room as suited her mood. Unbidden, from deep inside her, surfaced her own past. She had done well at school, but choked when she thought of some of her childhood thoughts. 'I wouldn't expect you to understand that. You can barely read.' What could ever have given her the idea she could think of anyone in this way? Her squirming increased when she recalled the accompanying feeling of superiority. What harm would she have inflicted had her thoughts been spoken?

On another occasion it was, 'Do it this way. I'm telling you.' Oh dear!

She recalled many arguments. Once she had an idea in her head, it was hard to shift it. Even when she had come to know she was in the wrong, she was unwilling to back down.

Slowly her past began to make sense to her. Different memories and different moods in different rooms, as if the walls themselves were turning the pages of her life.

Sometimes the phone rang, almost an alien sound from another century. Friends and family from the city, from London, from Germany, from the USA checking on how she was. At first they were an intrusion into the world she had escaped into, a world immutable, frozen in its own time. Gradually this changed. She began to return the calls, not out of duty, or courtesy, or even self-interest, but because she wanted to. The world outside began to draw her. This did not deter her from bringing back to life her forerunners in the house. On the contrary, they sat side by side with her living friends at different points of the day. She could slip from a conversation in the here and now, to listening to the chatter of the washerwomen.

In the past the occupants of the house did not have the easy access to the world Beth had. They had to wait for letters, and when they arrived, they contained news and perhaps views, but there was no dialogue. The phone made all the difference. Hearing the voice of a friend or a loved one dissolved the miles.

She thought of the people who had lived in her house, whose loved ones had made their lives elsewhere. They had their village community, but they did not have the wider community. Letters but no voices. How cut off she would be without the phone. How lucky she was to live in a time when it was possible to have both worlds. Isolated in her home, her world did not need to shrink.

'Thank you, Alexander Graham Bell,' she said as she picked up the phone and dialled her brother in America.

Chapter Twenty-One

Twenty years, nine months, nineteen days and eighteen hours after the end of the war to end all wars, Germany declared war on Poland. September 1st 1939. Once Adolf Hitler became the German Chancellor in 1933, democracy was abandoned. Elections continued to be held, but they were merely a charade. From her reading, Beth knew history to be littered with dictators who seek to legitimise themselves by holding elections in order to claim they are ruling by the will of the people. They do not; they rule for themselves, but they do so only when people collude in their lie. The gnawing need for the cloak of constitutional respectability is indicative of their inherent weakness, their vacuum of personal morality and political legitimacy. Hitler claimed the Third Reich would last a thousand years. It lasted twelve. But during these twelve terrible years, 55 million people were destroyed at the whim of one individual, who had not been held to account.

Throughout the thirties, Hitler had become increasingly aggressive in voice and action. The League of Nations had been unable to stop his appropriation of adjacent territory lost by

Germany at the peace arrangements in 1919. Invading Poland was different. This piece of land had not been part of these arrangements, and as such, attacking Poland was a simple act of aggression. The British government intimated that if Hitler did not pull back, Britain would declare war. He did not withdraw, and on September 3rd Britain declared war on Germany.

The atmosphere in Britain was very different from that of a quarter century earlier. There were no illusions now about cavalry charges and glory. This time it was about defending freedom from dictatorship. On that Sunday morning at 11.15, the Prime Minister broadcast that as the deadline had been passed for the withdrawal of German troops from Poland, and there had been no assurance that this would take place, 'consequently we are now at war with Germany'. The mood in the country was one of overwhelming sadness.

Mina and Iris went for a walk in the hills near Glasgow that day. It was a walk they often took, laughing and chattering as they planned their future. They were twenty-two years old, with a world ahead of them. They had grown up aware of the pain inflicted on society by the previous war, but they did not understand it. They had not lived through the fear and the grief, nor had they any reason to think they might live through another such catastrophe. But on that Sunday, they knew that their assumed future had disappeared. Something unforeseen had happened, which stripped away their expected tomorrows.

In the village those who had lost members of their families in the Great War gathered at the War Memorial. They stood in silent grief, not assuaged in two decades, wondering bitterly where the next set of names would be engraved.

Poland collapsed within a few days, and then came a strange uneasy period of quiet. Nothing happened; both sides waited for the inevitable next move. In the early spring, the lull was over. Germany struck north crushing Denmark, Norway, Sweden and pushing on into Finland. Then west; Holland, Belgium and into France. The tactic was new and devastating. *Blitzkreig* – lightning war – the bombers came first, raining death on the houses below. The people fled the buildings as the armoured trucks and tanks swept in. It was planned. It was co-ordinated. It was clever. It was brutal. It was unstoppable.

The British army was caught ill-prepared. An attempt to assist the countries of mainland Europe to withstand the onslaught was beaten back to the beach at Dunkirk, from which a flotilla of little ships rescued the British army. Retreat was rewritten as stoical victory.

Two of the German High Command urged Hitler to destroy the British army on the beaches rather than allow escape, but their advice was ignored. Hitler wanted to reach Paris to achieve what the Germans had failed to achieve in 1914; victory in the French capital. He was in too great a hurry to feed his need for adulation to bother with strategy. Hitler assured Field Marshal Erwin Rommel that, as the British would inevitably now surrender, wiping out their army was irrelevant.

Britain did not surrender. By then Winston Churchill was Prime Minister. Descended from a former Field Marshal, who had led Britain to military success by defeating the French in the eighteenth century, Churchill had waited all his life to lead his country. He dug in.

Hitler demanded surrender, and when that was not forthcoming, he launched attacks on the Royal Air Force. For *blitzkrieg* to work, the armoured trucks had to already be across the English Channel, and for that to happen, the RAF had to be destroyed so that they could not attack the German navy carrying the trucks and the tanks.

The Battle of Britain began, and when the Germans lost more planes and pilots than they shot down, they began to bomb the airfields in the south of England from where the RAF were flying.

When that too failed, in order to break the spirit of the British people, the cities became targets. Plymouth, Portsmouth, Coventry, Birmingham – the list went on and on. London and the area around it were bombed eighty-one of eighty-four nights in a row. Wee John and his young bride had made their home outside London in more rural Kent, but that did not make for safety. They were on the flight path of the bombers.

Wee John had gone to London to work on scientific instruments mainly for medical science. At this pivotal moment in history, the focus shifted to military instruments. He worked on detection instruments and early radar. In this highly skilled work he was not called up to the services, but living near London through the blitz, and developing the science which in the end was crucial to victory, he was on the front line, and he knew his role was essential. On the daily commute into London, he often thought of his home in Glasgow and of the holiday house he had always loved, but time off to make the long journey north was impossible.

The need for steel had increased with the need for weapons production. Like his son, John Connell was, as he had been in 1914, in essential war work. He wrote to his son every week, telling him of the situation in Glasgow, and of the effect the war was having at River View. Changes had come to the house and to the village.

Jean continued working in the dress shop. She had taken Marion's designs and shown them to the head of her department. Miss Mills was a kind lady, who was caring of her staff. She also had an eye for good design. Like Jean, she saw the merit in what Marion had drawn, and ordered two of the designs to be made up. They were chosen with specific customers in mind, and the customers loved them. Marion was paid for her designs, and Jean felt very privileged to bring her friend an envelope containing the money. To her surprise, Marion did not open it. She just sat looking at it and smiling. Jean urged her to open the envelope, knowing she had been paid a goodly sum. When she finally did so, she was surprised that Marion barely noted the amount. She still just sat smiling, almost unable to believe what had happened. To her the money, welcome though it was, was secondary. What mattered to her was that her designs had been good enough. As the war went on, she drew more and more, even though she knew it would be a long time before people would again be buying expensive dresses, coats, hats and blouses. What she drew was squirreled away for the future.

Before the war, Mina worked in the Railway Office. In 1938, the Railway Company had negotiated a contract with the government in Argentina for staff to go to South America for six months, working on setting up a railway system in that mountainous area. Mina, as a skilled shorthand typist with a geographical brain that she could attune easily to requirements for timetabling, applied and got the job. Her father would not countenance it. She was twenty-one years old and planning to go half way round the world to a country with only a rudimentary system of law and order, where she did not speak the language, accompanied almost exclusively by men. The adventurous streak which had taken her down the garden path aged four had not abated. Her father's consent was essential to her going, and, as that was not forthcoming, she had to stay in Glasgow.

Shortly after this, she began walking out with a young man who also worked in the Railway Company. They went to concerts and to the cinema. He talked of marriage. She changed the subject. As his family were comfortably off, he offered a very nice house just outside the city, and a settled future. She wanted excitement.

At work her boss had gone into the army and was replaced by a man who knew far less of what the job entailed than she did. He often asked her for her ideas, and then passed them off as his own. She was more than able to have been promoted, but that was not to be. The aspirations of the women trampling the sheets and blankets had not yet played through in the workplace. An incompetent man at work and a boyfriend pressuring her into a marriage, inside which it was assumed she would not work at all, were increasingly suffocating, and so without a word to anyone she joined the Women's Royal Naval Service – the Wrens, as it was popularly called. She broke off her relationship with Jim, she resigned her job, and she set off to become a naval electrician at Birkenhead.

Before she did so, she and Iris went to the old house by the river.

The village had undergone much change. Even before war was declared, children had been evacuated from the cities to safety. They arrived by steamer, many of them crying. They did not understand the danger that staying in the cities represented. They just knew they had been forced from their homes to a place that was completely unfamiliar. When they arrived, they were allocated to the houses where they were to remain until further notice. Some of the children liked it, and some of them hated it. For the people on whom they were billeted, a little group of women who had not had children were very happy to have this instant child to care for, while others saw the child as just another mouth to feed. The evacuees divided the village into two camps – those who thought they breathed new life into the community by it having to adapt, and those who saw them as an unwelcome intrusion into their idyll.

The little school was not large enough to accommodate all the young people who had arrived. The children were put on to a shift system; some had school in the morning, and others in the afternoon. This just caused another problem. The evacuee children were unsupervised in their free time, and some of them in their unhappiness simply ran out of control. They wanted home to what they understood, and they thought that if they behaved badly they would be sent back. Some also became quite ill. They saw the local children eating berries growing at the sides of the road, but as outsiders, they did not know which berries were poisonous.

In an endeavour to eliminate the outbreak of wild behaviour, the hall was used as an extension of the school. Classes were increased in size, and teachers from the city accompanied the children. The headmaster, Mr Muir, spent a great deal of his time cycling between the outposts of his school.

Many of the evacuee children were smaller and less well nourished than the local children, brought up as they had been on fresh air and fresh milk. Some of the local children sneered at the look of city poverty, but as time went on, the evacuee children grew healthier and the visual distinction was blurred. Friendships began to develop in the playground.

Mina knew the children were not wholly welcome, and that set her wondering how the village might have reacted to her own parents arriving twenty-eight years before. Of course her parents had not been forced to come, nor had they arrived in a large number, but when she thought back on her younger years, the house had been filled with people on holiday from the city. How had the locals really viewed this? She had always felt a part of the village, but for the first time began to wonder if she was seen as an incomer, even though she had first arrived when she was six weeks old. There was no one to ask. She did not feel she could ask Jeannie-from-over-the-wall, and Jack and Catherine Weir had, with heavy hearts, recently moved. Their family having grown up had gone their own ways, and the house had become too big for them.

As Mina and Iris walked along the road, they noticed another change. All the big houses had stone walls separating the garden from the road, but the walls had not been built high as that would have destroyed the view from the houses. The compromise was an iron railing rising from the stone wall. No expense had been spared on the railings. They were works of art in their own right. Why would one build a beautiful house and then spoil its outlook with a plain railing in front of it? Walking past the railings for years, Mina had her favourites. Now they were gone, wrenched out of the walls to be re-smelted into weapons. Most shocking of all was that the railing delineating the place of remembrance at the War Memorial had gone too.

Of the house tenants, John, Maggie and family were the only ones left. The tenants in the two very small houses had not renewed their leases, and Jack and Catherine Weir had moved along the road. The building briefly sat empty.

As the war went on, a new type of soldier was trained – a commando. Winston Churchill had been a soldier in the Boer War. The Boers had been unable to defeat the British army in a pitched battle, so had moved into highly successful guerrilla tactics. The kommandos, as they were called in Afrikaans, harried the British army and attacked it, not in full-scale encounters, but in unexpected carefully planned raids. Britain in 1940 was in the situation of the Boers forty years earlier. Evacuated from mainland Europe, it was not possible to launch a frontal attack on the German army. Churchill decided on commandos. Men from the existing forces could volunteer for training. This initially took place in the west of Scotland, and the men who were successful were assigned to different areas of the country before being sent to Nazi-occupied Europe.

The village had so many big empty houses that the Government took them over in order to billet these men. As the house was empty except for the Connells, Mr Leitch leased the other parts of the house to the government. Was this for the war effort, or was the increased rent the attraction? When Mina and Iris came to the house, they found the other parts of it akin to an army block. Secrecy abounded so the men had no names, just numbers.

During the day these men continued their survival training in the hills. The moorland, where people had always walked, was now fenced off for the Ministry of Defence. The shore was similar.

Areas of deep water were now in use for underwater training, and the development of tiny submarines known as midgets.

In the evenings the men devised all manner of activities to keep boredom at bay. They were not permitted to go to the local pub; they had to stay in their houses and gardens. When Mina and Iris arrived, all the faces at the windows peered in disbelief. Two young women had been sent to them. In no time, the self-appointed ringleaders were knocking on the downstairs door. It took even less time for them to be told quite firmly by the two women that they were not army issue!

The men had invented a game involving bottles. Despite not being allowed to go to the local pub, alcohol was not in short supply. That was army issue. But what to do with the empty bottles? Just beyond the flat piece of ground there was a definite slope, steeper than the rest of the garden. They lined up the bottles at the edge of the slope, and the object was to smash each bottle, but with minimal damage. The winner was the one with the least amount of individual pieces of broken glass. A variation on this was exactly the opposite; the maximum number of shards of glass with one hit. The ultimate was being able to throw a small stone into the neck of the bottle from ten yards. Hours were spent on this. At the end of each session a garden rake, which had been questionably procured, simply swept the glass onto the slope of earth and raked it in. The men were not in the least concerned with tidiness, but rather with no stray pieces of glass being counted in the next competition.

Although the garden was very steep, that did not stop the attempts at football. The men did not play up and down the garden but across it. Changing sides at very regular intervals was essential to equalising the stretch on the calf muscles.

Mina and Iris were fascinated by one of the soldiers. He was tiny and he could run. He refused to be addressed by his number so they settled on Shorty. Shorty did not wear shoes. He had come from poverty-stricken Belfast, where he had spent his entire life barefoot. He joined the army for the wage, and he liked all aspects of army life except one. He had to wear not only shoes, but worse, he had to wear boots. At the first opportunity, off they came. Here in the garden he could weave in and out among the other players like lightning. He seemed to be running in one direction, and then he would take off in another with no apparent turn. He could kick the ball with a strength in his bare feet often greater than his teammates with boots on.

One afternoon, they found Shorty sitting on the wall with his pistol.

'What are you doing?' asked Iris.

'I am going to try to hit the bus when it comes along. I'm gonna puncture a back tyre.'

'But why?' murmured Mina.

'To see if I can. I've been thinking about this for a while, and know the bus has to be at a particular point on the corner for me to get it. If the bus is going too fast, I will miss. If too slow, I will hit something else. Precision, you see. Precision.'

From barefoot Belfast, here was a latent mathematician.

'But suppose you do miss and hit someone?' said Mina.

'Well the bombers won't get them then, will they?' In his upbringing life was fragile; it had no certainties.

The bus came along. He took aim. He fired. The bus swerved and stopped. The driver got out and examined his tyre.

'Someone has shot my tyre,' he announced.

A passing cyclist was hailed to report this to the local policeman. Off he peddled, and in time the local bobby turned up. The three watchers on the hill lay hidden on the grass spectating.

'Someone has shot my tyre!' declared the driver.

The policeman laughed. 'Dinna be daft. Who could do that?'

'Well, it had to come from that house up there. It's full of soldiers. They're mad, these commandos.'

'Don't be silly. They wouldn't do that.'

'Oh wouldn't they? Are you going to investigate or not?'

'Yes I will, but not until this bus is towed out of the way.'

The passengers were by this time off the bus, offering their thoughts on what had happened.

'Very loud it was.'

'A bullet? I don't know. Sounds like one of his stories.'

One passenger had a more pressing concern. 'How am I going to get home with my messages? I want my bus fare back. I'm just going to sit here till the bus moves.'

'In that case you might be here till tomorrow.'

A search began. The bullet was nowhere to be seen.

The bus was removed, and the policeman came up to the house to investigate.

'Did one of you shoot the bus?' He realised how silly he sounded.

'Shoot the bus? What? Why would anyone do that? Shoot the bus? Not us, officer. Not us.'

And that was that. Shorty survived the war and spent his old age in Belfast regaling people of his exploits in Europe, in Africa, in Italy. But never was there a moment he was more proud of than the day he had hit the bus, an exploit no one believed but Mina and Iris.

Towards the end of their visit, conversation grew serious. They knew this was a unique moment. It would never happen again, and even if they were all to meet again, it would be different, because of the yet unknown experiences they were all about to go through. Iris was going into the Women's Auxiliary Air Force, Mina into the Wrens and the men into combat as commandos. Not one of them was yet twenty-five, and it was to them the nation had turned. Long into the night they talked of what they saw ahead. None of them looked very far.

The old house listened and shuddered.

Chapter Twenty-Two

The army had been rescued from France, the RAF was fighting in the skies over the south of England, and a significant portion of the Royal Navy had moved into the Clyde. The German navy were prowling British waters to prevent men, food and weaponry arriving from abroad. Merchant shipping protected by the Royal Navy was being sunk by the German U-boats on a terrifying scale. The Clyde became a major base. With easy access to the Atlantic, a number of very deep glacial lochs feeding into the river providing ideal harbours, and backed by the shipyards with their repair equipment, the Clyde was vital. To protect it, a boom was laid across the river. A form of netting, it was weighted down, stretching four miles shore to shore, to prevent enemy submarines penetrating the upper reaches of the waterway.

The village was outwith the boom, so crossing the river to reach it meant sailing across unprotected waters. This did not deter John and Maggie from visiting. They knew that inevitably the bombing would come to Glasgow, and as such they lived permanently in a potential target. In this sense, visiting the village was respite. Reaching the house safely was all the more attractive. From the window, where they had watched steamers quietly working the river, and liners carrying passengers across the seas, day and night they now saw warships. The river had become a war zone.

The evacuees were still in the village, the commandos gone. The Leitch family had moved back in. They felt safer than in Glasgow. The smaller houses were still leased by the Ministry of Defence, with the result that each time John and Maggie came there were different inhabitants, but with Mr Leitch living in the main house, the glass smashing game had dropped into history!

Another visible effect of the war was that there were no flowers. Every piece of cultivatable land was turned into crop growing. Because so much merchant shipping was being sunk, it was essential that people grew food. Girls from the city were drafted in – the Land Girls, they were called. Like the evacuees some of them liked living in the country, while others hated it. In the garden at the house there had been vegetables for decades, so there was no visible difference, but the gardens of the big houses, which had been croquet lawns surrounded by flower beds, were now a vast area of vegetables. Once again, the gardeners were essential.

In March of 1941, the bombers came. The aim was to both destroy the ships in the Clyde, and break the will of the population. They had set out from France, and on a moonlit night followed the sea off the west coast of England and continued into the Clyde. No blackout in the world could hide the river at full moon in a cloudless sky. The Home Guard of the village on the Clyde watched from up on the hill as the bombers flew beneath them, wave after wave in orderly formation. The river turns a corner about six miles from the village, and the towns beyond, from where the evacuees had come, were not visible. What was visible were the flames. The noise of destruction drowned out the spoken word.

The evacuated children were terrified. Their parents were amidst the fires. Desperate children screaming for their loved ones was the lasting memory in the village of that night.

The next day was no better. Children determined to go home and find their parents, but with no idea of how to get there, and no steamers crossing the river, were in the extremes of despair. The thin facade of coping had been gashed. That night the children did not go to bed. They waited in silence. The sound was slight at first, and then grew to a roar. Planes, swastikas painted on their sides, mustered at the mouth of the river. This time the anti-aircraft guns were ready. To avoid them, the planes broke formation veering towards the land, where the villagers huddled beneath this crazed struggle between life and death. The children did not hide. They watched and they waited their turn. It did not come. The village was not hit. The children were neither killed nor injured, but they were deeply, deeply scarred.

On the third night there were no bombers. They never did return. Only gradually did the extent of the destruction in Glasgow and the surrounding towns reach the children. Some of the very young, who could not remember their parents, adjusted to their orphan status better than the older ones, who did have clear memories. They had nowhere to go, the lifeline which had sustained them, that one day they would go home, was gone forever. Frightened and lonely, they lived in an isolated limbo with adults who could not reach them.

Mina went off to the Wrens and was stationed at Birkenhead. Across from it is Liverpool, where she knew her father had grown up. In letters she asked him about it. She must have relatives there. At first her father ignored her queries, until he could no longer do so. When she had asked him why he ignored her questions, he knew he had to explain.

He told her of his dead siblings, and of his mother disappearing. He could not remember her clearly, but she was an absence which had featured all his life. He told her of returning to Glasgow with his father, growing up there, and then becoming one of the shipyard nomads. He had begun his apprenticeship in Barrow and then, after a second family split, he had left and returned to Glasgow. At seventeen the split had been so serious that, penniless, he had broken his apprenticeship and walked the hundred plus miles to Glasgow. He refused to tell her what the split had been about, and she knew that he was immoveable, for the moment. She was quite sure she could coax the story out of him when she came home. And so, as she busied herself with her new life, she let the matter rest. Liverpool for him was a place of pain. Mina, on the other hand, liked the freedom and variety the city brought her.

As a member of the armed forces, she moved from naval base to naval base. She had been trained in electrics, and was drafted to where damaged ships limped into port for repair. On one of her drafts, she was sent to the Clyde. Down past the village she went to the island of Bute. Rothesay's deep bay was ideal for a naval base. In her time off, she walked along the sea-front, and up onto the hill to look to the lighthouse she normally saw from the other side. She enjoyed the companionship of the other young women in the barracks, but she also liked her own company. She knew she had made the right choice to leave Jim and the Railway Company for this new life, which she was fully aware would not last forever. It was that very factor of borrowed time in a temporary new life she found so attractive.

One day as she was walking along the sea-front, she stopped to watch a Punch and Judy show. A young sailor wearing the distinctive uniform of the submarine service spoke to her.

'I've seen you working on my sub,' he said. He had been drawn to the very fact a female was working on the electrics.

'Yes,' she replied. 'Almost finished. When do you put to sea again?'

'The orders have not yet come, but I expect next week.'

'It'll be ready by then.'

And so it began.

He asked her how she came to be learning electrics, and she told him of her life in Glasgow and joining the Wrens. He came from the north of England, and very soon she became aware, not through what he said so much as through what he didn't say, that he and his family were not at one. Something had happened at some point in the past. Shades of her father and that mystery. He was not rude in not telling her. He was just private.

For the next two evenings they met. She liked his humour. He could tell a good story, and he could be serious too. When she asked him why he had joined the navy, his answer was that he had trained as an apprentice painter, and one day he was on a roof and happened to look out to sea. A lone ship was making its way across the vast space of the North Sea. That, he thought, would make for a more exciting life. Joining the navy spelled adventure, places he would never otherwise see, and a higher wage.

She thought of Jim and the Railway Company. Had she met someone who thought as she did? She was not sure, but she was intrigued.

Three days later, Eddie proposed marriage. She was shocked; this was too much. She was not quite as adventurous as she had thought. She politely turned him down, and for the next four years they wrote to one another, and met when they could. Devonport, Portsmouth, Birkenhead, Rothesay, the relationship grew in different places and through letters.

Her job was relatively safe. His was not. Each time they parted, they knew he might not come back. The toll on the submarines was very heavy. He was posted to the convoys escorting merchant ships carrying support to Russia, a task which was referred to as 'the suicide run'. When Mina and Eddie met, they lived in their present. He did not talk of the danger at sea. She did not ask. She knew that when he was in port he wanted to enjoy the now, and think of a future beyond the war, as if by so doing, it might mean that he would survive.

Near the end of 1943, Mina had the opportunity to go to Newfoundland. The WRNS (its official acronym) were sending multi-skilled operators to work on the cross-Atlantic fleet. Electrician, shorthand typist, timetable planner. She was ideal, but once again she was thwarted. In secret, the planning for a European landing was taking place, and when that date was set, everything else went on hold. So she was transferred to the south of England. Bitterly disappointed, it made her all the more determined that one day she would cross the ocean.

Eddie came to meet her parents in Glasgow. They got on well. He came from the same impoverished background her father had come from, and, like her father, he had set his own course. The little group came to the house. She was nervous, as she knew that if he did not like the house and the village, he was not for her. During the time there they trod the well worn paths, and they sat in the garden, in comfortable silence.

'I can't imagine anything better when this war is over than to live in a place like this. My life would have been so different had I been born into this beauty. I wonder if the children living here know how lucky they are.' He sounded so sad.

He went on, 'How I would like to grow vegetables! I don't know how to do that, but I would learn. To watch seeds grow and turn into what we could eat must be wonderful. Week after week, I destroy. I have to kill. I kill young men just like myself, young men who happened to have been born elsewhere. It is so random; they try to kill me, and I them. I was too young to understand this when I joined the navy. It was just an adventure to me then. Not now. One time we sank a ship and then picked up the survivors. None of us wanted to kill them. They were just like us. We shared what we had, and brought them into port. I wonder if they came from places like this, or the kind of place I come from.'

She asked him about his home. Again there was no real answer.

'When this is over, if I survive, I want to live in a place like this. When I am afraid, and on subs we are all afraid, I will think of this house and this moment, and if that is my last few minutes of life, they will have been filled with thoughts of hope.'

No more was said. The evening closed in. The house listened, its old walls absorbing the sadness and the fear as they had done before.

He went back to sea, she to the barracks.

On his next leave, he took her to visit his family. They were polite, but they did not make her welcome. She was someone who would draw him away; they did not consider that he had chosen to leave. When she went home, her father listened to what she said of her visit, and then he quietly explained that if she married Eddie, she had to accept his family would not be easy. That was not a reason to not marry him, but rather to go into it aware of how difficult it might be.

'So long as I don't need to live there, it would be fine,' she reasoned.

'You don't need to live there. He is at sea, and so you can live here, or at River View,' her father pointed out.

She smiled. Yes, that would be a possible solution.

'Why did you not keep in touch with your family?' she asked, thinking that at last she would get the answer to the mystery of Liverpool.

As ever, his face closed over. 'Not today. Someday perhaps, but not today. Today we are thinking about your future.'

She wrote to Eddie, carefully choosing the words to make clear she would not live in the north of England, while at the same time trying not to hurt him. When the war ended, she would go back to

Glasgow, and spend as much time as possible at the house by the river. It was what he wanted to hear.

They were married in January of 1945 in Glasgow. On the evening of their wedding they took the train and the steamer to the village. They walked up the hill and laid the fire. It was a cold night, but it was too beautiful to remain indoors. They sat on the seat, watching the moon sliding along the river. The bare trees shivered round them.

The three days' leave sped by, and then they left, silently wondering if they would ever be there again. In their new life together, they were alone with the uncertainty of war.

He went back to sea, she to Birkenhead.

The European war ended on May 8th 1945, and by August, Mina had come home. Eddie was still in the navy, due to be posted to the Pacific, where the war against Japan was still raging. Before he sailed, they had a few days at River View. Happy together, they could not celebrate the end of the war as the rest of the country was doing. For them it had not yet ended; in the Pacific, he would still be in real danger.

She returned to her job at the Railway Company, and living with her parents. She was back to where she had been five years before, but with a difference. She had gone, she had experienced a different life, and now she was home again, as a married woman but with a husband on the other side of the world. The adventure she wanted now was for him to come home so that they could begin a life together.

In 1946, she left work to give birth to her first child, a boy. Towards the end of her pregnancy the doctor she attended realised the baby had not turned, and he urgently requested a hospital bed. None were immediately available, and by the time one became available, it was too late. The time in the hospital was the lowest point in her life. At that time there was no real understanding of the emotional impact of losing a child – infant mortality was still so common in the days before the National Health Service that it was regarded as normal – and she was allocated to a post-birth ward to recover. She was the only woman in that ward with no baby. The new mothers avoided looking at her stricken face. She could turn away, but she could not shut out the sounds of babies crying, nuzzling, gurgling, nor the sounds which flow naturally from a new mother to her baby. Still in physical distress, and in anguish, she went home. Her mother took her to the village.

She had always seen her father as the rock of the family, but in these days of grief she saw a quiet strength in her mother she had never before been aware of. Maggie talked of losing one of her twins.

'But you had the others,' Mina said. 'I don't.'

'That makes no difference, because the little girl was a person, and having two others did not replace the one who had gone. When I look at Jean, sometimes I see her sister too. When you have other children, as you will, you will understand this. Your little boy Robert will always be there. No matter how many children you have, you will always know you had one more. He is just not here, but you will never love him any the less.'

Mina lay in bed in the corner of the room with the sea view, sounds only semi-human coming from the depth of her being. Sometimes her mother sat with her, sometimes she was alone. One night as the moonlight found its way through the trees, it lit the room and Mina glimpsed a flicker of an old lady in nightcap and nightgown in the bed opposite, watching her with such kindness in her expression. The day before as she had walked up the path, she thought she had seen a young man in army uniform sitting on the garden seat. Was she going mad in her grief?

She had read of what such despair can do, and she was afraid. At the weekends her father came to join them, and one day she asked him about his mother. She had lost two children, leaving him with his father. Had she felt such despair, and had that pushed her into an act of madness? Had she just run away? Had she killed herself?

His silence was profound, and when he spoke his voice was strangled.

'I do not know, but I have never stopped wondering. When we lost our little girl, I watched your mother and at times she forgot what she was doing, or got lost in places she knew well. It was as if she wasn't there but searching for what she had lost. I thought then of how it might have affected my mother. When I was little I cried for her, and I could not understand why she was not with me. Why had she left me? Did she not want me? Was I worth nothing to her? I looked for her, and hoped that one day she would come back. I have never forgotten her, nor the emptiness when she went away. It did not get easier with time. Eventually I lost hope, and as I did so I lost part of myself.

'When I watched Maggie in those early months, I saw what loss and grief can do. Something terrible had happened that caused my mother to go. If she is still alive, does she ever think of me? I could not replace my brother and sister who had died, but I am still me.

'When you were born, you did not replace your big sister. You were you. At times the emptiness came back – why was I not that to my mother?'

Silence, heavy with pain, seeped through the room. Three generations suffering the same loss, and so little known about its effects.

Mina had to write to her husband with the news. It went by telegram, a form of communication which in his experience invariably carried bad news. There was no compassionate leave then, and so father and mother grieved their lost child ten thousand miles apart. They were isolated from each other, and although surrounded by people, they were alone. No one could reach their loneliness. They both feared the consequences of not only the loss, but also the separation.

Sixteen months later, Eddie came home on leave. He was not good at expressing his feelings, but what passed between them by the open fire in the downstairs house carried a deeper silent understanding. She described what their little boy had felt like. He was classed as a stillbirth, but had in fact lived for a few minutes, and during these precious seconds she had heard him struggle for life. She had seen him move, and she had felt his skin. As she talked she made him live again, and in doing so she was able to speak what she had not been able to do with her parents or her sister. It was to the father of her dead child she had wanted to say these words first; they were his by right. Together silently grieving, they were no longer lonely in their loss.

Trying to look forward, they decided on names for a sibling for their lost little Robert. If they had a girl she would be Beth, if a boy Ian.

Mina went through her next pregnancy almost denying it was happening. She was so afraid to trust that this time it would be fine that she made no preparations for the arrival. No cot, no knitting; it had been so terrible to put these things away that she refused to have them brought out. The only concession she made to her condition was to stay in Glasgow. She would not be away from the doctor who had diagnosed the previous complication. After her loss, he had made a forceful complaint to the hospital. They would not thwart him a second time.

The baby was born in 1948. She was healthy. All was well. Two days later, an epidemic sweeping through the Glasgow hospitals reached the maternity ward. Healthy babies died in the space of a few hours. Their mothers became ill. Mina became ill, Beth very ill. Her weight dropped, and she was unable to breathe without support. At four days old she was unconscious and attached to a tiny oxygen mask. Because she could not eat, a little incision was made above her left ankle, and she was fed through a tube pushed into her tiny vein. Her father flew back from Singapore, bringing a little blanket he had bought for her, when early naval electronics had brought the news of her birth.

On that day he had been ecstatic. The entire submarine crew had gone ashore and celebrated. On the way to the bar, he had passed a market stall where tiny blankets were being sold. On them was sewn 'Singapore 1948'. He had bought one for his little girl. As she grew up, she would have the blanket her daddy had bought for her on the other side of the world the day after she had been born. When the telegram arrived two days later, he was terrified. This time he was given leave to go home.

By the time he reached Glasgow, Mina was improving. Their daughter was in intensive care. She lay in a tiny incubator, kept alive by machines. Day and night they sat, holding hands across the incubator, willing her to live. And she did. On the twelfth day of her life, she opened her eyes and saw her parents. Hospitalisation was necessary for a while yet, but she gained in strength day by day, and then she went home. It was too risky to take her away from her Glasgow doctor, so she did not make the steamer trip to the village. That came later. Through the winter of 1948 and into 1949, Beth survived and developed; a miracle of science.

Her grandmother observed a few years later, 'That child has willpower. I wonder if that was what kept her alive.'

Her grandfather added, 'Aye, and if she uses it well, she'll be a fine lass.'

Once Mina and Beth were out of danger, Eddie had gone back to the navy, and Mina and Beth lived with John and Maggie. Mina spent more and more time at the holiday house. She wanted her wee girl to run on the grass and crawl among the flowers. Mina was always up early, pushing Beth in her pram along the roads. She had known a number of the women of her own age through the years of visiting the village, but now friendships grew as the young mothers talked of their children.

No decision was ever made that Mina would come to live there permanently. It just came to be.

One day she saw the local children walking home from school in a group. They looked so happy. She wanted that for her family. She wanted her child to belong in a family, and in a community, in a place she would love.

In 1952 Mina had her third child, a little boy to be called Ian. He was healthy, and there were no complications. Beth did not take well to no longer being the centre of attention. She looked at this little boy, and after a few days asked her mother when he would be going back to his home.

Eddie was still in the navy, and came home only for a few weeks a year. The house in Glasgow was crowded, so Mina with her son and daughter spent a great deal of time at the house in the village.

~

At New Year of 1952, the upstairs house became vacant. After the commandos had left, the Leitches had moved back in. When they returned to Glasgow, it was leased to a lady called Miss Power. Mina regularly went upstairs to visit her, and on this occasion Miss Power said she was leaving to look after her sister in England. If Mina wanted the house, this was the opportunity. She had not a second thought. She went straight to Mr Leitch who was on holiday in his house next door, and it was agreed. Mina would move in, just in time for Beth to start school. For the first time in her life, she was almost willing to believe in destiny.

She went back to Glasgow to tell her parents, and write to her husband.

They moved on Coronation Day. The whole country was celebrating the coronation of the young Queen Elizabeth as Mina boarded the steamer to begin her new life. She had Ian strapped on to her, and the pram piled high with their belongings. On top were a kettle and a tin of sandwiches. Beth wanted to help by carrying something. She was given a watering can. Mina had always taken an interest in gardening, watching and learning from Jack Weir. Once she knew she was coming to live at the house, gardening was her priority. She was full of ideas, and so her sister Jean had bought her a watering can. Beth carried it with pride. She knew she had the most precious item of all.

The house had two tables, four chairs and a bed. That is how the new tenants began. Two days later, a gas cooker arrived. Two tables, four chairs, a bed, a cooker, running water and a watering can – what more did anyone need? Mina had the riches of the world.

Chapter Twenty-Three

As the days slipped into weeks of solitude, the memories flooded back. Beth could recall so easily the pride in carrying that watering can almost seventy years before. It had served a long and dignified life until its age got the better of it, and it was pensioned off to become a plant pot, and there it has remained in its new life, in service still.

Beth had wandered around the house and garden amidst all the people who had lived here, and in this found great comfort. So many lives, so many stories and all of them lived inside these strong walls. Now she had come to her own life and her own story, filled with half-remembered conversations and half conversations remembered. What of her story would have echoes from the past? She had walked a very different path from those who had gone before, but she had come to realise that although her path was different, human experience did not vary so very much. The house, loved by so many, bound its inhabitants across the centuries.

In the weeks of isolation, Beth's loneliness had decreased. She had seen very few people, but with those she did meet out walking, conversations had developed. She often met up with William out walking with his dog. They had known each other for years, but only peripherally. In a small community knowing people for years means knowing their story, but not knowing who they really are. That comes only through conversation, and in the weeks of bumping into each other, gradually they had begun to talk of what mattered in life to them. He had not been born in the village, but had come decades earlier for work. Walk after walk, they chipped away at each other's views.

'How far do you think we are shaped by our environment? Does it shape how we think? Would we be who we are if we did not live here?'

He paused, but not evasively.

'Now that's a question for a future conversation,' he replied. 'Let's think about that one.'

They smiled as they parted, each knowing the other was going home to turn over this idea.

She was becoming used to balancing time spent in the present with time thinking of the past. Time linked not just the immediate environment and immediate past, but with something much deeper.

She thought a great deal of her parents when they had been young. To her, they were just her parents; she had never thought of them young with their dreams. She certainly had never thought of the loss of her older brother. It was as if she was meeting her family in a new way.

In August of 1953, Beth went to school. There were seven new hopefuls in her class. She was the one most recently arrived in the village, and so had to make her way in tentatively. There were only two other girls in the class, and they had been born into the village, so already knew each other quite well. Nevertheless they welcomed her in, and she settled into school very happily.

The infant teacher was Miss Scott. Born in the village in the 1890s, she had spent some of her adult years away. She returned to teach in the school in 1938, and educated a whole generation of infants before she retired. She was well liked by her charges. Once when the school pupils had been marched along the road to a church service, the minister talked about the Great War. Child after child caught sight of Miss Scott, back ramrod straight, silent tears running down her cheeks. The children sat horrified. A pillar in their lives was crumbling in front of them. None of the children spoke to each other of what they had just seen. It was too strange an event for conversation. When Beth went home and told her mother about what had happened, there was a definite pause before the answer came.

'Miss Scott may have lost a young man in that war. She would be remembering.'

Miss Scott did not marry and did not have children, but, Beth reflected, she did have children – hundreds of us. She was an extra granny in so many ways.

After the infants' class the little group progressed to what was referred to as the 'middle room,' which was exactly as the words suggest, positioned between the infants' room and the seniors' room. Here there were three classes. Years later in education, policies were devised to teach groups of pupils at different stages of learning, in the same room. This was considered a new idea. In rural schools it had been going on for decades. In the middle room the teacher juggled three age groups and multiple ability levels. Long division and fractions, spelling and reading, it all happened in the middle room, often simultaneously.

By Primary Six, the children were in the headmaster's room.

Here there were two classes to be managed. On Fridays they worked together listening to an educational broadcast on the wireless. The school did not own a wireless, but the headmaster did, and so it was carefully carried from his adjoining house every Friday morning. Sometimes the programmes were stories, sometimes new scientific developments, sometimes historical. They were invaluable in widening the scope of learning. This was not a school for a restricted curriculum. Mr Muir, interested in geology, taught the children rock formations. To this little group of eleven year olds, recognition of metamorphic rock was as ordinary as recognising a blade of grass.

The wide and varied interests of all the children were encouraged. Where one of her classmates preferred to spend dark nights lying on his back studying the stars, Beth was a reader. She would read all day long if she had been allowed to. She also wrote stories with never an audience in mind. She just liked to play with words. Page after page filled with tiny stories. She had chosen an exercise book because of its cover. It had a map of the world. She could write, and she could dream.

On the paths the children walked along, and in the fields, where they played, they learned botany. The river and the weather, as constant features of life, were also a source of inquiry. Tidal movements and weather patterns were as important as reading, writing and arithmetic.

Beth's brother Ian was an outdoors child. As he grew up, he loved to roam the hills, as the wee boys had done half a century earlier. He was in a boat as often as was possible, just as his uncle had been. One of Beth's earliest childhood memories of him was that he liked to build in the garden. He made all sorts of constructions, from wooden houses to tiny bridges. How to make a building stand up was for him both a challenge, and when successful, a huge pleasure. The old house watched this embryonic engineer embarking on his future career at the age of seven.

Mina ran their world. When Beth started school, the normal routine was that Mina accompanied her to school, taking Ian as a baby in his pram. In time Beth became more adventurous, and asked if she could walk the last quarter mile on her own. At the parting of the ways there was a seat, and so, as Beth set off to school proudly walking alone, her mother sat on the seat till her daughter reached the school gates. Then they would both wave, and off Beth would go to join her friends in the playground. At the end of the school day, waiting at the seat would be Mina with the baby in the pram, for it to be done in reverse. One day, Beth made a dreadful discovery.

'What did you do on the seat today, Mummy? Did you knit?' she asked.

'No. I walked to the shops, and then came home and planted the potatoes.'

Silence. Devastation. WHAT!

'But Mummy, did you not sit on the seat all day waiting for me? Don't you do that every day?'

The world was not according to Beth, after all! A lesson of childhood.

In time carpets arrived, and then furniture, an item at a time. The house began to take on a new look. The centre of the home was as ever the kitchen, the fire being the sole provider of heating in the house. At the kitchen table the family ate, Beth did her homework, games were played and stories were told.

Outside, Mina laid out borders of flowers edging the path. She turned over the earth below the only flat piece of ground, and laughed when she found a great deal of broken glass. The children were not allowed near it, but were greatly taken with the story of the glass smashing game. In time, Ian had to be forcibly stopped from recreating it with his pals.

Mina and Iris had been in the Girl Guides in Glasgow, and in order to allow Beth to have this childhood pleasure, Mina started a Brownie pack.

The Brownies went on an annual picnic. The Church also went on an annual picnic, and so steadily over time Beth's world expanded. She loved these trips. Going to new places was an adventure. At the age of nine she instigated a rebellion at the Sunday School, suggesting that the Church picnic did not go where had been planned, as they had gone there the previous year, and demanded instead it should be to pastures new. She was firmly put in her place, but there is no doubt she had a determined streak which needed careful handling. She was also a traveller in the making. In time Ian joined the Cub Scouts and then the Sea Scouts, and his world also grew with camping trips to locations twenty miles away. That was real adventure.

In 1956 after twenty two years service in the Royal Navy, Eddie left the submarine service and came home. He became the village postman. Eleven years after their wedding, Mina and Eddie set up home together. This was quite a disruption. To the children, their father had been a remote figure who came to visit every now and again. It was not unusual for naval personnel to be away for up to two years at a time, so each time he came home they barely knew him, with the result they were initially shy when he arrived. He always brought them presents. Beth was inseparable from the teddy bear he had brought from Gibraltar, but the connection rooted in a child being with a parent on a daily basis was just not there.

It was with some nervousness all round that Eddie came home. He worked hard, and as dreamed of a decade earlier, he turned over a large part of the ground for a vegetable patch. Some of the ground had run amok, so he had to start by cutting down trees, and then do the very heavy work of lifting all the roots. In time the land was prepared, and once again vegetables grew in the garden.

Eddie was strong. To get to work he had to cycle five miles

regardless of the weather. He then delivered the mail by bicycle. He dug the garden, and then to eke out his income, dug gardens for other people. He became a gardener, but unlike the other gardeners who had lived in the house, he had a full-time job and a ten-mile commute by bike as well.

On the dark nights, he taught the family a naval version of ludo called Barriers. He explained that this is played in pairs, and the object is to build barriers on the board to prevent your opponents reaching the end before you and your partner do so. It involves strategy as well as rolling the dice. A game could last for nights, and so, on each evening when it was time for the children to go to bed, the board was carried safely to the round table in the parlour, where all contenders could pass by it over the next twenty four hours and whisper strategy to their partner. Cheating by moving the counters was not possible, as each of the four had the board imprinted on their minds.

For all Eddie wanted his home in this beautiful spot, he missed the male camaraderie of the submarine. He found it in the local pub, a number of whose clientele had also been in the navy during the war. He was very good at darts, and regularly came home on a Saturday night with a chicken which he had won. Came the Saturday he did not win, the family had no Sunday lunch. Before the coming of the fridge, there was no proper substitute.

One night he came home with a dog. A mongrel he had acquired for the price of a whisky – three shillings and fourpence. The children were having their baths in front of the fire when a black-and-white puppy appeared round the kitchen door. Beth, terrified of dogs, screamed. Ian launched himself at it. The dog for his turn decided that the fun was to get into the zinc bath too. Through this watery baptism, Sooty moved in. The family went to bed, and in the morning awoke to discover that he had eaten laces, leather shoes, gloves, anything he could get his teeth into. After that, to the amusement of all visitors, before going to bed everything had to be lifted off the floor. Sooty quite rightly took the view that if the item was on the floor it was his, leading to a crisis which almost wrecked Mina's friendship with Iris, when some months later she came to visit and put her new leather handbag on the floor.

In time Beth's fear of him vanished, and she dressed him in hats and dresses. Ian chased him. The family could do anything to Sooty he was so good natured, but let another person in, he was a holy terror. Once Mina accidentally locked herself out of the house, and she asked a man working on the road to go up a ladder and into the house to unlock the door from the inside.

'Naw missus, no' wi' that brute in there. I'll hold the ladder for you.'

Up she went, in the window, and there was the tiny brute, wagging his tail.

Sooty had a fatal flaw. He would have sold his soul for chocolate. He was taken out for three long walks each day, but he did not roam free as he was deaf to all instructions when off the lead. If he escaped past legs when the door was open, having seen his chance because the owner of the legs had not closed the door quickly enough, he was off. Armed with chocolate, the children would run in opposite directions to find him. He knew the drill. He knew the chocolate would be forthcoming. Let no one say a dog has no facial expression. The tussle in his features between the freedom and the chocolate was spectacular to watch. The gleam in his eye followed that chocolate. Beth could hide it behind her back, and he would run round. She could lift it above her head, and he got onto his back legs. She reached forward, tantalising him with the smell. Eventually he would spring to snatch it, and she got hold of his collar. It was declared a draw!

He had a particularly odd relationship with the kitchen table legs. Normally he strolled past them, but if someone moved the table he was at these legs, teeth gripping them. It was as if they had become alive to him and he was defending his house. The family realised very quickly it was easier to put Sooty into another room if the table was going to be moved, than to search the inside of his mouth for splinters. The legs became a feature of that table, and had to be explained to visitors who stared in amazement, but were too polite to ask.

Village life was busy. The little row of shops had changed in nature over the time. Gone were the dressmakers and the wine merchant serving the big houses no longer owned by the very rich. Instead there were butchers, grocers, greengrocers, bakers and a post office serving the population. There was even a bank. Few people had fridges, so shopping was a daily occurrence. One day Beth was sent to the shops for a pound of potatoes. This was just at the time when she was learning weights and measures at school. Somehow by the time she reached the shops the pound had become a stone, fourteen times the weight of the errand, and almost one fifth of her own body weight. Mr Watt the greengrocer realised what had happened and sold her one pound, not one stone. She was determined, until she tried to lift one stone. Head hung in shame, she carried home the pound and the note he had written to accompany it. She was not amused by how funny her mother found this.

The highlight of the social calendar for a child was the Christmas party run by the Scottish Women's Rural Institute – a party for small children in the afternoon, and a separate one for the older ones immediately after. One Christmas Eve Beth's mummy had not arrived to collect her at the set time, and rather than wait, the adventurous spirit took a grip. She set off home. When her mother arrived minutes later, Beth was nowhere to be seen. There were of course no phones, so parents took care of each other's children while the search began. As there were few cars on the road, an accident of that nature was unlikely, but the weather was bad and waves were lashing the road.

By the time Beth had reached Mr Watt's shop she was not so confident, and as there was a light on, she knocked on the door. He was of course taken aback that this wee girl was out on her own, in the dark, in a storm.

'Anna, can you come here?' he called to his wife. 'Keep your eye on this little adventuress while I find her parents.'

'Thank you, Mr Watt.' As a child, she would never have called him Billy.

Mrs Watt made her cocoa and gave her a little cake, sitting her up on the counter so she was visible, while at the same time finishing what needed to be done. Mr Watt went off in his van round the village looking for the frantic mother who was looking for her child. Very quickly all was well. Beth was grinning when she saw her mummy, but what she heard was, 'What are you doing? Why did you leave the party?' Her mummy sounded so angry.

Beth began to cry. 'I was coming home. You didn't tell me not to,' came the little voice.

From nearly forty years before, Mina heard the terror in her father's voice. She hugged her little daughter, thanked Mr and Mrs Watt for their kindness, and set off home. Beyond any rationality, and despite the weather, but driven by Mina's childhood memories, they went the longer way, up the lane and up the steps, through the gate, over the sewage pipe, and along the magic path. As they walked, Mina told her daughter the story of the day she went exploring along that path. Of course, Beth took that to mean that going exploring and being adventurous was perfectly all right. That may not have been her mother's intention, but it was what was understood.

The little family did not go on holiday. Rather, people came to them. John and Maggie, Beth's Gran and Grandpa, came very regularly to their little house downstairs. Beth adored her grandpa.

He read to her when she was very young, and once she was able to read, she read to him. Out walking with Sooty, they told stories and played endless spelling games.

They always arrived by steamer from Glasgow, and one day he arrived carrying the metal structure of a garden seat. He brought it in sections, and once in place, it was bolted together. Wooden planks were then acquired, and they too were bolted on. John Connell loved this seat. After he retired he spent many hours sitting on it, smoking his pipe. Often one of the children sat with him. He had endless patience with their guessing games and non-stop questions. The seat had replaced its forerunner which was moved to another part of the garden, and there it resided till wind and weather finally destroyed it. Years later, Beth reflected that John Connell's seat had never been moved. Just as Beth had spent time sitting on this seat reflecting on the life of the house and all its inhabitants, she wondered if her grandfather had done so also. Had he sat there wondering about his mother's disappearance over half a century before? Did he ever discover what had happened to her?

In the cellar of the house was a maypole he had made. In 1959 the Guides, Scouts, Brownies and Cubs put on a Gang Show to raise money to build a hall. Mina, as Brown Owl, devised a dance around a maypole. Her father designed and made it. A metal stand held steady a single pole, at the top of which two horizontal wheels had been attached with holes drilled into them, from which long ribbons were hung. The six Brownies in the dance had two ribbons each, and had to move in such a way as to create patterns of shifting colour. It was mathematically complicated, but it was after many, many disastrous practices, a success.

Years later, Beth was to rescue that maypole. It too was an inhabitant of the house, and demanded more than relegation to a cellar. With a bit of ingenuity, it had become a garden feature. She always touched it so gently. Her grandpa had made this. His imprint was on it still.

Mina's sister Jean was another regular visitor. She had always been elegant. From flower dresses for her dollies to advising on design in a dress shop in Glasgow, she had an eye for style. She had married a soldier, John Wood, but there were no children. Beth and Ian thought this an ideal set-up as it gave them two sets of parents.

As an adult, Beth came to realise how painful this must have been. Her aunt and uncle loved children, and what to these two children was a delightful situation must have been a loneliness to these two adults. How envious of her sister Jean must have been, and yet Beth could not remember one single uttered word of that envy. Beth had never thought of her aunt and uncle as brave, but their silent suffering must have taken tremendous strength. She was sure her Aunt Jean would have found companionship with the Misses Cook.

Jean's friendship with Marion had continued. Marion had moved to London to work in dress designing, but she came home as often as she could, and always coincided her visit with Jean's.

From Kent came Wee John and his wife Wee Jean, another Uncle John and Aunt Jean. Designated by the adults Wee John and Wee Jean, and by the children Uncle John and Aunt Jean London, they travelled by motorbike. They left Kent in the early evening, and rode the bike all through the night arriving eighteen hours later cramped into position, barely able to stand straight. In time a sidecar was attached for their daughter Janet. The sidecar was packed full, not only with a child, but with more luggage than they had been able to carry in their panniers. Two years older than Beth, Janet was ten years more worldly wise.

The garden was their playground. The shore too was a place to spend a great deal of time. They swam in the river regardless of how cold, or indeed how dirty, it was. An industrial river, it was, in the fifties, polluted, but that did not matter. Nor did the weather. The holiday was one long garden and beach picnic.

Into the third and fourth sections of the house came a Glasgow family on holiday. A matriarch with a twinkle in her eye arrived with a seemingly never ending stream of family members. Sons, daughters, grandchildren and even great grandchildren were all squeezed into the tiny house. She was referred to as Mrs N, which the children decided should be written on her Christmas card as Mrs Enn. She loved her house and put up a little wooden fence, the kind Beth had seen in books. It was not that she was shutting people out, it was just that from the busy life in a Glasgow tenement, she loved the idea of living in a section of a house that could be marked off and had a garden. She called it a cottage. It was not a cottage, as it was attached to the main part of the house, but to her it was, and the name stuck.

For the whole of the fifties there were no changes in the house: Beth and her family in one section; John and Maggie, now more than forty years into their tenancy in the little house downstairs; and Mrs Enn in the section of the house once lived in by the coachman and the horses. For most of the year there was only the one family, but in the summer the whole place oozed energy. Visitors came to visit the visitors. They seemed drawn not only to the people but also to the house, and no matter how many people came, the house embraced them. It was almost as if the old house knew how much it was loved, and was determined to keep it that way. Photographs of the house and the garden, and sometimes the inhabitants, travelled home with the visitors to take up residence on sideboards and mantelpieces many miles apart.

The Leitches still owned the house, but the tenants cared for it. Winter after winter, it shielded its people from the storms. In the summer it smiled, watching all the comings and goings. The house demanded Eddie's skills from his former life as a painter. It was a large expanse of wall which had to be painted and re-painted against the winter weather. The three levels made for a high roof, but not a simple one. With the house built in sections, the roof had angles and elevations which gave the building its quirky look. It needed annual attention. The chimneys had to be swept, too. Each year the children watched their father, surefooted as a mountain goat, make his way across the slates way above their heads. They stood in breathless silence as he moved from one slope to another. His years on the high seas had taught him balance.

And watching over the inhabitants, high on the building, the lion had the tiniest hint of a smile.

Chapter Twenty-Four

In 1960, the house had stood for almost a hundred years. Built by old Mr Leitch, whose widow inherited it, followed by his son Alan, it had by now passed to his daughter Annette. A teacher in Glasgow, she came to the other Leitch house, Springbrae, just up the road at weekends and for holidays. The hatters' business had failed, because once again it had not moved with the times, and it was impossible to maintain both a house in Glasgow and a house in the village on a teacher's salary, even when supported by three rents. The old house needed improvements to bring it in line with modern standards, and that she could not contemplate. Miss Annette Leitch informed her tenants that either they must buy their houses, or leave. The tenants of the 1960s had no more rights of tenure than had those a hundred years before. At a whim they could be evicted.

John and Maggie were desolate. They had rented their house for almost fifty years from Miss Leitch's family. The strange political conversation which had grown into a friendship with Miss Leitch's father counted for nothing. Mina had loved this house all her life without really knowing just how much it meant to her, until she was about to have it taken away. Mrs Enn had not lived in her cottage for long, but her feelings for the building were no less sincere. Mortgages for people of their means did not exist. It had to be hard cash.

When Mina had gone into the Wrens, the wage was lower than she had been paid in the Railway Company. To encourage enlistment, the government offered to bank the balance, provided the employee returned to work for a specified period after the war. This she had done, and that money had never been touched. There was a tiny pot of gold. Eddie in submarines was well paid. After the war he had volunteered for service in the Pacific, simply for the wage. It was higher than in other sections of the navy. Beneath the waves there was nothing to spend it on, and so his money was sent home. Mina was careful and saved the extra. It too was in a pot of gold. Eddie and Mina were able to pay for both their house and for John and Maggie's. How Mrs Enn managed to pay for her house, they never found out.

And so the former tenants became reluctant house owners. The alternative had been unthinkable.

In the late nineteen forties and fifties, there had been major house building in Britain. So many people had been rendered homeless by the bombing that houses had to be built. They were built to a much higher specification than their predecessors. The bombing had inadvertently set in motion Victorian slum clearance. These council houses had indoor plumbing, electricity, baths. People who lived in Victorian houses both large and small, which had not been bombed, found themselves living in what was now designated sub-standard accommodation. Owners were given government assistance to upgrade, but only if they lived in the house. The government was not funding upgrades from which private landlords would benefit. It was into this bind that Miss Leitch had fallen.

This, however, worked to the advantage of the new house

owners. They could access government grants, and so, early in 1961, the house underwent major surgery.

The main house had had an indoor toilet and electricity for years. It needed a bathroom. The question was where.

As Jeannie-from-over-the-wall was almost blind by the 1950s, Beth had been dispatched on many occasions to read to her. The Wild West was still the preferred diet of reading, and by the time Beth was eleven, she was fully conversant with a significant portion of the works of Zane Grey. It was many years later that she discovered what a mythical re-write of the American frontier this was. Eventually Jeannie-from-over-the-wall had to move, as she could no longer manage even with Mina's help, and she went along the road to live with her brother and his wife. The house fell empty, but it was in such a state of disrepair that it was beyond renovation. It was condemned to be demolished. Mina and Eddie had a fraction of their pots of gold left, and were able to buy it, not for itself, but for the land on which it stood.

When Mr Leitch had built his house, he had blocked out the little cottage over the wall. Indeed, he had gone so far as to build a wall to hide it. Approaching the back of the house, one saw angles of the rooflines and pseudo battlements. All of this came down, and onto the footprint was built a bathroom. Out of the original foundations of the cottage over the wall came two pillars, on which was built a small brick box containing a toilet, a bath and a wash basin. The back of the house had always been one plain wall disguised by the little cottage and the wall battlements. Now there was a box. It was not an improvement visually, but it was a huge improvement over the zinc bath in front of the fire.

Ian was particularly fascinated with the building. Here was a real building going up right on his doorstep. He avidly watched and learned how the pillars were built, how the cement was mixed, how the box was built absolutely horizontal on sloping ground.

From inside, access to the bathroom was at the top of the stairs.

When Beth came home from school she discovered a hole in the wall, where house and bathroom would be joined together. She just hoped it would not rain in the interim.

When the bathroom was built in the downstairs part of the house, a slice had to be taken from the kitchen to create the necessary space. An artificial wall was constructed, and in so doing, the kitchen lost the big cupboard where the Misses Cook had kept their preserves. The bathroom was narrow, but into that space was shoehorned the delights of a bath, a toilet and a washbasin. A new world had indeed arrived when electricity and hot water were also installed.

Part of the floor was cemented. One night after the builders had gone home, Mina and Sooty went to investigate. Whilst Mina obeyed the sign 'Wet Cement', this was beyond the capability of even the smartest dog. Onto the wet cement he strolled. Summarily lifted off the floor, his paw marks remained. Next morning the builders roared with laughter. Sooty's imprint was on the house, where it has remained ever since.

The coach house, with the coachman's house above it, had been converted into two tiny houses, and now it was converted a second time into one house. It too acquired a bathroom and electricity.

When all the work was complete, Eddie painted the whole exterior. The building had not only internal surgery, but cosmetic also. Sometimes it was hard for twelve-year-old Beth to believe the house was inanimate. How could it have stood here all these decades and not heard and seen everyone who had lived here? She liked the idea that it had heard the whispers and known the secrets. How did it feel about this massive disruption to its innards? Perhaps it felt it had been good enough just as it was, or perhaps it was grateful for a helping hand. It certainly did not complain. It withstood all the hammering and the enforced removal of some of its outer layer.

As the house began its second century, it had a new feel. Still white, still edged with its roofline trim, chimneys still smoking, with a spring in its step, it was ready for another hundred years. It had a party. Music was provided by a gramophone. John Connell had always loved music, and while he no longer played in a dance band, he listened to music on records borrowed from a local library in Glasgow. He had access to great classical music for the price of a second-hand gramophone. It was a black box with a handle to wind it up to the correct speed at which the records should be played. As the wire which rotated the turntable unwound, the sound took on a grotesque slowing down, and so it was essential for someone to sit beside it, to keep it constantly wound up. Dance music was particularly funny as the machine slowed down. A slow-motion eightsome reel is a sight to behold. John Connell had brought the gramophone from Glasgow, and in the house it had remained.

As that party surfaced from the depths of Beth's memory, she found herself climbing the stairs and going into the two-door cupboard under the eaves where the gramophone lived. It had not been played for nearly fifty years, but out it came. The records were stored safely beside it. She wound it up. The table turned. The record went on, and the room was filled with the crackly sound of a polonaise waltz. There were her mother and father, her grandparents and her uncles and aunts dancing just as they had done that night. Her brother had been in charge of winding up the gramophone. Beth had danced with Sooty.

Decades on as she listened, her feet began to tap out the beat, and she began dancing with an imaginary partner. She smiled. She laughed as the music surged through her. It was not just the memories triggered by the music. It was the music itself. The sound quickened her being. She was dancing with the same energy as when she had been a young girl; at that time it was the twist, not the polonaise waltz. She danced as she had as a young adult, remembering halls and rooms decorated at Christmas, where she had spent many happy times dancing in her thirties. She had danced barefoot in Africa, the drumming pulsing through her in sync with her heartbeat. And here alone in her own house she danced from room to room with Chopin. It was good to dance. Her spirits lifted, she returned to her story.

The pot of gold was almost empty, but there was just enough left for three items; a phone, a fridge and a television. The phone was the least interesting to the children. They liked the television bringing new horizons into the house, but the star was the fridge. No more going to the burn to fill a bucket with cold water in order to stand milk in it to keep it fresh. Orange juice took on an entirely new flavour.

Stone houses are solid; humans more fragile. Ian was always outdoors, and one Friday evening he was playing with some friends near an old gate. He decided to climb the gate to venture into new territory. The gate had not been used in decades, and with his weight, its rotten hinges snapped. The gate fell backwards, pinning him underneath. Seeing him neither moving nor responding to them, his friends in panic ran for help, one to the nearest house in the hope of a phone to summon an ambulance, and one to his parents. Eddie was at work, and by the time Mina arrived to find her unconscious son, the gate had been removed, and Ian was being slid onto a board in tiny movements to minimise further internal damage which could ensue by lifting him. Into the ambulance they both went.

That night, Mina and Eddie sat by a hospital bed willing another child to live. By the morning Ian was conscious, but in terrible pain. His back had been damaged, and a lung had been punctured. Barely alive, it was possible he might not walk again.

When he came home ten days later, he was carried into the house. Once again the kitchen was converted into a bedroom for a sick child. There he lay in excruciating pain.

But Ian was determined. Life in a wheelchair was not going to be his future, if he had anything to do with it. He did exactly as he was told, and little by little his breathing improved as his lung repaired. Weeks later, the doctor decided it was possible for him to try to stand. Supported by his parents, he stood up. His back held. They inched their hands away and he stood alone. Day after day this went on; each day he stood a little longer. After a month he was able to take a single step. Once again his back held. Slowly one step became two steps, and then unsupported he crossed the room.

Then he moved from the kitchen to a ground-level bedroom. His friends arrived. At first they were afraid, but as he gained strength there was no keeping them away. His bedroom became quite a gathering place for the boys of the village. Whoops of laughter emerged from that bedroom, banishing the weeks of tension.

The next challenge was the gravel path. Slowly, surrounded by his parents and the doctor he made his way up the gravel path to the gate. The determination in his face turned into triumph.

Stairs were the last great challenge. Fifteen steep stairs demand a great deal of the spine, but slowly and steadily he did it. Day in, day out, he went up and down these stairs until he could do it unsupported, albeit not pain-free. That came later.

During these months, his schoolwork had not been ignored. The headmaster visited the house twice a week, bringing in the work to be done and taking away what Ian had completed.

Within the year, he was playing football again. This had been a regular Sunday occurrence. After lunch he had run along Mina's magic path, down the lane, and onto the flat stretch of ground used by the boys as a football pitch. Jerseys piled high were the goalposts. Ian had been doing this for years before the accident. When he went back, the other boys were afraid to tackle him, or attempt to outrun him, just in case, but the advantage this gave him was not indulged for long.

This terrible accident left invisible marks. It had exploded into the lives of these two children. Its very randomness frightened both of them. But it also taught them something they would not otherwise have learned. Sometimes we can overcome enormous odds.

Uncle John, Aunt Jean London and Janet arrived the following summer with Janet's boyfriend Alan. They were both sixteen. Janet had been determined not to go to Scotland that summer unless he could come too. When Alan arrived, the house and its inhabitants were dumbfounded. He was dressed in London style – suede shoes, a blue collarless suit and with a hair quiff that would never withstand the winter gales of this coastal village. Fairly quickly all this was dispensed with, and once in jeans, Alan fitted right in. Eddie decided he needed assistance with the annual exterior painting, and Alan was set to work.

He spent time fishing with Ian. Down to the pier where the steamers came in they went with rod and line, and back they came with their trophies. When the holiday drew to a close, Alan seemed genuinely sorry to be leaving. He liked the house, he liked the village, he liked the family. When Alan and Janet married, they continued to visit each year, bringing their children with them. Three boys, each one in turn fishing off the pier. Another generation of visitors had begun, carrying their memories away, and returning the following year to build on them.

At seventy, John Connell retired and spent more and more time in his holiday home, where he sat for hours on his garden seat with his grandchildren. Their ages were such that they were better dealt with one at a time. A few years earlier, when Beth had been in Glasgow, her grandpa had taken her for a walk to Kelvingrove Park, and they had stopped to look up to the university.

'You will go there one day,' he said. She had no idea what it was, or why she would go there, but if her grandpa said she would go, she would go. On the garden seat he taught her the history not taught at school. The old house listened and remembered the political discussions and arguments in the thirties. It was Beth's turn to be educated into class politics. In the thirties, a better world was over the horizon. By the time the old man and the young girl were on the seat, education for the working class was real. Beth had it drilled into her that she must work hard at school and go on to university, but never forget her roots. How could she forget where she came from? How could she forget this house? It was her home. Years later she came across people who had chosen to forget their origins, and she realised what he had meant. She never understood those people. By amputating part of themselves, they ceased to be whole.

In what turned out to be his last summer, John sat on the seat with one grandchild after the other. His walks were shorter and slower, but the children and Sooty slowed pace to walk with him. He told them the stories of the house over the years, and of all the people he knew who had lived there. They spent time examining each root crop as it came up. He watched them lay the gravel on the path as it was now too heavy for him to do. On wet days they sat by the old coal fire listening to its crackling.

Summer drew to an end. The children went back to school. The nights drew in. Gran and Grandpa went back to Glasgow.

One afternoon in November when Beth came home from school, her father was silent and Ian was crying. Sooty cowered in a corner.

'Where's Mum?' Panic rising in her voice.

'She's gone to Glasgow. Grandpa has died. Jean phoned to tell her.'

He had died of a stroke. The night before he had felt unwell. In the morning he had got up feeling quite a bit better, but then without further warning had collapsed. His death was instant.

The days that followed were hollow. Mina came home, while her sister in Glasgow arranged the funeral. The children did not attend, such was the thinking at the time. On the day of the funeral Mina and Eddie went to Glasgow, Ian was sent to school and Beth stayed at home with Sooty. This was not as uncaring as it sounded; what would happen if Ian was so distressed he could not remain at school? She was responsible enough to manage this, but she was still just a young girl who had lost her grandpa.

The clock moved slowly. The old house wrapped itself round her in her misery. She could hear his voice, and yet he was not there. It was the first time she had ever been alone in the house for more than an hour. She and Sooty lay cuddled together in front of the fire. She stroked his silky ears and his wiry back, and every now and again, he licked her hand. What was she going to do without her grandpa?

She never forgot that day, and for decades she did not speak of it. It was the confusion which overwhelmed her. She wanted him back, and thought that all she should feel was loss and emptiness. Certainly that is what she felt, but there was also a comfort. She had no idea how she could feel this, and in the months and years ahead was afraid to tell her parents, far less her grandmother, that that was what she had felt. In her distress she wondered if in fact the old house was providing the comfort. But how could it? It was a building; no more, no less. It did not hear, it did not feel, but because it had carried so much of him for so long, it seemed to her he was still here. He was in his own house, he was in hers. She felt the house protecting her, and although she was alone that day, she was not lonely. Without any understanding of how this could be, her relationship with the house began to change.

It was no longer just where she lived. It was no longer just her home. It was a place to be cared for, as a being which gave nurture and which needed nurture. It had become to her human. She did not dare to say this. People might think she was mad. It took her going to the other end of the earth ten years later, and finding other people who felt about their little corners of the world what she felt about hers, to know she was not mad.

After what felt an eternity, her brother came home from school, and then her mother and father with her grandmother arrived from Glasgow. Her father came down the path first, followed by her mother supporting her gran. Beth was frightened to look at her gran, afraid she would somehow look different. Maggie just looked tired, and her smile, while it was wan, was as warm as ever. Beth, Ian and Sooty ran to cuddle her and take her inside, where in silence the house began its role of comforting the old lady.

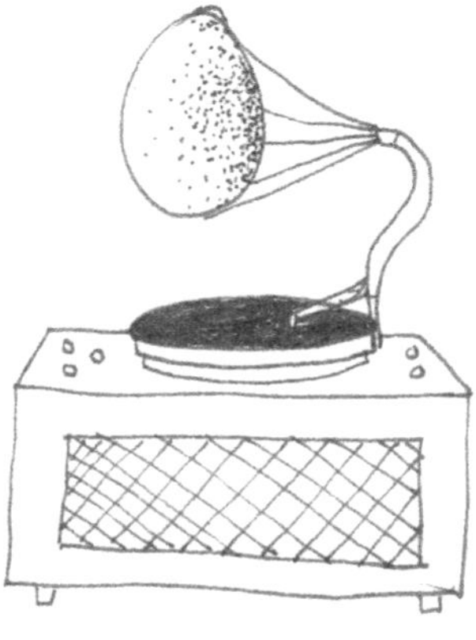

Chapter Twenty-Five

Half a century Maggie had lived with John Connell, and now he was gone. The children did not know what to say to her. They watched her, and they watched their mother. Both of them had become brittle. Nor could their father reach across the divide of silence. The children missed their grandpa and wanted to talk about him, as if by so doing they could keep him with them, but none of the adults were able to do this. He had just gone. Beth and Ian shrank into the shadows.

The days passed into an unhappy Christmas, and by the time the daffodils were coming up again, Maggie had given up her home in Glasgow and was living in her little house underneath Mina and Eddie.

While Beth struggled with her loss, her community had begun to change. Once again war affected this small, compact peninsula. This time it was not men going off to war, but weapons of immense destruction right at its heart. Beth's village, the nearest town and everyone who lived there were on the front line.

In 1945 the USA, the UK and the USSR ended the war against Nazi Germany as allies. Barely had the war ended when simmering fractures ruptured into enmity. The Cold War had begun. The USA and the USSR targeted their weapons on each other. Bombers carrying weapons became obsolete with the development of long-range nuclear missiles. In 1957, the USSR launched a satellite into space. If they could do that, they could launch a weapon from space. It became essential to the USA that their weapons were not easy targets and so a new system of weaponry, Polaris, was developed. From Polaris submarines, nuclear warheads could be launched from beneath the waves. So long as the submarines kept moving they could not be detected, as the USSR did not have the technology to locate submarines which were submerged. To make this possible, it was necessary for the USA to have a base closer to the USSR than mainland America in order to service the submarines. The UK was in the ideal geographical position. In return for the knowledge which would allow the UK to build its own nuclear missiles, the USA was granted the use of a Scottish loch in which to station a base. With no advance warning, this was announced in November of 1960. Four months later, Uncle Sam arrived.

In the intervening four months the small community was catapulted from its quiet rural way of life into a political battleground. Members of the Peace Movement demonstrated; they were carried away by the police. Protests took place increasingly regularly as the date for the naval base grew closer. By the time the sailors actually arrived, they were met by organised peaceful resistance.

The community was divided. The way of life would change forever, but there were economic advantages. Americans had to eat, and if their families were coming also they needed to rent houses. To many of the young children, this was also very attractive. Here were children coming from the world of Mickey Mouse.

The men of the US Navy had to wear their uniforms even off-duty and soon became a familiar sight in the village and in the nearby town. Next came huge cars designed for an American freeway, not single-track roads. Although their presence was visible, at the level of human interaction it was not threatening.

Not so politically. Even at the age of thirteen, were the situation to escalate into war, Beth knew she was four minutes from death. This was never more defined than one morning in October 1962, when Beth went to school. She had not done all her homework – why bother? She might be dead by the end of the day. The USSR was sending weapons to Cuba and the USA made clear that if the ships carrying the missiles to Cuba were not turned back by 3pm UK time, America would retaliate. Reciprocally the USSR would do so also and the naval base would be destroyed. Two miles from the base, Beth's school along with everyone in it would also cease to be.

That morning dragged and by early afternoon no one was talking. The teachers had stopped trying to encourage the children by then. They too were terrified. Beth sat watching the clock on the wall as the minute hand moved to 3pm. By 3.05 she was still alive but it took the wireless being turned on to announce that the Russian ships had turned back for her to believe she would go home that night. She was alive but she was not unscathed.

Conflict erupted at home when she challenged the presence of the US Navy. The Royal Navy submariner defended the situation. Her father dismissed her ideas as silly; in grim silence, a different Cold War took root in the house. Shaken by the experience of Cuba, Beth's political views began to form, but in secret.

Despite her misgivings about the presence of the US Navy, she liked many of the Americans with whom she shared a classroom. Real friendships began to develop; others came unstuck. When she invited friends to her house she was shocked one day to be told by one American that she could not come if another American was also invited. This was not teenage pettiness: this was racial conflict in the school playground. One day she overheard a child asking the teacher where the toilets were. The teacher pointed out the boys' toilets. There was a momentary silence and then she heard, 'These are for the white boys. Where do I go?' On multiple levels the presence of the Americans widened Beth's understanding of the world and developed her views from where her grandpa had left off. These years had an intensity which did not evaporate when friends went back to the USA at the end of their fathers' tours of duty. Letters flew back and forth, and years later so did Beth when she began travelling to the USA to see the land through the eyes of the residents.

The years passed and Beth left school to go to university. This had been talked about for years, but it was not without controversy. Her father had opposed it; what value was education to a girl? Battles raged. The silent war between Beth and her father erupted.

'Oh so you think submarines and we who fought in them are wrong, do you? Yet you want to go to university. What do you think would have happened to you if we had not fought that war? Would you be going to university if the Americans were not here to protect you?' As the ridicule went on, Beth's views became more defined. Her ally was her mother, who taught her when to stand her ground and when to keep quiet and allow developments behind the scenes. In the end, Mina was her father's daughter. Beth was going to university.

For this to happen, Beth had to leave home. She looked forward to doing so, as it made her feel very grown up, but as the time drew near, her feelings wavered. The uncertainty of the adventure which lay ahead was very attractive, but it was also frightening. She wanted away from the increasing friction with her father. Yet she did not want to leave her mother, her brother and her dog. As she walked the old paths she had known all her life, she realised also that she did not want to leave the house itself. So much of her life was written on its walls, that it had become a guardian of her story. It had comforted her on the day of her grandfather's funeral, and now as she was leaving, she felt she was deserting it.

On the morning she left home she walked round every room in the house, and across the garden, stroking her hand along the wall as she went. She sat on her grandfather's seat in the garden, and in his favourite chair in the downstairs house where they had told stories. She wondered what he would say about the military presence in this place he had always seen as comfort. He had held different views on the two world wars. Where would he have stood on this conflict?

Torn in two she spoke to the house, giving it instructions. 'I won't be gone forever. I'll come back often. Stay just as you are. I will live here again someday. Look after my family and yourself, please.'

As she went out of the gate to catch the steamer, she looked back at it. The sun glinted on the window, and the house smiled, wishing her well.

She settled into life in Glasgow, working hard and enjoying city life. As she walked the hard pavements, she often longed for the softness of the paths, for the garden and for the view. She lived in a tenement, and for the first time in her life she had no view. She had never thought of the emotional value of space, hills and sea. It had always just been there, and so she had taken it for granted. Being deprived of it left an emptiness. The house on the hill with its long garden sweeping down to the river belonged to a different life from that of the city streets. She wondered as she walked along if people who lived in the buildings she passed every day on her walk to university felt about their homes as she did about hers. She could not imagine that, hers was so much more beautiful. But even as she thought this, she knew that was not the point. The beauty was irrelevant. A home is more than the sum of its external parts. It is to do with how it shapes its inhabitants, their experiences inside it and what they carry with them. She knew with a certainty she could not explain, that while she had set out for a life of adventure, one day she would go home. Walking through the city in her mini skirt and black leather jacket, she looked every bit the young city slicker, but inside her the imprint of the house became ever stronger.

She studied English Literature, History, Politics and Philosophy. Very quickly she saw that they were not separate from each other. Writers are products of their time, and history can be understood though the poetry, as well as the facts. Why did things happen? What motivated people to do what they did? In came the philosophy with a dash of sociology and psychology. In studying contemporary politics, she knew she was living inside tomorrow's history. She took to the debates and discussions, and gradually her childhood stubbornness disappeared.

'I was wrong. I missed the significance of the point that was the nub of your argument,' she said with a genuine smile. To her amazement, she did not feel diminished by conceding she had been wrong; in fact, quite the opposite. She found a strength born in self-doubt and in being willing to consider new ideas.

She felt a kindred spirit with many of her contemporaries and had been spending increasing amounts of time with a young man. Daniel was very popular among her group. He seemed to share her world view, until one evening on their way to a party, she had wondered aloud about the moon. It had just come from behind the clouds, and was very full and very bright.

'Why can't we see the other side of it?'

He did not reply immediately, but then with a curl of his lip sneered, 'What a stupid question! Take my advice and stop embarrassing yourself with your idiotic ideas.'

She shrank into silence. As she had learned to curb her stubborn nature, she had learned to curb her tongue. Maybe she was idiotic, and no one had yet told her. In trying to fit in and keep her boyfriend, she learned to be silent, but all the while she watched. It did not take long to realise his was not an enquiring mind at all. He was not for her. When she told him, she spoke gently and kindly. The response was vicious. When he ran out of insults, she asked, 'If that's what you think, why have you spent months with me?'

At first he said nothing and then came, 'I was trying to save you from yourself, but I see I have wasted my time.' The arrogance was breathtaking.

'I believed you when you spoke of equality and shared ideas. To say what you have just said, you cannot have meant a word in all the discussions we have had.' As she walked away, she realised how lucky she was to live at a time when she had the freedom to do so.

Over time she began to realise what had happened with Daniel was not unique. For all the apparent radical thinking of her contemporaries, a number were thirled to convention. It just came in a different guise. When she tried to be part of the group by wearing that guise, she did not belong, and at nineteen found it difficult to find a path through this confusion. Rather than walk the easy path to acceptance, in silence she pondered. Who was she really? For the first time she asked herself that question and realised she didn't know.

Coming home for the holidays was always a joy. The house was smiling. Sooty was running in circles. Her family were happy to have her home again. Mina always had a meal ready; her father was more accepting of her now it was clear her university venture was going to be successful. At the first opportunity she took to the bench, regardless of the weather, just to sit and listen to the wind and the river. Despite her happy life in Glasgow, when she wasn't there, she didn't miss it, but sitting in the garden she always felt whole.

Within a few days she was working as a waitress in one of the local hotels. She enjoyed this, because there she met people who would never otherwise have crossed her path. In this quiet place, her life widened.

The village had changed with the Americans, but only on the surface. In many ways it still hummed to the same tune. Baseball rather than football does not erode community life. Despite the politics of the situation, the American families fitted in with village events and the two communities found kinship. This was different from Beth's experience at university. When people learned where she came from, it was assumed she had a negative view of all Americans. Slowly she grasped that the experience of growing up sharing her life with the 'friendly invaders', as they were sometimes called, was different from the experience of her contemporaries who had grown up elsewhere. They had not experienced the conflict between the American presence and the Americans as people. They had not learned that it is possible to carry two different perceptions of one situation. As she walked the familiar paths, she realised she was developing a question for a future Philosophy tutorial – to what extent can we integrate human experience in the formulating of principles?

Her brother had a few more years at school, during which the battle of education was less severe. Education for a boy was within their father's frame of reference.

Completely recovered from his accident, Ian ran the hills, played football and took up golf. He was employed on the golf course in the summer cutting the grass and clearing the greens of sheep droppings. Six days a week he worked for £1 – a fortune to a young boy. The greenkeeper, a drinking pal of his dad, took him on. An old Land Rover pulled a grass cutter behind it. This Ian operated, all the while watching and learning how to drive. Sheep roamed the golf course, and their deposits on the green had to be cleared away to allow the golfers a clear playthrough. Not the most glamorous of jobs, but vital to a dedicated golfer. Clearing the greens with a fireman's broom allowed him to wander into the rough, and find lost golf balls. With entrepreneurial spirit, these he sold.

To this, he added caddying. He watched as he caddied, and soon became a good junior golfer. His tips were turned into clubs. The golf club ran an annual competition, and on one occasion he was caddying for the eventual winner. That tip was a fortune, saved for the next dream – a motorbike. By the time he was in his mid teens, his lifelong love affair with these exciting machines had begun. How proud he was of his first bike. Over the decades which followed, he had a fleet of them, each one remembered for its unique sound.

Even as a teenager, he had to admit cars were more convenient than bikes, and four wheels became his next goal. Not a car that would actually run, but one on which he could learn mechanics. In time, one such did come his way; he paid £100 for a wreck covered in leaves and mould. Problem was, he had to move it. With the aid of pals, it was pushed two miles to sit outside the gate. The house seemed to take on a cockiness with the status symbol of a car, albeit one with no working engine.

Ian's next step was to spend time at a local garage washing and valeting cars, but always with an eye to watching and learning. Bit by bit he acquired what was necessary, and the old house looked on in wonder at this new invention as it coughed and then roared itself into life. Before he was old enough to drive, Ian had a car! The cosmetics came next. Lovingly painted and polished, it awaited the driving licence.

On the great day of his driving test, off Ian went. How could he fail? He understood how cars worked – he had built one! But the test adjudicator thought differently. Here was a teenage driver who had to be taught a lesson. Ian failed on a technicality. He came home enraged. He sat in the stationary vehicle with his friends who had come to have a spin in the car. Mina let them into the car, and then took the keys away, just in case they decided to be defiant. Little did she know, he could have started it anyway.

The weeks passed until his second test, and this time the same adjudicator decided Ian had learned his lesson. The old car roared into action, and the house waved it on its way on this first of many trips. When Beth came home from university, there was Ian at the steamer to collect her in the car he had built from a shell. Never having been picked up in a private car, she felt like a film star.

Mrs Enn in the Cottage visited more regularly, and in the holidays her family also came. Once again the house swelled its ranks in the summer. Beth, home from university; Annie, come to visit her sister Maggie; uncles and aunts from Glasgow and London. Alan, Janet and their boys were also fitted in each summer. As time went on, many of this group came at Christmas also. For two stretches of each year every chimney smoked, and lights blazed all over the building. When it was time for the visitors to go, the old house could rest.

One year, Mina decided to make wine. She gathered brambles from the hedgerows, and followed the instructions to the letter. However, in the middle of a December night, the family was shocked out of sleep by what sounded like gunfire. The explosions were happening inside the cupboard. The wine corks were popping. The bottles were still intact, but they had become fountains spraying wine all over the interior of the cupboard, now a delicate shade of burgundy. What a mess! What a waste of wine! What a story! And why? Had Mina made a mistake? She was adamant she had not. Nothing in the instructions had warned about the effect on the fermenting process of heat radiating from walls, warmed by a century-old coal fire and transmitted into its adjacent cupboard.

Ian went off to university in 1971, and Sooty went into a decline. Mina said he moped about the house, looking for Ian at his normal time of coming home from school. Perhaps the regularity of Mina's tasks told him the time, perhaps it was some internal canine time clock; it certainly worked. He was old and stiff by then, but he would hobble to the door and wait for it to open, and when it did not, he went back to his bed in the corner of the kitchen, his head, shoulders and tail down. In December Ian came home from university, and Sooty found a new lease of life. The fun boy who took him up the hills and played games with him was home. That Christmas, he was the happiest dog in the universe.

In the January Ian went back to Glasgow, and, Mina said later, Sooty just gave up. He slept more and more. He was listless. He even turned down chocolate. In the February he suffered a stroke when he was lying in his favourite place, right in front of the kitchen fire. He had always liked that spot, in the middle of his family, lying on his back, legs in the air, and warmed by the heat. Once again, Mina and Eddie sat with a member of the family gravely ill.

Sooty, at fifteen, did not survive. He was buried in the garden in a little grave dug especially for him at the end of the vegetable plot. His bowl and his water dish were put into a cupboard. Fifty years on, each year when that cupboard has its spring clean, the bowl and the water dish are washed and carefully returned to their place. Visitors still smile at the story of the chewed table legs.

Chapter Twenty-Six

Beth had no idea what she would do after university. As her friends planned for the future, she dreamed. She wanted to travel and wondered about applying to the Foreign Office. She loved the theatre and thought about a career on stage. Nothing felt quite right, and so she did nothing. Eventually, however, reality could no longer be postponed; she had to make a choice about how she was going to earn a living. Many of her friends opted for teaching. It was, they declared, a good safe job and ideal for marriage and children. Beth, however, did not see her future as a balance sheet.

The year when her group all turned twenty one was expensive. Presents and parties required an income. At that time, there was such a shortage of teachers that it was possible to get temporary work in education. She gritted her teeth for as short a time as possible.

To her amazement, she loved it. In a classroom, she discovered skills she did not know she had. On a hefty diet of humble pie, she trained as a teacher. Once qualified, from Monday to Friday she taught literature, and at the weekends enjoyed city life, or when the pull was strong she went home. Sitting on the garden seat one night, she wondered about applying for a job at home. A vacancy had come up. It was ideal, but something inside her rebelled at the idea. She knew she would come back one day, but the certainty of this idea was matched with an equally strong certainty it was not yet. Underneath her certainty, fear niggled that her education had changed her such that she could no longer fit in. Can our experience make us no longer really want what we think we want?

Nor did the city hold her. She wanted an adventure and so she went to Australia. Like her mother before her, she was not yet ready to follow the assumed route into marriage. Once more she had to separate from the house and her family. In some ways, it was easier this time. She had gone to university; her house and her family had continued. What difference 12,000 miles?

On the night before she left, she went up the hill and looked down on the house. She went to the shore and looked up at it. Its quirky angles had never changed; its striking whiteness and contrasting rooflines as they had always been. She fought down the panic of when she would see it again.

She wanted to go. She did not want to go. She sat on the garden seat, and realised that even if she could back out at this late stage, she would not. The old house listened to the same dilemma it had listened to in 1914, but it was not so uncomfortable, because while Australia was a very long way away, this time there were no guns. It sat, if not content, certainly not uneasy. The shadows moved round her. The birds fell silent. In the darkness, she did not need to be told she would come back. She knew it.

On the morning she left, her grandmother, who had said little throughout all the discussions, could contain herself no longer. In a strangled voice Beth heard, 'You're a brave lass. I shall miss you,' and in a whisper, 'I don't think you will see me again.' Beth was shocked. Of course her gran would be there when she came back, but these words torn out of the old lady hurled doubt at what she was doing. How could she have caused her gran such grief? Indeed, she might not see her again. As she left, she could not look anywhere but at the ground. Had she looked at her gran, her parents, her brother, the house, she might have faltered. She learned later that after she left, no one spoke for many hours.

In Australia she found a community of like-minded travellers, many of them Americans, with whom she explored the country. She wrote home every week, and she looked forward to the mail coming from home with the same regularity. Everyone in her family wrote, and these letters she treasured. In one of them came the news that another dog had arrived. Ian had been working on a farm during the university holidays. When pups had been born, and without prior discussion with his family, he asked the farmer if he could have one, picked up the one that appeared to be the smartest in the litter, put it into his jacket and cycled home. In Ian's words, this dog was on approval for three days. Geordie stayed sixteen years. He was a collie, and unlike his predecessor he did not eat everything. Rather, he chased everything. Sticks, balls, the lawnmower, children – he herded them.

Beth was furious. How dare they replace Sooty? From the other end of the world she wanted to influence events, and it was with quite a shock she realised she had no right to do so. She had left. She could not demand that life at home froze into stone. By the act of leaving and going so far, she had cut herself off. Home lay at the end of the adventure.

Everything she did reinforced this. Every young man she met who interested her, she knew was temporary. She went through boyfriends with a cake knife. No matter how much they liked each other, no matter how much fun they had together, no matter the similarity of thinking, careless of their feelings she discarded them one after another. She was passing through.

She liked Australia, and she was not homesick. It was deeper. She simply did not belong. If she had stayed there she would have been lonely all her life, as to do so, she would have had to destroy part of her being. She imagined marrying in Australia and going home on visits. The agony of each imagined leaving to return to Australia was visceral. She did not speak of this. She did not write it except in the diary she had kept, carefully wrapped with all the letters.

This did not stop her from enjoying the adventure. In fact, it enhanced it. She was determined to extract every moment of experience from this temporary life, so different from home. She taught in a small school in the bush. It did not have a bicycle shed, it had a stable; some of the children arrived on horseback.

The long holidays were pressed into use. She and her friend Carol travelled all over the country, usually hitchhiking. Not only was this cheap, it also provided the opportunity to ask questions of the people they met. Every new car they climbed into was an opportunity to learn. Every driver was interrogated. Instead of only talking to the people they knew in the little town where they worked, there were people everywhere they went, from all walks of life. Travelling was a daily exploration of places and people, ideas and culture. Sometimes they quizzed her, and occasionally she found their questions unintentionally offensive. She met people who drifted through life, never apparently making a choice, just going along a path that lay open. She knew this could never be her way. She met people with no self-doubt; people who would destroy whatever was on their path rather than admit they might have been wrong. She shuddered, recalling how in her early stubbornness and in the arguments with her father, that might have become her way.

Travelling a country, she discovered, is hard work. It takes effort, but the rewards of getting under the skin are immense. Without this level of interaction, a so-called traveller is just a visitor skimming the surface. There is no insight.

Australia's desert is stunningly beautiful. Throughout the day it changes colour as the sun moves across the sky; yellow, orange and at times flaming red. The sun and the land become as one; a vast empty kaleidoscope of colour. We humans shrink to tiny insignificant specks in this silent timelessness. At night, the desert finds its voice. Sounds of scurrying creatures, rocks cracking, the wind stirring the sand belong in a world stretching back an eternity.

She knew below consciousness that it was for this she had come. In the desert, it is the person who does not wonder about the other side of the moon who is out of place. Both day and night, watching the desert was a source of endless fascination. After she came back, she made one or two attempts at describing the constant shifting colours and shapes in the land by day, and the moving stars in the heavens by night. Sometimes people would say, 'But what's the fascination? There is nothing there. Is it not really boring?' If she had not known before, there was now no denying she saw the world differently, and very quickly she learned not to speak of what she had seen and heard and felt, not out of fear or shame but rooted in her own dignity. Only her travelling companions understood, for they experienced it also.

In conversation after conversation in trucks and cars, on stretches of open road and at campfires, Beth had learned the startling truth that we are shaped by our worlds without even being aware of it. It had taken her standing outside that world to truly understand.

From so far away, she could look back on her childhood almost as an outsider. Much of her life had been happy, surrounded by family who loved her, though her father's increasing hours in the local pub and the arguments they had endured had not been easy. She would not go back to that, but living on the other side of the world was not the only alternative. Ahead of her lay choices. What was not clear was how to make them.

Two years later, she came home overland. Ferries, trains, buses and two short flights. Darwin, Bali, Jakarta, Singapore, Bangkok,

Kathmandu, Delhi, Peshawar, Kabul, Teheran, Istanbul, Athens, Venice, Innsbruck, and all points in between; for months she and Carol were on the road. Each Wednesday she wrote home, where every detail was pored over and the location from which the letter had been posted carefully marked on a world map. Even more amazingly, letters arrived for Beth sent Poste Restante to her next destination. At one point the bus she and Carol were on broke down, and they were transferred onto a bullock cart, much as people had travelled for centuries. Yet when they reached their destination, found accommodation, and then set off to the post office, there was the mail. The old world and the new sat side by side.

On the journey she met a young man from Tasmania starting out on his journey across the world, as she was finishing hers. Their relationship deepened, and by the time they reached London, both knew this was not just for being on the road.

She had looked forward to coming home. In her mind she expected its beauty as it had been the night before she had left, a long summer evening a lifetime of experiences ago. Arriving in December, it was cold and dark. From the wide open spaces of Australia, it all looked so small. She made the acquaintance of the new dog, and disliked it on sight. Geordie was a usurper.

And thus began a very painful time she had not expected. Had she made the right decision to come back? Could she fit in again? Had this changed her forever, and if so where would she go? The relationship with the young man had begun to crack, because he too was facing crisis. He was on his adventure. He liked Scotland, and he was not homesick. It was deeper. He simply did not belong. He imagined marrying in Scotland, and going home on visits. The agony of each imagined leaving Australia to return to Scotland was visceral. He could not stay, and she could not go with him. They lived in a strange present, knowing one day they had to part, because they both had roots they could not tear up.

Strangely, realising this helped Beth to readjust. She was home, and the old house opened itself to her. On the day she came home, her gran was so excited she was waiting at the gate. In the look that passed between them, they both remembered what the old lady had said, and for the only time in her life Beth was glad to know her gran had been wrong. She was there to see her come home.

Beth spent many hours downstairs talking to her grandmother, absorbing her wisdom, and as the old lady's eyesight failed, reading to her. They had both kept all the letters they had written to each other, and often they would read a letter or two and amplify it with remembered details. Beth had gone to the other side of the world in order to come home.

Maggie died two years later at the age of ninety-one, in the house she had loved for over sixty years. One day she tripped over Geordie's bed and hit her head. Her decline was sudden and rapid. Her sister Annie, who had continued to live in Glasgow, followed shortly after. They had been born during the reign of Queen Victoria. They had seen the soldiers setting off to the Boer War. Maggie had fought alongside the Suffragettes. Their father had walked from the Highlands as a destitute Gaelic-speaking peasant looking for work.

When Beth touched her grandmother's face, she was touching a face which had first been touched by two adults born in the 1850s.

Her grandfather had never faded. When she had graduated from university she had walked down to the spot in Kelvingrove Park, where he had said to her, 'You will go there one day,' and she thanked him. Looking at her grandmother before the coffin was closed, she thanked her for her letters, her wisdom, her humanity, her strength. She had a duty to carry this with her. She went home to sleep in her gran's bed in the little house downstairs.

Chapter Twenty-Seven

When Beth came back from abroad, she settled down with her parents. She had been on the road long enough, and was eager not only to work full-time again, but to build the kind of relationships with pupils she herself had experienced; relationships which require years in one school.

Her grandfather had instilled in her a deep belief in education, and through her mother insisting on her going to university, she was the living embodiment of that belief. And now she was a teacher, imbued with the essential role of education in improving society.

She truly liked children, and so even the ones who caused trouble were to be worked with, not shunned or punished. They were people to be reached through the power of literature. When children took to reading for pleasure, that for Beth was the ultimate success. In time, the entire world of books would open for them. All she had done was sow the seed. She was particularly fond of Shakespeare, and very quickly realised that if she read all the parts herself, her students could see beyond the difficulties of the language to the essence of the meaning. She chuckled remembering the day she had taught the scene in Macbeth where Lady Macbeth persuades her husband into killing King Duncan. The class had looked carefully at her methods of persuasion, and then one young girl announced, 'Wants to be Queen of Scotland? Huh! She nags just like the woman next door to me.' Shakespeare was no longer remote.

Beth was back living in the house she loved, working at a job she found to be a joy, connecting with friends from the past, and making new friends. And yet there was something missing; she still sought adventure over more than one horizon.

In the long summer holidays from teaching, she went travelling. Before going to Australia she had not gone beyond western Europe, but now she was ready to go much further. She did not choose places. They seemed to choose her. Something she came across would strike a note, and she pursued it until it was not just a note, but a whole symphony to be played. Her holidays took a year; six months in the reading and the planning, then the going, and after that the follow-up. Sometimes she travelled with Carol, and sometimes alone. She became increasingly interested in physical landscapes. From her time in Australia she was drawn to deserts, and so began regular trips to North Africa and the Middle East. This caused her parents much anxiety, but neither of them had any argument against it – how could they, given the choices they had made?

As time went on, part of her also yearned for the city life she had known. Faint sounds became whispers. 'You know you can go away again. Come back when you're ready.'

She referred to this new restlessness as 'the Call of the Orient', but the east was the east of Scotland. She went to Edinburgh. This time leaving was not difficult at all. She would come home regularly. Only eighty-nine miles. After Australia, the mere blink of an eye.

She threw herself into her new Edinburgh life with great

vigour. She got involved in many activities, some political and some theatrical. Never a week went by but she was at the theatre, and it seemed a natural progression when she moved to the other side of the footlights.

It began very simply. She had small parts in plays, and while she dreamed of greater things, she knew she was just not good enough. But she also realised she had a talent for directing. Could she do this with amateurs? So often used pejoratively, Beth preferred the pure meaning of the word 'amateur'; people for whom this was not a job. That did not diminish their talent. Beth set out to try. She worked with small companies and then was invited to work with one of the best musical companies in central Scotland. She simply expected the cast to be able to do what she was asking, and as they did so in show after show, she raised the bar. In 'Dolly' she built a train scene out of human movement. In 'Fiddler' she put the spirit of Judaism silently onto the roof of the cottage, watching as events unfolded, until, when the family were forced to leave, the light was extinguished on the last beat of the music. It took hours of practice to co-ordinate the slow walk, all the characters in unison, to build the tension in movement, music and lighting until they were extinguished in sudden silence and darkness.

Scotland was changing and there was a new energy in the arts. A new generation of writers and musicians, sculptors and artists were making their mark. Like Beth, many of them belonged to the first generation of a family to go to university. They too were shaped by their childhood experiences with education layered on top of it. Pubs all over the city listened to every new idea. Beth was in her element.

Her circle of friends grew. Her great friend was Maggie, whom she taught with. Meeting her only a few months after the loss of her grandmother, Beth was drawn to having another Maggie in her life. A highlight of the weekly calendar was Sunday evening in the pub, Beth with Guinness and Maggie with Glenmorangie. Both in their twenties, they had their dreams. When Maggie bought a house with a garden, she decided she wanted a tree, and so the two of them set out to a garden centre one fine Saturday morning.

'We'd like to buy a tree,' Beth announced.

'What kind of tree?'

'Not sure. What would you suggest?'

The gardener rolled his eyes.

'This is not like buying a pair of shoes. I need to know where it is going to grow, how tall you want it to grow to, what kind of soil and what amount of sunlight.'

'Oh.'

The following week was spent acquiring answers to these questions. And on the Saturday they went back.

'We've come to buy the tree. We have the answers to your questions, except for the one about the soil, and so we have brought you a bag of it.'

He glared and then softened. They would learn. One hour later, the tree was bought. It was nine inches tall, a cherry. They were all set to leave, when the gardener who was by then quite taken with these two crazy young women, asked if they had a spade.

'No, will we need one?'

He hid the smile, which the previous week would have been a smirk. Armed with a spade and a tree, off they went.

'Come and tell me how you get on,' he called as they left, and indeed they did. About once a month, they went to see him armed with a chart, on which were the growth measurements of the tree. He always had advice. One day he turned up at the house.

'I have just come to check on the tree.' He looked, he prodded, he shook it and then pronounced.

'Aye you've done well. Any chance of a cup of tea?'

Beth went back to her flat with a pinprick of envy that she did not have a garden and a tree to measure. Of course, she had a garden of trees at home; momentarily she wondered if she was now being tugged in the opposite direction.

City life suited her. But it was undeniable that every month when she came home for the weekend, there was a real sense that that is precisely what she was doing. She was going home. Often she took her washing home, not so that her mother would do it, but so that after drying on the washing line, it went back to Edinburgh with the smell of home.

In the summer holidays she continued her travels, but at Easter and Christmas, back she came. The elastic kept pinging.

In travelling alone she met a great many people, and in conversations in bars and cafes and souks, on park benches and sand dunes, on trains, buses and ferries she found people like herself, people with the travelling rat gnawing inside them, but who also had a strong sense of where they belonged. They were not rootless wanderers, but explorers whose minds were opened by what they saw and heard. Travelling alone, at times she was isolated, but she was never lonely. Her community were the people she met along the way. Every year she came back with threads of many colours weaving a tapestry, not only of what she had seen and heard of the world, but into her thinking.

Time rolled on, and as her friends married and had children, she became less settled. She was not at all sure she wanted this new chapter of living, but began to wonder if she was perhaps out of step with what she ought to feel. She liked her life, but was increasingly isolated from her contemporaries. Her holidays became less of an adventure and more of an escape. Into the tapestry crept fear. If she did not follow the pattern, would she one day regret it, and if so what then?

She often thought wistfully of her relationship with Alex the Tasmanian. That had been a relationship of equals. She had learned to hear the timbre of truth in a voice. When he spoke of going home because that was where he belonged, she knew he was speaking from his soul and he could no more stay than she could go. They had parted in Glasgow's Central Station. He was taking the train to London to fly to Australia; she was going back home. The parting was so sharp that she unconsciously protected herself by almost being outside of it. She could still see herself standing beside the seats on the concourse of the station wearing a green and white beret, her face rigid with misery. His eyes were wide, staring as if frozen. Neither could speak. As the years passed she longed for another relationship with the same sense of belonging, but it was not to be. Reluctantly she accepted that the choices she had made had exposed her to a wider world and it might not be possible to fit into the world she had now chosen. The alternative choice was to become a permanent traveller. She shuddered at that idea. Yet no matter how much she turned over this new dilemma, she could find no regrets about the choices she had made. But how to make different choices now? That was the question.

In the end she got married, but in doing so, she dug a deeper hole. She knew it was a mistake, but how did you say that in the 1980s? She wanted to really want what she had chosen, but she could not, and in the end they parted. Neither of them were wrong. They just wanted different things. Her trouble was, she was not sure what she wanted. How do you ever know if you are making the right choice until after you have made it?

She began to wonder if each generation fights a battle from which the next one benefits. Her grandmother had fought for the right to vote, her mother for the right to education. Was it her generation's battle to have the right to choose a lifestyle, and resist the pressure from within? Was it her generation's battle to beat a path of relationships rooted in the silence of the soul rather than in selecting someone to march beside through life? The women's movement had done much to change the externals of society, but little to challenge the internals of human conditioning.

Into this was built the powerful force of nature. She wanted a child. She had lost a baby early in her married life, so that when the marriage ended, she lost not only her present, but also her anticipated future. The pain was almost beyond enduring. A gynaecological problem, easily corrected ten years later, was at that time damnation to infertility.

In that summer when her life went awry, she had no interest in travelling. She came home. Like an injured animal, she moved by instinct. Her relationship with Geordie had improved by this time, and in these weeks he was devoted to her. They walked the hills together, and when she lay on the couch crying, he climbed on top of her to lick her face. That dog did not of course understand what had happened, but he did sense misery, and brought what comfort he could. One day when she felt very low, she went to him. He was under the table, and, her misery reaching the point of a physical ache, she got under it beside him. This he did not like one bit. He got up and walked from under the table, turned and looked at her. She did not move. Back he came, and taking her sleeve in his mouth, he set off to the couch. He waited till she got onto it and up he climbed. He could have licked her face under the table, but that was his territory, and she had to go where befitted his canine programming. What in an animal can trigger such empathy? He could have ignored her, but he did not. He knew his role.

As the long daylight hours faded to darkness, Beth went out walking. She wanted no one to see her. She had failed. The expectations of society had not changed from the days of the Misses Cook; they were different only in that they were unspoken. She dreaded pity. Mile after mile in the darkness she trudged. Sometimes she slept on the hillside. Sometimes she came home. Every time she opened the gate, and saw the lights her parents had left on for her, she felt not pity, but the warmth of comfort. Not only her parents, but the old house too, was offering safety. It drew her home, and she was able to sleep.

One night she came in about 3am and heard sounds from her

parents' room. She went to speak to them, and as she looked into the room, she stood stock still at the scene in front of her. Her father was sitting on the edge of the bed, holding the little Singapore blanket, sobbing.

Beth crept away. They had not seen her. Wrapped in her own misery, it had never occurred to her that her pain was theirs also. She would not cause them more hurt if she could help it. In such a moment, she had a choice to become a victim or to become a survivor. Both routes carry a burden of pain, but once the immediate shock had passed in the ensuing months, Beth's life force knew only one way at that crossroads.

She had survived when she was only days old. No longer a victim, she would survive now... somehow.

By the end of the holidays she was as ready as she was going to be to go back to the city, and as the autumn settled into winter, week by week she recovered. The pity she dreaded came only from people whom she barely knew. They sought her out, but their words were empty. She was puzzled by this, but gradually became aware there was a pattern to how they spoke; their words were uttered in smugness.

From her friends it was comfort and help and endless listening; sympathy not pity. As the year turned, drawing on all the threads of her life, she began to forge a new path.

Ian had gone from home by then, too. After university he worked in England, and then was offered a job in America. He was a civil engineer who had become involved in bridge building, just at the time a new style of bridge was being developed. He had been in the right place at the right time. After that it was not luck, but sheer skill and hard work.

Like his sister eight years before, he found going away difficult. He wanted the career and the adventure, but he too loved home. Crossing the Atlantic on an annual visit at that time was not possible, so once he had gone, he would be away a goodly time. He had no intention of living across the ocean permanently. Going for a few years and coming back was the plan.

Over the wall, beyond where the bathroom sat on its pillars on the site of the old cottage, there stretched an extensive wood. It had been the Victorian orchard where the fruit trees had grown, long since gone to seed. Ian bought the land, so that on his return, he would build his own house there. He too was on a piece of elastic.

He wanted to go. He wanted to stay. In the end, Mina said to him what she had learned from her father.

'I have given my children roots, and I have given them wings.'

And off he went to his new life. However he did not go alone, not quite. For some months before the offer to work in Florida, he had being seeing a young woman in England. Jacqui was a Drama student, flamboyant and well read. When Ian brought Jacqui home to meet his parents, all the way from England on a motorbike, the visit had been a success. She had also to pass the test of the house and the village. Beth remembered Jacqui many years later telling her that right from the beginning she had thought the house 'a little piece of paradise'. Its quirkiness, its location, its view. The third test she had to pass was his idea of building over the wall sometime in the future. Jacqui's parents lived in the north of England, and going to America was only possible if she thought she would one day be able to come back. Her family were to her as strong a pull as Ian's was to him.

Ian went off to America. Jacqui followed and they married in 1980. In 1983 Kate was born, and what a bundle of excitement she was when she was brought home. As she grew up, she was devoted to Mina, her 'Grandma'. Grandma by this time had a greenhouse, and spent hours cultivating plants from seeds.

One day she said to Kate, 'Would you like to hear how this greenhouse came to be here?'

Kate nodded enthusiastically.

'A few years ago, before he lived in America, your dad came

home on holiday. He was working in Yorkshire at the time, and had driven north in a mini, which, as you know, is a very small car. He did not come on his motorbike that time, because he was carrying a present for me. Can you guess what that present might have been?'

'A big plant pot?'

'No, something much bigger.'

'A very big plant pot?'

'No, it was this greenhouse. He knew how much I would have liked to have a greenhouse, but they were too expensive for me. Your dad saved up and bought me one. When he came into the house, and told me he had a present for me in the car, he was very excited as we went to the gate. All I could see was a car packed with boxes. What on earth, I wondered. And then the boxes were carefully carried down the garden, and he told me to open them very, very carefully. I did so and can you believe with all that glass there was not a single breakage.'

'This must have made you very happy, Grandma.'

'Oh yes. It was a wonderful present. But I was a wee bit worried because how was it going to be built?'

'Daddy would build it,' announced Kate, no other option even to be considered.

'Indeed he did. He laid the foundations you can see over there, and then put in the metal poles and lastly the glass. It was very exciting to watch. This was in late summer, but through the winter I planned and I bought seeds. I grew them in the house to keep them warm, and it was a great day when they were strong enough to be brought out here. And they grew until they could be planted outside and others could come into the greenhouse.'

Kate smiled. Even as a little girl, she could see how much her grandma loved the little glass house.

Together they also walked Geordie. Kate threw sticks for him to chase, so that for every journey they made, he made at least three, running backward and forward to collect the sticks from where they had landed. Mud, burns, fields, gardens, nothing deterred him on the stick chase. Kate was forever raising the bar of his ingenuity to find the sticks she threw in all directions. She worked out that Geordie could count, but only up to four. If there were four sticks and only three were thrown, he pestered Kate to get the other stick, but if she had five sticks, he seemed to not realise when only four had been thrown.

She was a great reader, and so another generation sat out on the garden bench reading aloud to anyone who happened to be passing by. The old house listened to this young voice, fascinated with the very different accent.

One evening Ian and Jacqui went out, and left Kate sleeping upstairs in the room Ian had slept in as a child. It was an odd shaped room, an L shape with its short leg stretching over the staircase. It was a room very difficult for placing furniture. The L shape, the deeply sloping ceiling angles, and the fireplace left little wall space against which to place items. Unlike the grandness of the main bedroom with its huge bay window, this room was small and cosy. It was also the warmest room in the house, as its walls were heated by the kitchen fire below.

That evening, Beth went upstairs to check on her niece. Kate was a beautiful child, her red golden hair spread over the pillow as she slept. Beth sat at the end of the bed, looking at her. Why could she not have this too? Silent tears coursed down her cheeks. And then beside her was Mina. She had heard her daughter go upstairs and not come back. She had guessed the torment going on in the room above. Nothing was said. They just sat, Beth turning to her mother with all the helplessness of a child.

Back downstairs, her kindly old eyes calming Beth, Mina spoke, 'You know you are unlikely to ever have this, but you can still have her. Spend time with her. Listen to her. Be her aunt. Think of what Uncle John and Aunt Jean did with you. Don't focus on what you don't have, but think on what you can do with what you do have.'

For days Beth turned this over. She tried, and slowly found she could spend time with her niece without scorching anguish. She played the spelling games Grandpa had played with her. She told the stories he had told her. They read stories to each other. The child responded, and the relationship grew.

Gradually she saw that her mother's wisdom was a maxim to apply right across her life. One day as she was dusting the lily of the valley on the ceiling, from somewhere she heard, 'You are lucky you have choices. Trust yourself and don't waste them.' The limbo she had been living in began to evaporate, and she was able to look ahead.

In time Kate, had a sister. Rosie was a very strong-willed child. She too loved the greenhouse. She had never seen anything like this little glass house hung with plants. She loved the smell inside it, the humidity, and she loved its warmth. She happily planted seeds and watched the careful watering that went on. She tenderly touched the plants, but then as if seized by a demon, one day she snapped off the heads of all the flowers she had been carefully tending for weeks. When Mina asked her why she had done this, her answer was, 'To see you get mad. You don't ever get mad at me, and I wanted to see you get mad.'

Mina did not concur, but quietly explained to the child that what she had done was wrong. Rosie's response was to become devoted to her. Night after night she asked her grandmother not to read her a story, but to tell her stories of her dad when he had been small. As Grandma told the stories, the old house smiled, remembering.

A favourite moment of every visit was her arrival. Rosie loved to open the gate and make her way down the gravel path. The house was always the same. To her it was from a fairy tale with the sheep on the hill, the river beyond, the wet smell in the air and all the greenness which on dull days contrasted with the grey of the sky. She had an artist's eye for this kind of detail.

Her least favourite part of the visit was the bathroom in winter. The house had no central heating, and the bathroom, punched out the back of the house, was surrounded by cold air on three sides. Having a bath was not for the faint-hearted. The water, heated as it was by the coal fire, was of limited amount. Bathwater was rationed to two inches.

She was at her happiest in front of the fire, sitting cross-legged poking at it to incite the blaze. It was not just for her a visual pleasure. She loved the smell of the coal and the logs. Generations may come and go, but the fire remained at the centre of the life of the house.

Always when Ian, Jacqui, Kate and Rosie were setting off back across the ocean, they took with them the most precious of souvenirs, their memories. The house watched the quiet sadness of departure, but with its long memory of all those who had lived here, knew it would not be long before these little girls would once again run down the path shouting, 'Grandma! Grandpa! We're here.'

Chapter Twenty-Eight

These years of the late seventies into the eighties brought other changes, also. After Maggie died, the downstairs house sat empty. It needed to be lived in and cared for. It was also a financial drain, and so reluctantly Mina decided it had to be rented and pay its way.

At the American Naval Base, sailors with families needed accommodation. Once again Beth and her father disagreed. She could accept the Americans as people while opposed to their presence, but that did not mean she agreed with making an income from the situation. This time her mother opposed her. The house had to be lived in to fend off the dampness and cover its costs.

It was not big enough for a large family, but it was for a couple. Mark and Brenda arrived. They were twenty years old, and had known each other since high school. Mark was already stationed in Scotland, living on the ship, but, as he was going home to marry, he had to find accommodation for himself and his wife which would be ready for their return. He had heard from his friend about this little place, and came to see it. He loved it on sight, and as a dog lover, he was particularly taken by the fact that clearly Geordie ruled the roost. Years later he said that the pull was the garden, the dog, the building, Mina's welcoming smile. The little house underneath was like a hidden secret. He took the lease and went back to Minnesota to be married. A week later, he returned with his bride, who at that point had never been out of her state.

And thus began a forty-year friendship. On the long winter nights, when Mark was on the ship, Brenda would appear at the door upstairs with cakes she had baked. In she came, and drew up her seat by the fire with Mina, Eddie and Geordie. She just became a member of the household. Mark and Brenda were in the little house downstairs for less than two years, but during that time parents came to visit, her sister came to visit, and when they left, they carried the imprint of their visit back across the ocean.

Beth came to know Mark and Brenda when she was home from Edinburgh. She may have disagreed about them being there, but she could not be rude and ignore them. Over time conversation developed and what struck her most forcibly was not the differences between her and them, but the similarities. They were two rural farm kids from the Midwest who shared many of her beliefs and values. In town the sailors looked daunting. Mark in his uniform did too, but on the bench in tee-shirt and jeans talking of their hopes and dreams the friendship grew. This was a new dimension.

People she had met on the road who shared her world view did so, she assumed, because they were on the road, but here were two people, one in the military and the other a vet's assistant, with the same quiet strongly held beliefs. This threesome spent hours on the garden seat. Once again she experienced the conflict of the political situation with the reality of the experience. This time, however, she understood that she could hold both opinions.

In the decades that followed, Mina went to Minnesota. So did Beth. Mark and Brenda with their family came to River View.

Their daughter Jessica at the age of twelve drew the garden gate, a picture which still hangs in the entrance to the house.

Mark and Brenda also gravitated into the greenhouse. Tomatoes, courgettes and cucumbers were grown and metamorphosed into chutney or soup, as well as tasting delicious on salads. The pleasure was in the growing; Mina grew far more than she needed. She was happy to give it away. In time she grew fruit, and this, added to the berries gathered in the hedgerows, she made into jams, jellies, pies and crumbles using recipes from two very old notebooks she had found in the house when she moved in.

~

Annette Leitch had a very big garden at Springbrae between her house and River View. When she retired from teaching, she eked out her pension by selling off part of the land. A young couple bought it. Ann was a teacher; Alasdair an architect, living the architect's dream of building his own house. The two houses, which had sat side by side for a century and more, suddenly had an incomer. Alasdair built a modern house; it too had angles and twists and turns which made it as unusual as its neighbour. The defining similarity was the sloping roof, essential in the west coast of Scotland.

In time children were born, and the houses watched over them as they played in the garden on hot summer days. Adam and Nina were both very attached to Mina, and spent hours in the greenhouse helping her with the plants. How much help they gave is debatable; what is not debatable is the love that grew up.

One holiday the family went to the island of Colonsay, and Nina sent back a postcard. The picture was of an old man in a flat cap walking along a country road with his collie. Nina wrote on the back, 'This is just like you and Geordie.' The postcard had pride of place on the mantelpiece in the kitchen for over twenty years. Beth could not for the life of her remember what had happened to that postcard. Such treasures are important. They are not just postcards; they are memories of people and places and feelings.

A real friendship grew up between Mina and her young neighbours. Many a day Mina and Ann sat drinking tea, putting the world to rights. And so it seemed quite natural that when Nina went to school, and Ann went back to work, Mina became an after-school childminder to the two children next door.

History, however, was not repeating itself. Mina was not walking along the road to collect another little girl. Adam at nine years old was in charge of bringing his sister home. The two children collected Mina, and off the three of them went next door. Adam was in charge of making the cups of tea, and then he took himself to his room, leaving Mina and Nina playing games.

Time passed, and Alasdair and Ann decided to build an extension to their house. At one point there was only a temporary entrance, and access to the cup of tea required walking across a plank to the front door. In Adam's words, 'Walking the Plank' was far too risky for the old lady, so the arrangement was temporarily altered. The children went into Mina's house rather than their own. This was not at all to Adam's liking; he could no longer escape to his room, but rather had to suffer games he had decided he was far too old for. It was all change again; Adam delivered Nina, and then went to his own house feeling very grown up. Thirty precious minutes till his mother came home, and he would once again become a wee boy, rather than the boss of the building work that was going on.

Nina had a favourite seat by the fire. It was a very low seat, just the size for a child, and there she would sit with a glass of milk and a little cake, and regale her listeners with the events of the day. The time was put to use, as well. She did her homework. This was entirely her choice; she was an organised little lady, who liked to get things done. The adults were roped into this, as was everyone else who happened by. One day a man came to read the gas meter, and he too was drawn into the doing of the homework.

Once Ian was settled across the ocean, Mina and Eddie went to visit. What excitement that generated! She was finally going to cross the ocean to the American continent. The plan was to go for Christmas, but this was not without concern to her, as her brother and sister, Wee John and Jean with their spouses Wee Jean and John, had in recent years come to visit at Christmas as well as in the summer. Mina was afraid that if this pattern was broken, it would not repair. She devised a plan. Beth would do the whole Christmas event. To facilitate this, Mina bought a freezer. She could cook and freeze for weeks before setting out, and Beth simply had to run the meals as her mother had laid down on the menu plan she had written.

The meals were cooked, bagged and labelled. John and Jean from Glasgow arrived first to take care of Geordie, as Beth was not yet on holiday. Then came John and Jean from London, and finally Beth. It was a very cold winter, but all went according to plan until two days after Christmas when there was a ferocious snowstorm. The electricity was cut. The freezer went off. Nobody knew how long before there would be damage to its contents.

Then Beth hit on an idea. They would bury the food in the snow. Years before she had heard of souterrains; mediaeval freezers. People dug a hole in the ground, packed the food in with ice chipped from rivers, and it kept quite well. Out she went and hauled up her mother's beautifully kept borders of carefully tended plants. In went the provisions, wrapped in foil and plastic bags to ward off hungry animals. Ice from the burn was piled in on top, boulders on top of that, and all of this done by torchlight.

The hours crawled by, but still no electricity. Anyone looking at the village might have wondered which century it was; every house lit by candlelight. Eventually the household went to bed, but Beth kept her light switch on, so that immediately electricity was restored, she would be awakened and could bring all the food back in.

2.28am, the lights blazed forth. Clothes on, out she went. She dragged back the boulders and the ice and began lifting the soup, when suddenly the whole place plunged into darkness once again. She waited, hoping, but no. It had been a false alarm. Back went the ice. On went the boulders. Back to bed shivering.

4.31am, on came the lights. She knew better this time. She waited. She made a cocoa. She waited until she considered it might be safe to uproot the food. By this time she had a plan. Only half would be brought in until the storm died down. The snow had abated by this time, but it was very cold. Wrapped up as if for the Arctic, she dug up the soup again, and the remains of the turkey. They would depart Mina's menu and eat these items that day if need be. The planned steak casserole would remain interred, along with all the vegetables. Hours later, the five of them decided it was safe to risk the freezer again. As she was bringing in the last of the food, Beth was sure the old house had seen this happen in its youth.

One evening after her uncles and aunts had gone to bed, Beth sat by the fire. The flames were too high to leave it unattended. On impulse, she turned off the harshness of the electric light. Reds, oranges and golds danced across the ceiling. Through the window, a shaft of moonlight glided across the room. The fire whispered.

And still she sat and watched and listened. The flames became embers still glowing with life. The room rustled, and she saw herself in the years ahead, an old lady smiling by the fire.

Hours passed and the glow became faint – it was time to go to bed.

At the end of the holiday, she went back to the city. She had made her choice... for now.

Wee John and Wee Jean had come home every year for four decades, firstly on the motor bike, and then a motor bike with sidecar, and latterly on the train. As Beth's Uncle John grew older, he had a very set pattern. Each evening he would take himself downstairs and sit for hours on his own. He liked to just remember. After the downstairs house was rented to Americans, this was no longer possible, so he moved onto his father's garden seat. He never spoke of his reminiscences, but the time spent on them was clearly very important to him. No one disrupted his thinking time. How many memories he must have had! From when he first came here at two months old, through his fascination with the ladybirds to his friendship with the Weir boys, there were memories deep down that his family did not know about. Had the old house seen him climbing the trees, meeting girls in the wood? Had it heard his thoughts on living so far away? He was not an unhappy man at all. He was very jovial, and sometimes he sat on the seat laughing away to himself as he turned over a particularly rich memory.

His health was deteriorating as the summer trip north in 1985 was planned. Wee John and Wee Jean were coming by train. A week before they were due to travel north he was really quite unwell, but flatly refused to go to a doctor. He feared the diagnosis would mean no visit to Scotland.

Wee John and Wee Jean were driven to Euston Station by their son-in-law Alan and their daughter Janet. Alan dropped them off with the luggage, and went to park the car. When he returned to the concourse of the station, Wee John had collapsed. The station master had arrived and a nurse, waiting for a train, had abandoned her plans and followed her calling. She was attending to him. She advised an ambulance. John refused. He kept repeating, 'I must go home. I must go home.' Of course both the nurse and the station master thought he meant his home near Euston Station, but Wee

Jean, Janet and Alan knew better. Wee John was coming home to die.

Janet could not leave her parents to travel alone in this situation, so she travelled with them. It was an overnight train, and in the morning they reached Glasgow. On to the next train and then the steamer, they travelled in silence. What was there to say? As they neared the village, Wee John's appearance began to change. He became his old self.

Into a taxi, through the gate, and down the path they came. It was not the usual happy homecoming; the mood was one of sheer relief that they had arrived. Wordlessly, they knew he would never go back south.

Mina had insisted on summoning the doctor, and when he arrived the two men met as old friends. The doctor recalled the time decades earlier when Wee John, Alan and Ian had gone fishing near the pier.

They had hired a motor boat. They were so intent, they did not see the storm clouds gather, and suddenly they found themselves in a downpour. They made their way to the pier to shelter under it, but the power of the motorboat was such that they reached the pier at an alarming speed. In panic Ian leaned out to prevent the boat crashing into the pier, but even as they avoided the boat hitting the pier, they could not prevent his head crashing against it. Shells clinging to the pillars of the pier lodged themselves in his skull. It could be dangerous if they got into his bloodstream, and so to reach the doctor, speed was of the essence. As the surgery was closed, they had gone straight to the doctor's house. He was sitting in his garden when this blooded threesome had turned up. Painfully each piece of shell was removed with tweezers, and even more painfully, the wounds wiped clean with iodine. They had gone home, looking like the survivors of a pitched battle.

As Wee John continued to slip away, he sat for hours on the old seat. Days passed into weeks, until he had to go into hospital. As he left the house, he stopped for one last look to take with him.

When Alan and his sons arrived for the funeral, the whole group sat round the table as they had done so many times, but this time the seat beside the fire was empty.

Geordie too had grown old. Mina took him walking three times a day, and for years he ran double and triple the journey. In time he ran less, and then he walked sedately, until the walks became really quite short. At seventy, Mina was not slowing down as he was.

In his young days Mina had taken a particular route for his morning walk, during which she had befriended a little boy whose family had recently moved to the village. Whenever she approached his house, he seemed to just pop out and walk with her on his way to school. The little boy was very attached to Geordie, and in the course of these morning walks to school, he decided that when he grew up he would have a collie. The daily meetings of this little group ended when John went to secondary school, but he would regularly come along to visit Geordie.

As John grew up, he began to do outdoor work for Mrs H, as he called her, work that Eddie could no longer manage.

One day she went to his house.

'I need help,' she said. 'I need a grave dug. Geordie has gone.'

He came at once. Mina explained that Geordie had been ailing for a few days, but on the previous night his legs had given way under him. She had sat with him all night, and in the morning had called the vet. He had come, and said the dog would not live long, and a choice had to be made – let him die slowly or let him not struggle. Neither she nor Eddie could bear for him to struggle. The vet took him away, and later brought him back ready to be laid in the ground.

As John dug the grave, the collie, which sixteen years earlier had come on approval for a few days, lay in his bed wrapped in a blanket. He was buried beside his predecessor. His bowl and his dish found their place beside Sooty's, and his lead hung on the hook it had always hung on. Like so many treasures from the past, it hangs there still.

Mrs Enn had also passed on, and with her no longer at the centre of the holiday house, the rest of the family seemed to lose heart. Perhaps it was just too painful to come when she was no longer there. The Cottage began to deteriorate. Drain pipes fell off, window frames fell off. No re-painting was done, and that section of the building did not just show its age. It looked the truth of what it was, uncared for. To those who loved the building, it was painful to see. As the building became derelict, it ceased to be the Cottage and became referred to as the Ruin.

By this time Eddie was not able to do the maintenance on his own building as he had done before, and it too began to look its age. The old house, which had been looked after for so long, was beginning to fade. Beth and Ian did what they could, but they had houses of their own. To Mina and Eddie living there, they seemed not to see the problem, but to their children when they came home it was a wound. Their memories jarred with how it now looked. For the first time they began to doubt their dreams of coming back. It was not the value of the property which concerned them. It was the sadness. In desperate need of nurture, the old house seemed to be dying.

The garden, too, was not as it had been. Eddie just could not do it now. Where the vegetables had grown, now there was a patch overrun with ferns and brambles. This once proud house now had a Ruin and a Wilderness.

Chapter Twenty-Nine

As her father aged, Beth's conflict with him gradually resolved. Once he saw the satisfaction she derived from her work, he had finally acknowledged he had been wrong opposing her education. He was also quietly proud of her determination to travel. In conversation with her mother, she judged the time was right to ask him about his young years. She had never known her paternal grandparents, uncles, aunts and cousins and she was intrigued. As children she and Ian had been told of his navy days, but had been too young to understand what he had to say.

She asked him if he would speak his life story onto a tape recorder. At first he flatly refused. But then one day he asked her how the machine worked, and she explained it. She went back to Edinburgh, leaving him with the recorder. The old house watched what happened next. He tried to make it work. It worked. He spoke into it. He played it back. To his surprise, he sounded fine. He was willing to try. He found he could not do the recording with an audience, and so every night he went to bed early, and then got up at two or three in the morning to record his story. 'Back on night shift at my age,' he would say with a wry smile.

When Beth heard of this late night/early morning experimenting with technology, she feared he would erase some of what he had recorded by taping over the recording of the previous day, so she instructed her mother to buy a number of blank tapes and put into the machine a fresh one each night, carefully numbering what had been taped the night before.

Weeks passed, and the pile of tapes grew. Beth became increasingly anxious about coming home and listening to them, in case after all his effort, they were part erased or inaudible. She knew that if it had not worked, he would not do it again. She wanted to take them away, but he insisted she sit at the kitchen table and listen. In great trepidation, she turned on a tape. From the machine came his voice clear and confident. He was proud, and so was she as she listened.

Sitting at the kitchen table was how the recording was completed. She made supplementary tapes, asking him further questions. In time they would be spliced together.

Eddie had always been a good storyteller, and once he had got started on this, the old flair had come back. He recounted details of his poverty-stricken childhood in the north of England and going into the navy. Then some of it became funny. One of his best stories was in India. He had been ashore and had taken a rickshaw back to the docks. He had cut the time too neat, and the undernourished rickshaw owner was not going fast enough, so Eddie suggested they took turns pulling it. Thus he arrived at the dockyard gates pulling a rickshaw, whose owner was reclining in it!

Another tale came from war-torn Malta. He and a friend had found a piano amidst the buildings destroyed by the bombing, and decided a bit of music was needed in the mess. They pushed the piano through the streets to the dockyard gates. Neither of them could play it, but that did not deter them from stopping on every corner in an attempt to squeeze out a tune. They failed, but when the piano reached the mess, it was seized upon by those who could play. Hard-bitten Royal Navy submariners then ate their meals to the gentle sounds of waltzes and concertos.

Seated at the kitchen table, he described the conditions on submarines, the cramped nature of such limited space, the sanitation, the smell, the food, the male world, and Beth began to see her father in a very different way. Here was a man who had left behind a world of such danger and such interdependency, to live with his family in this house. No wonder there were strains in the adjustment. He wanted the life here, but he could not erase the life that he had spent there. Nor did he want to. It had shaped his life for over twenty years. Sweeping it aside was a form of betrayal of the good times he had had, of the war he had fought, of close friends who had not returned to port. It was part of who he was, and could not, should not, be cut out.

One day Beth asked her father to talk about depth charging. She encouraged him to begin by explaining what this was.

'Submerged submarines can be detected by a ship on the surface, and then little bombs are dropped into the sea in the hope that they will destroy what is underneath. For those on the submarine, they can only listen as the ship passes above them, and they can do nothing. They have to wait and hope. They cannot move, for even the slightest movement causes a tremor in the water which might be visible on the surface.'

As he talked, the memories of those days, long suppressed, came back. His voice became strangled, reliving the terror. Great wracking sobs, and then silence filled the kitchen. Beth's mother was at the cooker making the lunch, and she stopped. This moment demanded the respect of complete attention. Only the recorder continued.

He died in 1995, his drinking contributing in no small measure. It had been a problem for many years; the lot of many ex-servicemen. Years later Beth would realise that the experiences of her father's generation had come to benefit those who came after him with the provision of much better understanding and support; the pattern of one generation benefitting the next.

The Royal Navy sent a representative to his funeral. That would have made him very proud. His medals were framed and hang on the wall of the parlour, along with photos of Mina and Eddie in the uniforms they had worn when they met. And occasionally, just occasionally, in the days after the funeral, Beth and Mina would still hear Eddie call, 'Mina!' It was not a morbid call from beyond the grave. It was the call of the years as his health failed. The family would be sitting by the fireside, and the calm would be broken by the yell from the bedroom, 'MINA!' Long after he was gone, it remained a family joke.

Three weeks before this, Mina had lost her sister Jean. John in Glasgow had died some months before, and so in the space of one year Mina lost three of those who had known her when she was young. Wee Jean in London too had passed on the previous year, and with the death of each of her family, Mina lost part of her shared past. She was, as she kept saying, the lone standing stone. Beth had been terrified of how her mother would survive this, but like a standing stone which has stood for millennia, she had that grit.

The Ruin was more ruinous, the Wilderness more wildernessy, the downstairs house not let, and Mina the sole resident of the building. She was isolated, she was alone, but never once was she lonely. She was in the house where she had been young, where she had brought up her family. By then the American base had closed and so the downstairs house was empty and she could go downstairs and sit thinking of her very early years with her parents, her brother and sister long before she met Eddie. These memories lifted her, but valuable as they were, she did not wallow in them.

Free of all responsibility, she was determined to make the most of the years left to her.

She and Beth began to go on trips together, places Mina had long wanted to see, the Western Isles of Scotland, the Highlands and the Borders. Then they set off to the areas of England and Ireland where they researched her father's family tree. The hunt for the missing grandmother began. She went to America every year, spending time with her grandchildren. She was also determined to see the sights. As she approached eighty, she became a traveller.

During one of her visits, Ian had to go to a conference in Washington. He took her along, and while he was at work, armed with a ticket for the tour buses, she set out. Over the next few days she hopped on and hopped off at every stop, to the extent that the drivers and the guides came to greet her as a long lost friend. They were very taken by this sprightly old lady, who knew exactly where she was going.

One day she experimented with a taxi. When the driver took the direct route and not the tour bus route, Mina in her soft Scottish voice gently asked if he knew where he was going.

'Lady, I'm a Washington cab driver. I know where The White House is.' Suitably chastened she explained her mistake, and by the time they arrived at 1600 Pennsylvania Avenue, his feathers had been smoothed over by her asking about the buildings they were passing, all of which she had learned about. She added his information to what she already knew. As she paid him she smiled, and then tipped him in sterling, as a wee reminder of the lady from Scotland who thought he had got lost. No doubt he has been telling that story for years.

On a later occasion coming back from Boston, the plane had to put down in Newfoundland, as a passenger had taken ill. Mina asked one of the stewardesses if she could get off the plane for a few minutes. The woman stared in astonishment at this request, and then Mina told the story of how she nearly reached Newfoundland in 1944, and here she was over sixty years later. Could she just walk outside?

'Give me a minute,' the stewardess said, and off she went. Very quickly she returned. 'Yes. I will need to go with you for security reasons, but we can do it.'

And off Mina went! She finally stood in Newfoundland. Returning to her seat on the plane, her grin was the grin of the little girl who had set out on the adventure along the magic path over eighty years before.

Kate and Rosie came with their parents every year. They played in the garden from dawn to dusk. They had a garden in America, but not one on a slope. One of the great games of their childhood was rolling down that slope. The potato growing had still been going on when this game started, and that had caused much uproar when Kate had rolled into the potatoes, crushing them to death. Grandpa had not been pleased about that at all. But with him no longer there, and the potatoes no longer growing, they could roll wherever they liked.

Kate developed a friendship with Nina. One summer they set up in business. They cut the flowers from Grandma's borders, made them into little bouquets and sold them at the gate. Flowers put into water and transformed into 'perfume' was their next product for sale. No one was spared. The coalman, blackened by his trade, went home one day carrying little posies of flowers for his daughters.

On wet days the call was for grandma's lentil soup; Maggie's recipe. Lentils, carrots and onions boiled in meat stock. Mina resisted all attempts by her family offering her a food processor. The carrots had to be grated and sliced by hand to get the consistency right.

And in the corner of the kitchen a big old chair now into its fourth decade, fought over by everyone, kept watch.

Around this time the cooker gave up. It resisted all attempts at repair, and a successor had to be summoned. Mina could not bear for it to go. She had been cooking on it since the coronation. Her solution was the greenhouse. 'Why not?' she declared. 'The oven will make a fine cupboard and the burners a shelf.'

Beth's life in Edinburgh was happy. She enjoyed her job, she had a wide circle of close friends, and lots of activities. After her marriage she had other relationships, but as time went by they never seemed to be quite the right fit. Her love of travelling was a bone of contention. It was all very well to go abroad, but only to certain places. Expressing her views was acceptable, but within limits determined by the relationship. And as for this pull to her childhood home, well was it not time to grow up?

More often she found her thoughts turning to Alex in Tasmania. She knew there was no point in pursuing this, but she was bewildered by not being able to replicate such a relationship. Did it only belong on the road? She found that hard to believe, but as the years passed, the more she concluded this might be so.

She had adjusted to not having children by spending time with the children of her friends. She never pretended it was what she had wanted, but it was a very good second best. Her life was full. Holidays were spent at home and abroad, and it was for her a varied and happy life. Edinburgh, alongside very regular visits home, was her future.

'Events, dear boy, events!' Harold Macmillan, British Prime Minister in the mid-twentieth century, once said in response to a question about what can blow governments off course. They can blow people off course, too.

~

In 1996 she and Carol set off to Alaska, a trip they had been planning for over twenty years. It was a holiday, exploring by car, bus, plane, ferry as far as they could in that vast space. It was also an event, which Beth did not anticipate, or indeed realise, until she came back home.

She loved Alaska, the space, the light, the water, the trees, the small communities which welcomed the two travellers. In the town of Nome they were booked at a bed and breakfast. When they arrived, there was a note on the door telling them which room they were to occupy, and where the breakfast would be. On the last evening, there was the invoice with instructions where to put the cash. They never met the owner, as she worked night shifts and slept all day. Beth asked one of the locals how the proprietor could be sure she would not be cheated. The answer was simple.

'There is no way out except by plane. The pilot would be told, and you would be stopped in Anchorage.'

What a system! Neighbourhood Watch by air!

Beth had been living in the city for so long by then, she had almost forgotten what small community life really was. Here in Alaska she found herself more at ease with the world around her than she felt in the city streets. It came to her that in visiting her parents she was only skating over the top of village life, popping in and out, and not seeing that what was in Alaska was in her village too. She began to question her city life. Perhaps there too she just popped in and out. She went to work, she went to play, but she did not have a sense of belonging in the city. It was too big. People did not greet strangers in the street as they did in Nome, and as they did in her village. People did not belong to the place in quite the same way.

Walking in the emptiness of Alaska, she and Carol had talked about this. Carol lived in the house where she had grown up, and understood this feeling of belonging to a place and a community. In Carol's words, 'It is not so much *belonging to*, as *belonging in*.'

At one point in the trip, Beth and Carol went on a tour of Denali National Park. The ranger guide was very good, and talked at great length about the bears.

'This is very interesting, but could you say something about wolves also?' Beth asked.

'Yes,' came the reply, 'but I don't know a great deal about them. I will do what I can, but if you are not in a hurry when we get back, I can arrange for someone to come and talk to you about wolves. I can radio back and arrange that now if you like.'

The guide was as good as her word. She did incorporate wolves, and when the bus arrived back to base, there was indeed another ranger waiting for her.

As Beth walked away at the end, she thought what a wonderful gift it was to offer information to visitors to one's country. She had no intention of ever stopping teaching. Jokingly she had said that she would die in her classroom, but after this experience, a thought crept in. If she ever did stop teaching, re-inventing herself as a tourist guide would be a superb way to spend her time and earn a living. The idea was tucked away.

When she flew back to Edinburgh, she took a sudden dislike to the street she lived in. For years she had enjoyed living there, but all she saw now were tenement buildings as cliffs hemming her in. Her thoughts turned to the wild emptiness where she had been. She had a few days before she went back to work, and so went home. There she felt the same calm as in Alaska, the open vista, the water, the trees, the space. As her dilemma surfaced again, the house just shook its head and smiled.

Back to the city. Back to her work and her life. She loved the Old Town of Edinburgh, the narrow wynds and closes, spires, turrets and the castle. She walked the centuries of the city's life; Edinburgh, once tiny and then overcrowded, for a thousand years at the epicentre of Scotland's story. Visits to the theatre, dinners with friends, conversations of real depth. These were the stuff of her life. She truly valued them, but try though she might, she could not shake off the change in how she felt about the place.

And so the idea of one day going home for good became more

real. She was blown off course onto a new one. The idea had been there for so long, but it had existed only as a vague idea inside her city life. Feeling stifled by the city, she began to look hard at what a new future might be. This scared her. She had a good life in the city, and it was a frightening thought to start again. It was terrifying to leave her friends, the theatre, her life there.

During the years in Edinburgh, when she had come home, she met up with friends both from childhood, and from the three years after Australia. They walked in the hills, they met in their homes, they sat in the pubs. Sometimes she went to plays or concerts in the village hall, sometimes to dances. The hall had not changed in all these decades. From the tiny stage where she had performed as a child, the ceilidh bands played. The toilets still did not have heating. The chairs were hard. But Beth was happy there, every bit as much as in the city theatres. When she talked with people from so long ago, and with the new friends she had made, the conversations were different from those in the city, but they were no less sincere and no less valuable. Despite the different paths they had walked, there was the same sense of belonging. At home she was no stranger. Some Sundays when it was time to go back to Edinburgh, she stood at the back of the ferry watching the coastline receding. Always for the first few days back in town, she was homesick.

But leave the city, and all she knew there? Panic welled up in her at the thought. And yet the event of Alaska was undeniable.

As the century rolled on to its close, Mina travelled to America, Beth lived in Edinburgh, and the Ruin deteriorated further. But unbidden and below consciousness, changes were beginning to crystallise. The old house quietly waited.

Chapter Thirty

December 31st 1999 was a beautiful winter day. It was cold, and it was bright with not a breath of wind – the ideal weather for a bonfire to mark this particular New Year. For weeks neighbours had been gathering flammable material and Mina had been making soup, mince pies, sausage rolls, essential ingredients for a winter garden party.

People began to gather from houses stretching along the road. The fire blazed, and with no wind the smoke rose vertically, very unusual in the west of Scotland. Even the weather was playing its part for this symbolic turn of the clock. The older people sat on the chairs they brought with them, the younger ones on waterproof sheets and tartan blankets.

The bonfire was set down the garden, and from that angle the house looked larger than indeed it was. This could not have been the first bonfire in this garden. It occurred to Beth that the inhabitants of the house a hundred years ago might have marked the occasion in the same way. She looked at two old ladies sitting side by side at the edge of the blaze, and put them into Victorian clothes. Yes the Misses Cook might have sat here, having soup handed to them by one of the village children. Had Hugh Weir come back for a visit to bring in a new century with his two old friends? Had any of the Leitches come?

Beth's own grandparents were only twelve years off arriving here. She counted back twelve years in her own life. It had sped by in a flash. Was it really twelve years since the crisis in her mid thirties? Losing a child, followed within a very short time by separation and then divorce, had only been a prelude to the misery that had come next, the medical problem which made having a child almost impossible. There was no compassionate time off work or support when that catastrophe had struck; she just had to carry on, knowing that the future would be very different from the one she had come to hope for. Even speaking of it was too painful. She had had to make the best of it in silence.

She had been asked if she would consider taking part in research in order to find a cure for the same problem in other women in the future. At first she was unwilling; she did not want to set foot in that hospital again, but gradually she changed her mind. As her mother quietly pointed out, it was medical science which had kept her alive as a baby. Night after night Beth had touched the mark on her leg, where she had been fed all these years before, and knew it was payback time. The research had been straightforward, and in a strange way comforting. Medical science was indeed advanced. One generation benefits the next.

It was nearly midnight, and on the stroke of twelve that painful period in her life would slip into a previous century. It was not that she wanted to forget it had ever happened, but she had learned how to move beyond its impact, and when better for a moment of reflection than going into a new millennium?

She fastened her jacket. Back then she had long hair and flowing flowery skirts. Her pupils had nicknamed her The Gipsy. No gipsy clothes at that winter bonfire, but wrapped in her old motorbike jacket.

She looked across to where her mother was sitting, and realised just how unusual it was for three generations of an ordinary family to have been in one place spanning almost a century. With the more fluid living patterns of today's society, the pattern of generation after generation in the same house, that ordered nature of society for centuries, had almost died out. What made this situation even more extraordinary was that the house had been rented for so many of these years, and that during all that time, her grandparents had struggled to maintain two rents, this one and the one in Glasgow. This was not a family passing on inherited wealth. The years of Mina's childhood had ingrained her attachment to the house, and for so many years this had been her home first as a tenant, then as an owner, and lastly as a landlady.

In the moonlight the house looked proud. Its deterioration was not visible. That would be there for the revellers to see at daybreak, but for one night it looked its old self. As the moon moved slowly across the sky, the lion was smiling.

Chapter Thirty-One

In 2002 Beth and Mina were setting out across the ocean, and in preparation Mina had gone to the local bookshop to buy a holiday read. Without any warning her eyes darkened, as if a curtain had been drawn. She left the shop and walked to the optician, who sent her to the local hospital. There she learned that she had macular degeneration, a condition she had never heard of. She drove home, hung up her car keys, and decided that until she was treated, she would not drive again.

They went to America, and on their return, attended the specialist hospital appointment. Mina was technically blind. The pace of the deterioration varied from person to person, but the limit this placed on her life was profound. She was provided with appliances to improve the quality of her life, reading magnifiers, speaking clocks, television glasses, but the change in her life was irreversible. Her car keys were hung up forever.

Everyone knew, but nobody said, that the time would come when she could no longer live alone. It was unthinkable that she would go into care. Her life was this house. Her life was this garden.

'Events, dear boy, events!'

Not in her wildest imagination had Beth ever considered that her mother would go blind, and that that would be the catalyst for going home. The idea began to take hold, but she repeatedly shrank away. The thought of giving up her work spread tentacles of panic. Her mother would be ok. She could see a bit, at least enough to manage. Going home would come at the right time, she kept telling herself, her retirement age. Once again, it was not yet.

One day in school something happened, and she realised the moment had come. She just no longer wanted to be there. It was not a major event; indeed it was quite minor, but her reaction was undeniable. The new intake of children at the beginning of the school year was grouped in the foyer at the bottom of a staircase. When she looked at them, she knew she did not want to see them through their years of secondary education. She did not want to go on teaching for that length of time. In a relationship there can come a moment when a person knows it is no longer what he or she wants. Beth was only too familiar with this moment of uncomfortable truth, and she also knew that nothing can re-invigorate emotion once it has gone. Thus it was again. Her long love affair with education had run its course; it was time to move on. No matter how she looked at it, there was no reason to stay, except habit and convenience, and they were no reasons at all.

The realisation was terrifying. A coldness swept over her. Then it was sweat. She had been coming downstairs when it happened, and she had to grip the railings for support. As the day wore on, she regained her equilibrium, finding excuses to push aside what she had felt. She was tired. It was just a bad moment. She would feel better tomorrow. It was just a rogue notion.

'How can I stop teaching? It is who I am. Take it away and what is left?' Words torn out of her one evening as she sat in the house of a friend; the rogue notion was going nowhere.

Gently her friend said, 'That is not all you are. Don't fall into the trap of defining yourself by what you do for a living, no matter how much you enjoy, or enjoyed, it. Are you a teacher when you go travelling? Are you a teacher when you sit here? Are you a teacher when you are on stage?'

'I suppose not.'

As the weeks went on, she lived with a gash inside her. When she thought of leaving, she was light and reinvigorated. When she thought of staying, her stomach knotted. She had made a choice a quarter of a century earlier. Could she make another choice? What if going home was merely a fantasy?

One day a colleague said to her, 'Are you ok these days? You are not walking as you used to. You have always walked like a dancer. Now you seem a wee bit hunched. Are you in pain?'

'No I'm fine thanks,' was all she said, her stomach tightening at the lie.

She found herself looking at her reflection in windows, and she saw the truth. The person in the window was fading. The unhappy eyes looked at her. 'Why are you doing this to yourself?' they said.

One Saturday she was walking through Edinburgh to meet a friend for lunch. It was cold, but a bright sunny day. As she walked the sun caught metal flashing on a roof, and, as the sudden light caught her eye, she straightened her back and looked upwards. Blue sky, the golden orb, the light; she had seen this combination once before. When she had been struggling with the dilemma about whether or not to go to Australia, the same combination had come into play. She had never regretted that decision. She knew she was not ready to stop walking like a dancer. She had to leave her life in Edinburgh. She waited for the pendulum to swing to panic. This time it did not.

Lightheaded, she skipped along the road. Approaching a bus stop it occurred to her to slow to a sedate Edinburgh walk, but no, she decided. This was a day to skip. Drawing level with the silent group awaiting the bus, gleefully she uttered, 'Lovely day isn't it?'

Not a word. On she skipped, remembering that earlier time of dancing with Sooty to the strains of the gramophone, and then moved into a variation of a pavane, and finally arrived at the restaurant to a waltz.

'I'm resigning,' she announced.

'Yeah yeah, we've been hearing that for years.'

'No you haven't. You have only heard of it as an idea. Now the moment has come.'

'What's happened?'

She talked of dancing when she was young, in rooms filled with light streaming in the windows; as a young woman taking flamenco lessons in Granada; and of the ancient dance of Egypt, raq sharqi, in a village on the upper Nile. Even further back in her life, she had danced skimpily clad as a part-time job when she was a student, immersing herself in the sound to express joy and sorrow, surely the origins of music and movement. She loved the freedom of expression in dance. When she danced, she felt herself to be moving inside the sound. She was convinced it loosened the subconscious from which self-doubt arises. Long ago she had learned that self-doubt is painful, but also a vital positive if we learn from it. She knew she was ready to dance again.

Dancing, however, would not pay her bills. She had to earn a living, and so she plucked from the back of her memory the idea of training as a tourist guide. This could work. She could go home, look after her mother, and change career.

Into the mix she would live in the little house downstairs, and by selling her apartment in Edinburgh could free up the cash to tackle the Ruin. By this time the damage had migrated through the building to the point that something had to be done.

Soozie had arrived in the village from Edinburgh College of Art, where she had trained as a jeweller. She had taken tenancy of a house down the road, and as she settled into the village, she walked everywhere. One day she was looking over the wall and saw Mina working in the garden. Mina spoke to her, but she did not reply. Mina spoke again. She still did not reply. Instead, the young woman looking over the wall announced that she was deaf. Mina simply moved up to the wall to talk to her. Over the months, a friendship grew. They talked about the stillness of the land, of the birds and the plants and Soozie's dog Sam, and of course Sooty and Geordie. Sometimes on the dark winter nights Soozie came to visit, and they sat beside the fire watching the flames. Two people, fifty years apart, explaining to the other the loss of one sense, and how they had found ways to compensate. Soozie talked of her deafness, Mina of her blindness. Soozie, deaf for decades, taught Mina a great deal about acceptance.

One day the downstairs tenant announced he was moving out. This was the moment Soozie had been waiting for. She, her dog and all her jewellery moved in.

John, the little boy from along the road, had continued to help Mina with tasks she could not do. No longer a little boy, one day he was cutting down the Wilderness, uprooting all the brambles and the ferns in order to lay grass, when he met Soozie. An introduction, a gentle smile, warm honesty in these vivid green eyes; very soon John and Soozie became a couple. The little house was not big enough for the two of them and their two dogs, so they moved to the farmhouse along the road, and the downstairs house was once again empty.

It was at this point that Beth had looked into the sun, danced along the road and took the leap into the future. In Edinburgh she had had central heating, and she was not going to live without it. Downstairs needed heating, a shower, new flooring, kitchen units. An old coal cellar, which from time to time housed a frog coming in from the cold, had to be converted into a computer corner. The work began. Every weekend she came home to watch progress, bringing a carload of belongings as she did so. Clearing out decades of education was a very slow process. Now and again she wobbled, but after her resignation was handed in, there was no going back. The weight of indecision lifted, as the little downstairs house moved into the modern age.

It began to smile. It seemed delighted with its makeover. Shelves were strapped to the wall and the books, carload by carload, found their new home. Pictures likewise made their way westwards, and only at the end did the furniture arrive. The downstairs house was ready for its new inhabitant. Beth had indeed come home.

She embarked on training as a tourist guide, and took to the studying with great zeal. She particularly liked the new disciplines she had never encountered before.

'How do you get that castle to stand on that rock?' led to studying the techniques of medieval engineering.

'Why is that rock pink and that one black?' It was the turn of geology. She was way outside her comfort zone, and she loved it.

Mina lived in her house, Beth underneath her. They ate together and spent evenings together, but during the day, Mina went on with her life in the garden, and Beth went on with her studying. When Beth set out to learn the routes for tours of Scotland, Mina went too. She could see hazily, and it was good practice for Beth to learn that she had to describe what visitors were looking at, to ensure those with visual impairment could 'see' what she was going to talk about.

Every year, they crossed the ocean to Ian. Mina was as determined as ever to explore. She may not have seen much, but she heard plenty.

Ian crossed in the other direction with a regularity not dreamed of when he first went to the USA. His life too had changed; he had remarried by this time, and it was with some trepidation that Viola made her first visit to Ian's childhood home. She recognised it instantly – how could she not? From a photograph she had crafted a model of it as a gift for Mina. Using paint and fabric, stones and thread, she had built a three-dimensional house mounted inside a frame. It was a remarkable piece of work, and after Beth admired it, Viola created one of a classroom to mark Beth's retiral from teaching. For almost two decades they have each hung in place, distinct and unique.

In 2007, Mina turned ninety. A garden party was the plan with everyone who knew her invited. The postman, the builder, the neighbours, old friends, they all turned up. Many of them gave her plants. 'I'll watch them grow and then they'll be here long after I am,' she was delighted to say as the weeks went on, and the intended destination of every plant was debated. Gardening that summer took on plans for decades ahead.

One winter evening she announced to her daughter, 'I think I will come and visit you in your house tonight.' A week or two later it was, 'I think I would like to have a bath in your house.' Beth puzzled over this, and then it dawned on her. The attraction was the central heating. Tentatively she brought the subject up, and her guess had been right.

'Maybe I should install it,' announced Mina. 'Let's find out the cost.'

Beth moved fast. If her mother was going to install central heating, not a moment was to be lost. She might just change her mind. But no, the plumbers were booked and the great day came. Mina moved out. Downstairs she came. Beth was determined she would not see the chaos, and this suited the old lady nicely. She walked out of the old house with its sole fire, and she walked back in again three days later to central heating, but with the fire still glowing at the emotional centre of the house.

Two of the three sections of the house were looking very

spruce, but the Cottage continued to disintegrate. Legal battles raged year on year. As Beth built her village life, with friends from the past and friends new, always the question came, 'What's happening about that Ruin attached to your house?' What indeed!

Every Wednesday she phoned the legal team to verify progress. Every Wednesday she came away disconsolate. Nothing to report. Sorry. No progress.

One Friday morning, the phone rang. The voice was unmistakeable; she had listened to it every Wednesday for years. The tone was new.

'It is concluded. The Cottage has been transferred into the hands of the local authority. It's yours to buy if you want it.'

Chapter Thirty-Two

The winter of 2009/10 was vicious. For weeks Scotland was in the grip of Arctic cold, but no drop in temperature, no amount of ice and snow, could suppress either Beth or Mina. The relief they had felt when the phone call had come had given way in hours – nay, minutes – to the excitement of the project ahead.

Once the paperwork for the Cottage was complete, Beth found herself to be the proud owner of a Ruin, but work could not begin until the weather improved. One day as she was walking past it, she noticed ice bulked at one of the windows. Next day there was more ice. In horror she realised that for that to happen there had to be running water. Although she owned the property, she did not have a key. With the building in such a state of dereliction, it would have been dangerous for her to enter it. The local council were holding the key, until the builders were ready.

She made a frantic phone call. The local authority engineer came. When they opened the door, they came face to face with a wall of ice. From floor to ceiling, there was an iceberg. Remaining furniture was encased in it. A pair of slippers, not worn for fifteen years, was frozen inside this mountain of ice. An unwashed cup balanced on the edge of an icicle. Above it was the sound of running water. The pipe bringing the water into the building had burst, allowing water to gush in.

The two of them stood and stared.

'I have never seen anything like this,' said the engineer.

The builders arrived next. They too stared in disbelief.

The first thing to be done was to turn off the water. One of the builders climbed onto the treacherous roof, tied himself onto a chimney, and then as the anxious watchers held their breath, he lowered himself through an upstairs window. The water was stopped.

This success only dealt with the developing crisis. Of enormous concern was how to get the ice out. A thaw was not imminent, and as the sheer weight of the ice could destroy what remained of the Ruin's structure, time was not an option.

The builders used picks to break up the ice and throw it in chunks into the garden, where in time it would melt. Getting it out was a race against time. Would the old building withstand this? Beth lived through these days in terror. She was alert to every sound in case the house was finally defeated.

But no! The builders of over a century before would have been proud, had they been watching. The ice was hurled out bit by bit, and the pressure on the walls was removed. What remained was an empty sodden shell. The upstairs floor had been brought down by the weight of the ice, and so Beth could stand inside the Ruin and look up through a hole in the roof to the stars.

Duncan the builder took Mina and Beth to pick their way through what resembled a war zone. Hard hats on, they surveyed the destruction wrought by fifteen years of neglect, followed by a flood. Nothing could be salvaged. Everything had to be stripped back to the stone.

The thaw was followed by a very dry spring. The door was

locked to keep out the curious but with no windows, the building was open to the elements, and the wind began its work of drying it out. Months passed as the architectural plans were drawn up.

Eventually, the building began. Where once there had been a coach house with the coachman's house above it, where next there had been two tiny houses, where latterly there had been one house, now there stood an empty space stripped back to stone. Even that had to be taken back further. One wall had to be removed. A crack wrought by neglect was irreparable. The roofless Cottage stood as just three walls, like the ruins of many a mediaeval building Beth visited on her tours.

The whole village came to see what was happening. The Ruin had been an eyesore for so long, that watching it being rebuilt was a source of great interest. The daily dog walkers watched the minutiae of the progress. Children intrigued by construction came to ask questions. Down the path to visit Mina came the people she knew, all of them seeing how pleased she was.

It was a fascinating process. The foundations and what was left of the building were secured. Mina's house had to be protected against the invasive rot. The fourth wall was built, and then, inside the structure a wooden house began to take shape. When the roof went on, it became a house again. Gone were the walls blackened with damp. Gone were the holes in the roof. The whole building began to smile, as the daily surgery went on.

Inside, insulation was inserted between the wooden frame and the exterior walls. The floor joists were laid. Just before Christmas, the staircase arrived. It was a stair with a turn in it, so the steps were not identical. Each step had been calculated exactly to fit between the walls, the turn and its neighbouring steps above and below it.

Beth had owned flats in Edinburgh, but she had never owned a real house, a house with a stair. The day of the staircase was very exciting. It arrived in two sections and was taken into the house via the window opening. The tension was palpable. She got on very well with the builders, but this morning they just did not want her watching. Back she went to her little house downstairs, pacing anxiously. What was happening about the staircase? She took her garbage out in order to hear what was going on. She took her mother's garbage out in order to hear what was going on. No voices, but much hammering. This boded well.

She decided she might clean her car, a task she normally would not dream of in December. Fortunately, she did not have to reach this desperate measure. Duncan came looking for her, beaming.

'The staircase is in. Do you want to go up it?'

'Oh yes. Let me get Mum.'

In mounting excitement, the threesome made their way to the Cottage. Hard hats on, as it was still a building site, through the old door, part of the cosmetics which would be replaced later, and there it was. Tucked perfectly into the corner, the staircase, each step numbered, with its calculations pencilled onto it. They climbed the stairs, savouring every rise. The stair, every bit as much as the destination, was the thrill.

At the top and then along the landing, they walked into the room which faced in the same direction as the rest of the house. The view was different! The view they knew so well was strange seen from a slightly different angle. Beth described to her mother what she could see. The lighthouse, the river, the hills beyond.

'I remember being surprised at how different it looked from here,' was all she said.

'What were you doing in here?'

'Now that I don't remember,' was the enigmatic answer.

Going down the staircase was another adventure. Beth stood at the turn, stroking each step. It was a fairy-tale cottage.

With electricity installed, and the building equipment lying dormant for the holidays, a Christmas tree went up positioned such that everyone passing along the road would see it. Onto it were hung flashing lights, vivid and stark, the kind which might have been irritating inside a house, but were ideally suited to a Reborn Ruin. The windows were fitted, and inside them Beth anchored sheets of cardboard, on which in illuminated paint she wrote, 'Now I am being cared for, I am a very happy house and I wish you a Merry Xmas.' Messages were sellotaped to the exterior of the windows by people passing by. 'It's great to see you getting better.' 'Long live the new house.' 'When will you be open to visitors?' 'Happy 2011.'

Stewart, the plumber, was a local man whom Beth had known since schooldays. The electrician was new to her. The men worked collaboratively, each in lockstep with the others. All the electrics and the piping had been done before the floors were laid. That had necessitated measuring the furniture to establish where it would be placed, so that the wall heaters would be installed accordingly.

One day all three tradesmen were there when this was being discussed, and Beth said she would draw a plan for the furniture with all the measurements attached. If she was not here when they needed it, the site manager would have the drawings.

All three heads shot up. Site manager? Who had Beth appointed to oversee them without them knowing?

'Mum,' she said with a smile. 'She'll have it.'

And so Mina became known as the site manager. Certainly she managed the daily tea break. Duncan liked dark ginger biscuits, Jonathan oatcakes, Bruce chocolate of any sort. And as for Stewart, he would not drink skimmed milk in his tea. 'White water,' he called it. The weekly shopping included the tradesmen's preferences. On hot days they sat outside. On cold days, they came into the kitchen, jostling each other to warm themselves at the fire. Village news flowed across the table.

Mina was very happy throughout. As her eyesight became weaker, her life was more restricted, but with the constant activity she felt her little world had been stopped from further shrinking. She made the teas, doing it all by feel. Her hearing had begun to go also. Even when the hammering was very loud, she heard it as gentle tapping.

The Cottage had a porch which had to be taken down and rebuilt. Beth wanted to be involved in the destruction. Armed with a sledgehammer, she started to swing. It hurt. Even that porch was solid. She tackled the door instead, ridding the proud old building once and for all of the Ruin. In its place a new porch went up with a slate grey roof.

The village hall had been re-roofed by the same builders some years before. Duncan's son Bruce laid the slates in such a way as to create the design of a diamond. Beth had admired this, and one day she came home to find Mina and the whole team of builders waiting for her. They pointed to the roof, and there it was – a diamond design.

The winter of 2010/11 was also vicious, and during it, first Stewart and then Beth broke a leg. Both were in plaster, communicating by phone as the bath and the shower were put in, the heating tested and the taps run. Stewart's son John, along with Tommy, another lifelong resident of the village, worked on. With a leg in plaster, Beth was unable to see the daily changes, and on many evenings as the work of the day ended, she asked the tradesmen to take photographs of the day's progress. Digitally, she watched her house being completed. She was not checking up on them; she just wanted to see her house as it grew. One picture of John examining the boiler he had just attached to the wall makes for a wonderful record. Thinking back on the unknown architect who had designed the house, and the unknown tradesmen who had built it, Beth was ensuring that their modern equivalents would not be unknown.

She enjoyed having every decision to make, even down to the type of door handles. It occurred to her, that while this amount of care would have been lavished on the main part of the house, it would not have been spent on what had been designed as a coach house. This added to her zeal when it came to the cosmetic choices.

White rendering matched the Cottage to the rest of the house, and then came the final touch. The rendering was lined to make it appear as slabs of stone. The old structure looked as one house. It was grinning in delight.

Under the Cottage was the cellar, but it too had fallen into disrepair, and had become the haunt of numerous animals seeking shelter. The walls were in their original form, layered slabs of whinstone mortared together. In one corner was a fireplace, large enough to stand inside and look up to the heavens. The earth floor was permanently damp. The unknown architect of the past had devised this place for storage and for large-scale boiling. The water for the laundry was boiled in here. Old shelves hung off the walls. Hooks had been driven into the stone, originally to suspend the ropes essential for drying the washing on wet days. In Beth's time, non-rusting garden equipment was stored here. Her father had chopped sticks in here. The water pipes for the entire building ran through it. Everyone who had ever lived in the house must have been in that space. It was only after it ceased to be so heavily used that the animals had moved in.

It was a big enough room to stand up in, and Beth wondered if this could be converted into a library. Again there had to be time after it was emptied for it to dry out. A different stratagem had to be devised, involving a chemical to prevent damp seeping through. The old chimney was blocked up. If inside the Cottage, Beth's favourite part was the staircase, the cellar became her pride and joy. She did not really believe that it could be done, and had to be reassured on an almost daily basis.

'No you won't need welly boots to go to your library,' Bruce said in response to her constant questioning.

'Won't the pages curl?'

'I promise you they won't.'

In time the cellar was rechristened the library, and the books moved in. Beth waited, but Bruce was as good as his word. Not a single page curled from dampness. Into the cellar along with the books went Christmas decorations, pots of homemade marmalade, wine.

By June 2011 the house was finished, and Beth decided it would be officially opened. The builders came, and Mina, as the site manager, made a speech wishing a good life to it, to all who live in it and all who built it. She cut the ribbon Beth had tied onto the door handle, and inside they went.

And then came a shock. It looked exactly as it had done the day before, but there was something out of joint. To Beth it was not her house. It was theirs. Their skill had built it. Her bit of paper and her cash did not give ownership over their work. It was not that she did not like it, that it was a disappointment. Not at all. She thought it perfect, but there was none of her in it. She had not created it. It took quite some time for her to reach a balance. Duncan, Stewart and their teams would always have a form of ownership born of their skill in its construction. But as the weeks passed and her books moved in, and her pictures went onto the walls, Beth gradually came to own it simply because she loved it. She valued it. She cared for it. Ownership is much greater than a legal nicety.

The whole community came to see the Cottage when it was finished. Not once did Beth see this as an intrusion. She was happy to show people round and then say, 'Would you like to see the cellar?'

Years later, Beth was with friends in the city. One of them was talking about the problems she was having with a building project. She turned to Beth and said, 'You must know all about this nightmare with builders. Regale us with one of your horror stories.'

Beth thought for a moment.

'Actually, I don't have any horror stories. It was very straightforward. The tradesmen were great. I'll tell you a funny story, though. When I came back from the hospital with my leg in plaster, I had to get downstairs to collect everything I needed to go upstairs to live with my mum. I had to live in her house, you see, as I couldn't move between the two houses. To get downstairs was impossible as I was struggling with the crutches. So the builders carried me. Half an hour later, in convoy they carried me and my belongings back upstairs. We must have been a funny sight.'

'I suppose that is part of small community life.' The comment was not meant as a compliment.

'Yes indeed. And very glad I am that I live in it.'

The summer rolled on. Beth settled into the Cottage, and worked as a guide on a very part-time basis. In the autumn she and Mina would begin to prepare the downstairs house for letting towards the end of the year, but rather than embark immediately on what that entailed, they would just enjoy the summer, having attained what at times had seemed unattainable. They spent hours in the garden just looking at their renewed building. They had done the house research by then, and on those long summer nights they sat on John Connell's bench and brought the story to life. They were part of the community who, for almost a century and a half, had enjoyed this view, walked on this grass in bare feet in the cool of the evening, and built their own memories.

Out of nowhere, one evening Beth said, 'One day I will tell the story of this house.' She had written a factual account of the history of the village. She had written educational documents, papers and a textbook, but the story of her house was a new challenge.

Her mother smiled.

'All houses have stories worth telling,' she said. 'I hope you do. But wait until you are ready.'

On a calm evening in late summer, Mina announced she wished she had gone up the river by boat.

'But you did,' Beth said. 'You were always travelling to Glasgow by steamer.'

'No, I don't mean that. I mean beyond Glasgow where the river begins to narrow. People used to do that in small boats.'

Beth thought. She had a friend who had been a rower, and was still involved in a Glasgow rowing club. 'Why not?' she thought. 'It's worth a try.'

When she phoned Bob and explained what her mother wanted, she finished by saying, 'Is this completely crazy or is it possible?'

'It is completely crazy, but why not? Let's make it happen.'

When Beth told her mother the boat trip was a real possibility, she was thrilled. The little girl who had gone adventuring along the magic path had never changed.

On the appointed day, Beth and Mina set off to Glasgow. They met Bob and his fellow rower at the boathouse. When Beth saw the boat, she was horrified. It was so slim and light. Was this safe? The two men saw the panic in her eyes, and reassured her all would be well.

Beth waved her mother goodbye, and watched the little boat disappearing up the river. If anything went wrong, how was she ever going to tell Ian she had sent their mother up the river in a wee boat?

But of course nothing did go wrong, and an hour later the boat returned with a delighted ninety-four-year-old passenger. She may have seen almost nothing, but the experience of being in that little boat was everything. On their way home, Beth asked if next year it would be paragliding!

Four weeks later, news came that Ian had to have heart surgery. This blow struck hard. Mina seemed to retreat into herself. She did not give up, but she spent a great deal of her day not tending the tomatoes in her greenhouse, or weeding her garden. She just sat on her father's garden seat worrying about her wee boy.

The day of the operation was endured in almost complete silence. Conversation was impossible. The house too held its breath. Nothing mattered, but what has happening across the ocean.

And then Viola phoned to say he was through the operation, and it was a success. They were too exhausted to celebrate. Next day the news was better. He was on the mend. No relapse. He would be fine. By the third day they could talk to him. And then he went home, and desperate to put this behind them and grasp normality, Beth and Mina began planning the letting.

~

Two weeks after Ian's operation began as an ordinary day. By midday, Beth and her mum were preparing to go to the village hall for the regular Thursday lunch.

'Where's my comb?' Mina said.

'In the drawer at the sink.'

'Where is the sink?'

Where is the sink? In a house lived in for sixty years. What was happening? Beth failed to force down panic.

They went to the lunch, but Mina was not her usual self. She either did not speak, or she spoke loudly, interrupting other people.

'I think you need to take her to the doctor,' was the advice.

They went home, and a doctor came. He diagnosed an infection, which with medication would get better, but he warned Beth of a very hard night ahead. He was right. Whatever was happening, Mina became a fiend. She was aggressive in a way Beth had never known. She was demanding. Beth could do nothing right. She could see that her mother was frightened, but in her own terror of what was happening, she had no idea how to cope.

She tried reading to her mother, something she had been doing for years after Mina's sight had gone. Mina ridiculed the story. She tried reading the newspaper to her mother, but it was snatched from her.

'I can read it myself.' Seizing it, she put on her glasses and proceeded to hold the paper upside down.

By nine o' clock, Mina decided she was ready to go to bed. Beth made up a small bed for herself on the floor of her mother's room in case the old lady got up to go to the bathroom, turned the wrong way and fell down the stairs. It was a grim night.

In the morning, Beth made breakfast for them both. As Mina came down the stairs, Beth listened to her footsteps. They were steady. The medicine she had been given seemed to have done the trick. Beth had to go to the doctor's surgery, and as she was leaving she said to her mother, 'Go to bed till I get back. I'll only be forty minutes.'

Mina's gentle hazel eyes were as they had always been. 'I'll be fine. After all, we're going on holiday next week, so I'll need to be.' She smiled her lovely warm smile. Gone was the violence of the previous night.

Beth went to the surgery, and came straight home.

'I'm back.' No answer. Her mother was not in the kitchen. She raced up the stairs. She was not in her bed. She was unconscious on the bathroom floor.

The ambulance came quickly, and the old lady was carried down the stairs, up the path, and out the gate. The old house watched its longest-term inhabitant leaving.

Mina had had a massive stroke. For three days she lingered, Beth never leaving her side, talking to her, reminding her of places they had gone together. Beth was sure her mother heard her because when she told the funny stories, the old lady seemed to twitch and grip Beth's hand tighter. John, the little boy from years ago, now married to Soozie, came to see her. Exhausted by then,

Beth slept in the corner of the room, while John talked to the unconscious old lady he knew as Mrs H. Tiny movements at the memories he related of their walks along the road told him she could hear.

She died in the early hours of the third day. Her breathing had become more laboured, and then it became weaker. With instruction from the nurse, Beth touched the pulse in her neck as it became fainter and fainter, and then as it stopped, her mother seemed to have taken wings and flown away. The body in the bed was not her mother. Her spirit was in the room, but no longer in that body.

A friend had come to take Beth home. Barely able to walk, she was terrified. Mina had worn two wedding rings, her own and her mother's. The doctor had taken the rings off and given them to Beth. Afraid she would lose them, she hung them on a chain round her neck, alongside a gold kangaroo set inside a wishbone, a gift from her brother from decades earlier when she was setting off for Australia. Three generations now hung on that chain.

From the hospital she had made phone calls. Ian was distraught, but recovering from surgery, it was not possible for him to travel.

An hour after she had phoned Alan, he called her. Although he had always lived in Kent, he had been coming to Aunt Mina for over fifty years. Other than Ian, he was the member of the family who had known her the longest. He could not stay away.

'You should not be alone with this. I'm coming up. I've booked a flight and I'll be there on Tuesday.' He had thrown her a lifeline; an act of kindness she knew she would never forget.

In the days that followed as the funeral arrangements were made, she and Alan talked. He had lost Janet some years before, and understood grief. They sat by the fireside in conversation, and in silence. He took over the practicalities, and he listened as Beth cried. His patience was infinite.

In all the years Alan had been visiting the house, they had never really come to know each other. In these days together they learned that although they had trodden very different paths, they looked at the world through much the same lens.

At one point during that week, they had to blanch tomatoes. The tomatoes, grown so carefully all summer, were ripe for picking, and Beth would not allow her mother's tomatoes to rot. Neither Beth nor Alan knew how to do it. In the village it is customary to visit the house where a death has taken place. People came all day long, and the well known village cooks were consulted on how to blanch tomatoes. Alan and Beth managed this without mishap, and Mina's tomatoes were blanched and frozen. All through the long winter ahead, every time Beth took a packet of the tomatoes from the freezer, she thought of the astonished faces of the people who had come to offer their condolences and found themselves being interrogated about how to blanch tomatoes.

Jacqui, Kate and Rosie came from America. Alan's family came from Kent. The house once again needed elastic walls. Friends in the village lent mattresses and bedding. Food magically appeared on the table. The garden seat was permanently occupied. As one person got up, someone else sat down, each reliving their time spent here. Mina's light had not been extinguished.

The church was full. Many of the people of the village came. The builders came in the working clothes Mina had seen them in at the three o'clock teas for months. Beth's friends from the city made the long journey. Even though many of them did not know Mina, they had all heard of her.

Missing from this was Ian. Terrible though it was to be here, it was more terrible to not be here. He had tried every possible way of coming home, but it was too dangerous to his health. Would Mina have wanted him to make the journey under these circumstances? Absolutely not. Beth applied for special permission to film the service. Brother and sister consulted on every detail. Ian's daughters read the eulogy he had written.

Simultaneous with the service in Scotland, Ian and Viola held their own service for Mina in their garden. Viola had suggested planting a tree, a small tree, small like Mina; a dwarf pine, an evergreen never fades. The Mina tree has grown, and every year it becomes stronger.

Chapter Thirty-Three

Next day everyone left and Beth had to face the emptiness. Never had she lived alone in this house. She was isolated, she was alone, and she was lonely. She was also terrified of being at home. No matter where she looked, her mother was missing. People told her she would feel better in time, but she was not at all sure of this. Perhaps this was just too big. She had lost her mother, the person she shared her time with, and the person who had become dependent on her; her mother and her child.

Sometimes she slept in her mother's bed. Sometimes she sat by the fire and cried. She held her mother's clothes and handbag, hoping that this had not happened, and her mum would suddenly reappear. She did not wash the dishes her mum had used on that last morning. At night she sat at the kitchen table and wrote to her mother, pleading with her to come home.

Friends came to check on her as word travelled round the village of how unkempt she looked. Her friends from the city came, and were shocked at what they found. It was useless trying to tell her that someday she would be as she had once been. She did not believe this. Part of her did not want to be happy again; that seemed a betrayal.

It was at that moment that Beth 'saw' her family; her mother, young again, standing at the door, her hand on the doorknob; her aunt, never a hair out of place, with a dishtowel over one shoulder at the sink; her father as an old man in his chair at the table, cigarette in hand; and through the window she could see her grandfather on his bench, her granny standing near him on the path, holding Sooty by the lead. All exactly as they had been in life. For a moment, just a moment, her torment evaporated, and in the instant she felt this tiny glimmer, they disappeared. She pleaded with them to come back, not to leave her like this, but they were gone. Strange as this experience had been, Beth could not deny it. They were urging her to take the reins, and live again.

She tried! Oh how she tried! And every day the struggle just seemed to magnify. How had she not anticipated this and gathered strategies to cope?

Time dragged on. Mina's house sat cleaned but unlived in, as if she had just gone out for a walk. Her slippers sat waiting for her. Going into it took on the feel of entering a shrine, comforting to begin with, but then a symbol of death.

As the house could not sit empty indefinitely, changes had to take place, but Ian had to see the old house before they began. It was part of his rite of passage. When he was able to travel, he and Viola came home. Months on Beth had become at least partly used to Mina not being there, but for Ian this was just the beginning of that stage of grief. She watched her brother doing what she had done, constantly looking for his mother to come round the door. She watched him sitting on the garden seat, deep in his memories. Viola watched him too. She did not sit with him; she watched him as she tackled the gardening. As a keen gardener she saw what needed to be done, and set about bringing order into the borders. To her surprise, the soil had the same rich softness of their garden in the Pacific Northwest. The palm tree also surprised her. They were so far north, how could this be?

When the time came for their return to America, Ian was both desperately sad, and also relieved to escape this constant pressing loss. Beth was once again left scared and alone, afraid of tomorrow. For as long as she could remember, this house had been her haven. When she had come home to look after her mother she felt her life had fulfilment, but now it had no meaning and no purpose. She was paralysed. What on earth was she going to do? How long could she put off making some kind of decision? Most frightening of all was how to make a decision when she was in so much pain. It would be simple to run away; in her worst moments she wondered if her attachment to the house had died with her mother.

As she agonised over this hour after hour, there were practicalities to be done. The downstairs house had to be rented. The upstairs house had to be renovated for Beth to move into, and allow the Cottage also to be rented. The kitchen needed upgrading, and the bathroom needed a shower. With weary heart she began renovating again; unsure if this upgrade was in preparation for staying or for leaving.

One day Stewart the plumber was moving a heater, and when he sat down for his three o'clock tea, he was uneasy.

'What's wrong?'

Reluctantly he said, 'I've found dry rot.'

It was extensive in the upstairs bedroom, and to remove it, a metre had to be stripped back from it in all directions. This meant that underneath it, the ceiling of the parlour with its lily of the valley had to be removed. The devastation to the house was nothing compared with the devastation to Beth. In her mind, the old house, unwilling to live without Mina, had decided to die.

When the work began, Beth stayed out of sight. It was just too awful to watch. One night after the builders had gone home, she went round to the house and stood in the parlour. She looked up, and could see the ceiling of the room above. Walls had been stripped of plaster and skirting boards, shutters had been taken off, choking clouds of dust stirred as she moved.

She sat on the stairs and began to cry, uncontrollable wailing. There had been just too much pain, too much worry, too much fear, too much desolation. Consumed in her misery, she did not hear the door open.

'I left my glasses. I've come back for them,' Duncan said.

She barely understood his words, so locked as she was into her own despair. He read the situation precisely.

'I can't bring back your mother, but I can fix this.' There was such kindness and common sense in these words. Beth smiled wanly.

'Thank you,' was all she said.

Time passed and the house began to smile again. Slowly Beth came to like what was happening to it. Friends who came to visit fell into two camps.

'It is so different,' followed by, 'no actually, it is really just the same,' or, 'It is just the same, with a facelift.'

The house had been modernised, but had kept its self. The original features with the exception of the lily of the valley were still there. If the Leitches or the Weirs had come back to see it, they would have seen few real changes. The anonymous architect's work still gave the house its character. In removing the lily of the valley and the cornice, the builders had been very careful. Large pieces of it were positioned as a wall feature in the transparent ceilinged outside space known as the sitooterie.

As Mina's furniture went out, and Beth moved hers in, the house began to take on a sense of being alive again. She let the downstairs house and the Cottage. With people arriving, full of excitement about a new place to live, the old building was no longer cloaked in sadness. It was once again buzzing with activity, but one which barely touched her. When people asked her about the house, she answered, but her voice was flat.

The garden needed attention. She had always viewed gardening as housework outside. At first it was a chore, but very gradually she began to learn that her mother was right. There is pleasure in nurturing plants. Beside the two old notebooks of stories and recipes, she had found a gardening diary belonging to her mother and read in her steady handwriting,

To me as a child there were two types of gardens – beautiful gardens and beautiful, fun gardens. The beautiful gardens belonged to wealthy people who had gardens large and small, perfectly kept and a riot of colour. An extension of them were public parks, a beauty to behold! But 'behold' was the operative word. To tread on the lawns, or touch the flowers was beyond contemplation.

The other type of gardens, and by far my childhood favourite, was the natural woodland of family holidays and picnics. Here a child could wander barefoot through the cool grass admiring AND picking the wild flowers, flowers which were for days to come a lingering reminder of the beauty and freedom of nature's garden. So when I say there will always be a place in my garden for daffodils, bluebells, primroses and wild margaritas, you could say I have no intention of losing sight of my grass roots, nor the very special association these flowers have with my childhood, and later with the childhoods of my son and daughter, and later still my grandchildren.

When I came to live here permanently, the garden was still showing the effects of the 'Dig for Victory' campaign. There was no colour. I set out to rectify this with forsythia, mahonias, flowering current, primula, monbretia and lupins.

Beth smiled, thinking of her mother happy in her gardening hat, hoping she would learn enough to keep the spirit of her mother's garden alive. It had to continue to be a beautiful and fun garden.

Beth described her life as lived in three parts – her working life, her city life and her village life. She guided tourists, she stayed with friends in the city, and then she came home. Coming home had been so difficult. Putting the key in the lock, knowing there was no one there, stabbed her anew every time, but eventually that too receded, and coming home slowly developed the same pull it always had.

'What is your favourite part of Scotland?' visitors would ask.

'Home,' she always replied, and when she did so, she saw her home and her garden and despite her pain knew that someday she would find peace there again.

The village was changing also. The shops had declined in number as people travelled to the supermarket, but one remained as both a village store and that vital part of village life, the post office. The village hall continued at the core of the social life of the community. Dances, carpet bowls, art classes, children's parties were as frequent as when the hall had first opened over a century before. For Beth, the glitter over the horizon which had drawn her for so much of her life had been replaced by the authenticity of this small community.

In 2015, Ian and Viola came home to mark their fifth wedding anniversary. A few days into their visit the old house looked on in wonder, when first a photographer arrived, and then the couple emerged in their wedding finery; Ian in kilt and jacket, and Viola in a beautiful burgundy and silver filigreed gown. The sun shone. Photographs: moments in time marking life's passage. Over a century had passed since the house had watched a wedding in its garden. It now had another memory to add to its long story.

Before Mina died, Viola's son Adrien had come to visit. Living in busy Boston, he found the quiet strange, but like so many before him he was captivated by the view. He too found his way into the greenhouse, fascinated by Mina, by then over ninety, working with her seedlings and plants. On his next visit along came his partner, for whom the garden and the beach held happy echoes of childhood. When the old building heard this, it smiled; it knows the pattern. Soon they will bring their son, another generation with memories to carry home, ripples in time spreading across the ocean.

Tenants came and went. The first tenants in the Cottage were a couple of Beth's own age. In the hot summer days, they sat and talked. Different paths in life, many similar experiences. In time they moved away, but the friendship did not end.

One day Soozie came to visit. She often did this, but on this particular day there was something slightly unsettled about her.

'Would you consider John and I renting the Cottage?' she asked.

Beth was stunned. She had wondered why they had never suggested this before, and that was all she could think to say. One part of her saw it as a wonderful way forward, another part of her was afraid. Suppose it went wrong? She would lose their friendship, and in that moment she realised that if she said no, she had lost it anyway.

John and Soozie and four-legged Max moved in. Soozie with her tiny blowtorch makes jewellery in the cellar amidst the library and the pots of marmalade. John looks after the garden, and has prepared a vegetable patch. Once again the house will watch potatoes, onions, and cabbages grow. Soozie moves the flowering plants around, and has succeeded in a blaze of colour all summer long. Max keeps a watchful canine eye on everything that happens. Once a month they gather to eat together at what came to be referred to as the River View Supper Club. Sometimes when Beth has been away, she comes back to find John has come into her house and put the fire on. In the dark winter days, this homecoming is a true delight.

A young couple moved in downstairs. Many a long summer night, they sat in the garden watching the moonlight on the river.

Their friends visited; John and Soozie's friends visited. The sadness which had cloaked the house for nigh on five years lifted. The sun shone on the lead flashing.

Alan comes from Kent every year, and he too works in the garden. Often he sits on the garden seat and lets his memories wander. Over a bottle of red wine, Beth and he spend hours talking. He has travelled extensively, and they often compare places they have visited almost half a century apart.

Ian comes home regularly. At one point there was a mix-up in dates, and Beth had to be away for two nights of his visit. He was in his childhood home entirely on his own. In all the years, he had never been alone in this house. The old house looked after him, as it always does those who love it.

Kate and Rosie come to this house of memories from their childhoods when they can, bringing their partners with them. Kate has found her niche in a classroom, or in a garden, or in a hall, any space where children can use their imagination.

Rosie's artistic leanings have been channelled into hairdressing. Rosie always loved stories. She listens to her clients for three hours or more as they tell their stories. 'No matter who they are or what they believe in, they have a story and if I listen with an open mind, I can find similarities,' she said one day. When the old house heard this, it beamed in agreement.

Jacqui's mother, Doreen, also visits regularly. On one visit she bought Beth a white hydrangea so that she would always be there in the garden. That white hydrangea has grown into a proud plant.

Former pupils visit, and friends from decades ago visit, drawn not just to see Beth but by the place itself.

Americans who rented downstairs come back to visit. Their children come. Friends from across the world come. They see the beauty, and they often ask, 'Do you know the history of the house?'

'Oh yes,' Beth will say, and then launch into Hugh Weir and his son Jack, the Misses Cook and David McLean, as well as her own grandparents.

Sometimes they ask about things in the house.

'What happened to the table legs? They look as if they have been chewed.'

'Yes indeed. That was two dogs ago. Sooty objected if the table was being lifted, and got his teeth into it. He did much the same to the hoover.'

'What are the stories behind that leather stool and the wooden one?'

'The leather stool I brought back from Egypt. I bought it in Luxor at the beginning of my visit, and carried it attached to a rope handle for the whole trip. It was very handy when waiting for a bus or in an overcrowded train. What a carry-on I had trying to bring it back home as hand luggage! I was determined as I knew it would never have survived the hold. The wooden one next to it was my grandmother's. Her father brought it from the Highlands when he came looking for work in the 1870s. It is a milking stool which he thought he might be able to use. It never was used for that again, but his daughters loved it and then his granddaughters did too. The stools are both perfect size for in front of the fire.'

It is not just people or pictures on the walls that have stories; every item had its story too, and these stories could no more be removed from the house, than could those of the humans who have inhabited it since it was built.

With Beth in the house; John, Soozie and Max in the Cottage; and downstairs waiting for the right person to move in, Beth dared to hope that a less painful era had begun.

Chapter Thirty-Four

As the second decade of the 21st century rolled to a close, Beth was once again happy with her life: it had taken nigh on ten years. How glad she was that she had not left in despair. Now over seventy, she continued working, because she enjoyed it. She guided tourists round Scotland telling its story. Suffering and success; the story of human beings and of nations. Many of her visitors were contemporaries, and this led to an unexpected aspect of the work which afforded immense pleasure. With them all having lived through the second half of the twentieth century, they had a shared experience of major events. One evening in the bar, conversation flowed onto the assassination of President Kennedy.

Towards its conclusion, Beth remarked, 'And all this on such a horrible wet Friday night.'

'No it wasn't. It was a beautiful hot sunny afternoon,' came a response. The whole group had remembered that terrible day both the same and differently. The visual images were the same; a hot day in Dallas on black-and-white screens, but they remembered it differently, through the lens of their own time zones and their own weather.

The particular aspect of working as a guide Beth enjoyed most was being able to make connections between Scotland and from where the visitors had come. So many Scots have spread across the world, and their descendants return seeking their origins. It is not that they reject where they belong now. It is that they want their family's past, too. She once asked a group why this was so important.

'You are all Americans and proud of being so, so why do you want the Scottish origins also? Why does it matter?'

For days there had been no reply, and then it came almost simultaneously. Individually, they had been deep in thought. The answers were variations on the same theme.

'Yes I am proud to be American, but it is not enough.'

'I want to be connected more than one or two generations back.'

'I want to know where my family came from, and what shaped them. I want to know why my grandmother's mother passed on the stories she told.'

When did people feel they had become Americans, and stop looking back across the ocean? When and how does identity begin?

Beth knew much of her story, rooted in the land where it had happened, and watching the visitors carefully as they expressed their thoughts, she began to realise she had never lived without that connectedness. She had taken centuries of European history for granted. It was just there in the background of her world, in the form of stories and ideals, buildings and memorials. Identity reaches beyond family and place and nationality. Across continents and centuries, we are bound by pain and joy and by morality.

This was true also of her work in some of the major battlefields of twentieth-century Europe, guiding school groups of teenagers through the obscenity of the trenches, the Normandy bocage and the gas chambers. As the young people confront these events, they are brought face to face with a responsibility to carry into adulthood; to ensure that such terrible events would never happen on their watch.

The serious side of guiding was offset by the fun, of which there was plenty amidst a random group of people with enquiring minds. To Beth in her eighth decade, it was a wonderful job. People often asked when she intended to stop working, and her answer was easy.

'When I no longer want to do it.' When she came to feel the same as she did before she left education, the time would have come.

In the summer she worked, and friends came to visit. In the winter she visited them elsewhere in Britain, in Ireland, in Germany and in America, always exploring new places on the way. And in between she came home to the house, which always welcomed her back.

She was involved in village life and particularly liked going to the dances in the village hall. She could never go there and whirl around it without thinking back to her early days in that hall, and to those who had been there in the half century before that. As she walked home, she often thought of the Misses Cook being driven that same road in Mrs Leitch's carriage. It takes a long time to be a community, and for sure this hall and this village were shaping up nicely.

What was even more remarkable was that her contemporaries who had never left had lived by different choices, and yet she and they were all bound by a shared childhood history. During the arguments with her father she had felt constrained by the smallness of the village, but now she had found its richness.

Mina never did learn what had happened to her father's mother, the missing Jane, and Beth increasingly wanted to solve this mystery, this time for her own satisfaction; it annoyed her that she had not found it in almost two decades of searching. Use of the internet made such investigation easier. Brick wall after brick wall until one day, in response to a plea for help on a genealogy platform, she was thrown a clue. Jane had left her husband and her son, and then remarried. Why had she done this? What had driven her to such a drastic choice? Had Jane, like Beth, seen a glitter over the horizon? Once she had reached for it, her options would have been limited. Had she ever wished she could have come home?

Beth and Mina had searched death records, emigration records, divorce records, asylum records to no avail. It never occurred to them to try marriage records. But there she was. Married bigamously. The hunt was on again. Death records under a different name, and lo and behold, again there she was. Next it was the burial records, and once again Beth went to Liverpool. Armed with the plot number and the map of the cemetery, she found Jane, and then came the next surprise. She was not buried with her second husband, but with her sister.

A grand headstone, and also remembered on it were her parents. Who had paid for that headstone? Why were her parents on it, when they were not buried there? Why her sister, and not her second husband? And why on earth had she left her husband and son in the first place? How had she lived with the choice she had made? Who really was she? Beth had thought she was drawing the story to a close that day, but not so. A whole new one had just opened up.

Most surprising of all was that fresh flowers had been laid at the grave. Beth took from her bag a bottle of water to give the flowers a drink, and then attempted to dry the inside of the bottle. She wrote a letter on paper torn from the notebook she always carried, and left it inside the bottle, placing it neatly beside the flowers at the gravestone, asking that anyone who comes to tend this grave contact her. She is still waiting and hoping.

When John and Soozie moved into the Cottage, the friendship deepened. If the cellar lights are on late into the night, Soozie is designing. Occasionally Beth will go to the cellar/workshop for a chat, and to watch the jewellery being made, but if Soozie is in full creative mode, the chat will need to wait for another evening. Sometimes Beth watches through the window, as Soozie wields her tiny blowtorch with the exacting precision of a surgeon with his scalpel. One day Beth opened the cellar door and Soozie shrieked, 'Don't come in. I've just dropped a diamond!' Oddly by the very act of Beth opening the door, the diamond was easy to find; there it was on the carpet glinting in the light.

Even as her friendships in the village grew, those in Edinburgh did not wane. They strengthened by the years. Every few weeks Beth went off to meet up with friends, go to the theatre, and enjoy city life. As in the years she lived there coming home charged her batteries, so too did moving in the opposite direction. She still needed both places.

Alan came regularly and when she travelled to Kent they visited places they were interested in. Canterbury Cathedral, Dover Castle, Hastings – new places each visit. At Christmas of 2019 Beth went to Kent, dragging a suitcase full of the Scottish foods he and his family associate with all their visits north. Wrapped in plastic, to prevent a disaster in her luggage, was a large jar of her homemade marmalade.

2020 was shaping up well. She had tours booked for part of the summer, with friends and family coming for the remainder. Her friends in Ireland, much younger than her, have two young boys. How those boys loved this garden and the path with its old magic gate at the end. To them it was a portal to another realm. When Beth stood at the door and watched Callum and Euan running down the path, she saw not just them but generations of children for whom this was a playground. She chuckled remembering Steph and Neil apologising for their children chasing each other in the cupboard under the eaves, not knowing they were simply doing what Beth and her brother had done. There was no case for an apology. Beth was delighted these young children had found for themselves the delights of the house. The grim months of January and February would be a mixture of visits to the city, and quietly living at home.

January is marmalade month, a ritual Beth has known all her life. Her grandmother had passed down her recipe to her mother, and now it was Beth's turn. Who knows from whom the recipe originally came? Seville oranges were not readily available to the less well off, so there would have been no call for a recipe, and yet one such had found its way into the older of the ancient notebooks which sat beside their modern counterparts.

From her reading Beth knew that Scotland had had a long relationship with Seville oranges, much prized by the aristocracy. There is written evidence of the Seville oranges arriving in Scotland from the 17th century, but there is also anecdotal stories of even earlier. One rumour is that Mary Queen of Scots sent for marmalade when she had the cold, 'pour ma malade'. The word itself is derived from the Spanish word for jam, 'mermelada.'

The oranges leave Spain just after Christmas, and arrive in the shops by very early January. The community of marmalade makers go into action. Beth was of course aware that the oranges arrived by containers and lorries, but preferred the version of their travel arrangements she had been told as a child. They come in galleons in full sail, almost a latter-day Spanish Armada.

The oranges are very specific. No substitute will do. Their bitterness is the basis of the delicacy. The gelling agent is the pectin in the pips. The chunkiness is the rind. Every part of the orange is essential to its texture and flavour. Each individual's recipe is regarded as Truth.

One year, Beth's marmalade had turned out a little runny. This had puzzled her greatly. She had followed the timings exactly, and then it struck her that the timings had all been worked out for a house with no central heating. The ambient temperature of the room might be a factor. For the next batch, she reverted to there being no heating on, and indeed all was well. If people dropped in for a visit when the production was going on, they were amazed to find Beth wearing a coat and hat, but with all the windows and doors open, even amidst a snowstorm raging outside.

'With so much steam, the windows and doors have to be open or the walls run with sticky liquid. I can't put the central heating or the fire on, as that might unbalance the precision of the operation,' she explained to the onlookers.

She had also learned through trial and error not to make it on windy days – the wind swirling round the room caused a great deal of trouble.

Beth loved making marmalade. Replete with childhood memories, there is also the smell which evokes hot sunny days in Spain. Once cycling near Seville, she had smelled the orange groves; definitely the place to stop for a rest. On a cold day in Scotland, that memory is part of the ritual also.

In 2019 Britain was poised to leave the European Union, something Beth was deeply disturbed by. The community of Europe had come about as a response to the tragedies of two world wars, and it saddened her that the essence of co-operation was being swept aside.

On a personal level, she had been concerned about what impact leaving the European Union might have on the arrival of the oranges. In January of 2019 she had made the marmalade, and then stored frozen kilos of them just in case there would be no more. A summer visitor to the house had accidentally turned the freezer off, and in order that the oranges did not go to ruin, she'd had to make the marmalade in July.

This was all wrong. Marmalade should be made in January. The smell and the golden glow belong to the long, dark nights.

Part of the process is skimming off the froth. It is then wrapped in newspaper, put into plastic bags and dispatched into the garbage bin outside. Going out with household garbage a few days later, Beth was horrified to open the lid, and find the bin swarming with wasps. She banged down the lid, and raced off to get wasp killer. How had this happened? It had never happened before – well, of course it hadn't. She had never made marmalade in July.

When it came to bin night, Beth was worried. She could not have the men who emptied her bin exposed to the wasps. She resolved this by putting the wasp killer on top of the bin along with a note written in very large letters, so they could not possibly miss it. She explained what had happened and suggested they opened the bin just a fraction, squirted in the wasp killer, collected the garbage further up the road, and by the time they were back, the wasps would be dead. They followed her instructions to the letter, and when she came home found a note beside the can. It read, 'Thank you. You are a very kind lady.' There would be no more July marmalade.

As soon as 2020 dawned, she awaited the oranges tackling the Bay of Biscay under full sail. It was so much more attractive a story than a truck crossing from Bilbao to Portsmouth, that she embroidered it by anxiously watching the Met Office reports on the Atlantic weather.

Marmalade month was always good fun. Time to read as the concoction bubbled away. Fiction, non-fiction, she read by the fireside in a room full of the smell of oranges.

Since writing the tiny stories in her treasured notebook as a child, Beth had as an adult wanted to try writing fiction, but had never set aside the time to try. In summer she worked, in winter she gallivanted. She knew she had to have an unbroken stretch of time to tackle what to her was an enormous challenge. There was truth to this given the choices she made about how she used her time, but it was, she knew, also an excuse. She could justify it on the grounds that if she took a year off from guiding she might not be offered the contracts the following year, and she was not willing to take that risk. Fancifully she told herself she would write when she retired from guiding. A sensible explanation; an excuse. She knew that the truth was she was afraid she could not do it, to the extent she was afraid to even try. She spoke of this to no one, concealing and running away from both the compulsion growing inside her, and the accompanying fear. Someday, but not yet.

Looking forward to a January of marmalade and reading was altogether much easier.

The old house watched and waited.

Chapter Thirty-Five

On New Year's Eve in 2019, Beth, John, Soozie and four-legged Max had a bonfire. The downstairs house was between tenants, so only the long-term inhabitants were at the garden party in boots, coats, gloves, scarves and hats. The night was as clear as it had been twenty years before. In the moonlight, the house was silver. The trees were still, and the river reflecting their bare branches a palate on which squiggles had been drawn. Beth could see her mother with the other old ladies as they had been, not so long ago. And now she was the old lady sitting there.

The conversation at the bonfire wandered onto a small item on the news. A strange virus had just been reported in China.

'How awful if it spreads, and people have to be isolated in their houses, not allowed to go out.'

'Surely that won't happen.'

'You would hope not. That is how it was dealt with in the past. In the Middle Ages whole villages were cut off to prevent the spread of the plague. Surely we have better ways of managing such a possibility.'

The conversation moved on. It was happening a long way away. It had nothing to do with the three bringing in the New Year in the garden.

January and February rolled on, and the virus spread to Europe. Italy was not so far away. Then it was Spain. All over the continent, hospitals were overwhelmed by this terrible disease. Then it was France. Inevitably it would cross the Channel. People went on with their normal lives, but with this unseen killer approaching, seemingly unstoppable, there was a sense of unreality.

Beth made the marmalade, but for the first time in her life it was a chore. The time was out of joint, and the annual ritual of marmalade and reading by the kitchen fire in the evening, as the amber nectar cooled in its jars, had neither pleasure, nor the comfort of familiarity. What was happening in the wider world was unknown and terrifying. With the doors and windows open to let the steam out, she could see snowdrops coming up through the hardened ground. The flowers, unaware of what was happening in the human world, symbolised a normality felt nowhere else.

In February, Beth booked her winter holiday to America for November. Surely whatever happened, it would be all over by then. Two weeks later she went to visit her friends in Ireland. Ironically, they had planned to go to the Titanic Museum in Belfast; even in late February, the metaphor of going to a museum marking a disaster, which could have been averted with less human arrogance, did not at that point strike them. This strange virus was not an iceberg.

In March it became clear something dreadful was about to engulf Britain, and in shock, all the more acute because it happened so quickly, people adjusted their focus. Beth was no exception. She prepared for the possibility of her life being in some ways restricted, but of course it would not be for long. By May she would be out on tour.

In the short term she thought she had better fill her freezer with soups and casseroles, but in order to do this, she had to take out the remaining oranges she had stored. For the second time in two months, she began to make marmalade. Unwillingly she began again; cutting and mincing the fruit and the peel, soaking the pips, boiling and skimming. Compared to the threat in the real world, wasps were minor.

As the casualties came ever closer, the full extent of what was happening was still incomprehensible. Nothing on this scale had happened in a century. Scientists and doctors struggled. One wrong analysis could lead to the death of thousands. Politicians struggled. One wrong decision would have the same terrible outcome.

On March 23rd the government ordered virtually everyone to stay in their homes. The entire country just stopped. This simple instruction made explicit how dangerous a situation the world was in. Simple words: unspoken terror.

On that first morning of the lockdown, when Beth woke up she was terrified, and not only of the virus. It was the isolation, the emptiness, the purposelessness of existence. What was the point of getting up? What was there to do? What did the next twenty-four hours hold? What was the point of doing anything as this silent killer approached? Doing anything contains the expectation of a future, and for the first time in her life she was not so sure there would be one. She thought about the plagues of past centuries, and how helpless people must have felt at the steady approach of death. Despite all the advances of medical science, was the human population of 2020 facing exactly what people had faced centuries before? It was unthinkable, but it was possible.

She lay there, her body warm and snug, her mind cold and frightened. Her gaze went beyond the window. Would the world outside look as it had yesterday?

The sun was shining, the trees swaying with a gentleness of breathing. The river beyond was gleaming. She shifted onto her elbow to see the garden. Vivid green from all the winter rain, the grass released from its long winter sleep had begun its annual rebirth. Scattered randomly across the grass grew the daffodils. Last week she was busy, and had only glanced at them as she hurried by. They had not yet bloomed, she recalled, or thought she recalled. Were they mere green shoots then, or had she just not paid attention? Now determined to be noticed, they were announcing the arrival of spring. She looked closer. In the flower border edging the path, a primrose and a primula had suddenly emerged. Purple, yellow, bold colours she liked. Nature did not come back stealthily every year. It arrived in colours to be reckoned with.

Like the flowers she too surged with life at the coming of spring. January 1st meant nothing. A new year began when the flowers came up. A new year of adventures lay ahead.

But not this year. Life had just been stopped by an invisible killer.

The virus struck in a variety of ways, but what most frightened Beth was that some of its victims became unable to breathe. She had no idea how long it might take to reach that stage. Was this like the sweating sickness of past centuries, when a person could be fine at 9am and dead two hours later? Living alone, her greatest fear was the nights, lest she woke up gasping for breath, and was unable to phone for help. She took the phone to bed just in case. She left the main door slightly ajar, afraid that even if she could phone for help, she might not be able to reach the door to let the help in.

Cancelled arrangements. Hours, days and weeks ahead lay empty. What on earth was she going to do? Her carefully built life of friends and work and holidays and home was swept aside, leaving a vacuum of time. How would she ever manage to fill the lengthening days?

And then from deep inside her, it came. 'Now is the time to write your story. You always knew it had to be an unbroken stretch of time at the kitchen table. This situation is exactly what you need.'

She recoiled in terror. She had no plotline. She feared trying and failing. Could she write description and dialogue? Could she create character? A teacher of literature for over thirty years, could she do it? With her analytical mind and her non-fiction writing, she had no confidence she could. But this was no random fanciful notion. This was a compulsion fighting its way through her carefully constructed busy life. She was being driven to the blank sheet of paper. If she tried and failed, well, she reasoned, she had tried. She could swallow her disappointment, and accept that. What she knew she could not live with was not trying.

She cast about for excuses. What about her tours? They had been cancelled. What about friends and family coming to visit? That was now illegal. The house needed a good spring clean. It almost snarled at her – you did that last month in preparation for the spring and summer. No matter which way she looked, she had no excuse.

That did not get her closer to a plotline, and rather than see that as a welcome excuse, it set off a panic. Perhaps she would fall at the very first hurdle.

In Scotland people were permitted one walk a day, and in an attempt to build up her health and stay safe, off Beth went every morning into the hills where she would be unlikely to meet people. Quite the contrary. Many people had taken to the safety of the hills. Shy conversations with new acquaintances gathered strength two metres apart.

Between the conversations on the hill she struggled to find a plotline, but no glimmer felt right. Maybe it had all just been a ridiculous idea.

One morning, a flower emerging from its bud caught her eye. She had never made time to really look at flowers in detail, but today she did so – what else did she have to do with her time?

Unbidden, she found herself intrigued by looking at the stages of the different buds. She remembered someone once telling her that a European philosopher had written, 'A seed looks frail, but it conjures the earth's power to do its bidding.' She had liked that idea – from something so tiny and fragile, something of beauty can spring, driven by its own lifeforce.

If only she could have a seed of a plot.

And then the idea came to her, but from where she knew not. She turned it over. Yes, that was possible. On she walked, building the story as she went along. Parts of it even made her smile. This seed grew stronger. It was demanding to be written. She had to summon her power to do its bidding. As she walked there in the hills, her story began to take shape.

Home. Computer or pen and paper? She tried the latter but the scorings out became such a mess they made her feel incompetent. She tried the computer, checking paragraph by paragraph as she went. Definitely better. After two pages, she was exhausted. Next day she read it over, and grudgingly admitted it was not a disaster. This spurred her on.

Her characters came alive. Every morning she went for the daily walk and sketched out the daily writing, talking it aloud as she went along. She wrote in the mornings after her walk, and stopped when she knew it was weakening, sometimes in the middle of a sentence.

It was trial and error, but the story grew chapter by chapter. One day she took another huge leap into uncertainty. She would let someone read what she had written. She sent the first section and waited anxiously. A few suggestions and many positive comments. She tried someone else. The response was the same. On she went. The pleasure of the act of creating had become a daily joy.

The virus raged on. Week after week, every morning she walked, and created her story.

She kept hoping that there would be a flash of velvet and a grey cap and a young man in uniform come to watch her writing, but she knew they only came when a person the house loved was in distress. Conversely, that gave her hope.

She watched the flowers come and go. On the hills was the gorse, in the garden the bluebells and the azaleas, the yellow and purple irises and the pure white snow-in-summer, one of her favourites. Then came the rhododendrons. Each day she searched the borders and the bushes for new buds. As the flowers grew, so did her story.

She often met William and his dog. Conversation between them was never stilted. One day she told him she was writing a story. Gently, he asked her why. She had no difficulty talking to strangers on her travels, but doing so where she would meet the person again – that was new. There was a humanity about him which she had glimpsed, and trusting in the truth of this, she began to speak of her long-held carefully hidden desire to write.

'Of all the dreams I had as a child, it is the one that has always been just too big.'

In the silence that followed, the sense of being out of step welled up from decades past. Had she once again made an error of judgement? She waited for the ridicule, but it did not come.

'The biggest dreams are the hardest because they are the biggest. That's why we must pursue them.'

As they walked along he asked about her story, and listened with increasing interest. When they parted at the end of the lane, she walked home neither embarrassed nor afraid. Next morning, she felt a little more confident as she began to shape the sentences.

A few days later when they met she asked him, 'Why did you come to live here?'

She expected a simple answer. It did not come. She waited.

'When I was a student, I was wild. Parties, pubs, girls were putty in my hands.'

She winced, and sensing it he continued, 'Looking back on it I cringe at how I behaved. It is what I did. I knew no better. The strange thing is, it never made me happy. I was always searching. I was always lonely.

'One day, I watched a student who stood apart from our group. He did not do so in a superior way, just in a dignified way. He did not belong to this wild lifestyle. And I felt envy. He had a sense of self which I did not.

'A few days later, I saw him across the road. Almost driven by something other than my conscious mind, I approached him and asked him why he remained so apart. He waited for the insult, but instead saw I was genuine in my question.

'"Because it's not my way," was the answer.

'He had no arrogance, no sneering superiority. He was just himself. Over time I learned that he came from a Highland village, growing up in a house where his father and his grandfather and his grandfather's father had lived. He was living out his time at university in the city, knowing that one day he would go home.

'I went hitchhiking as often as I could, seeking increasingly remote places. I preferred vans driven by local people to tourists on holiday. I liked listening to the people who drove them. I asked questions. I walked the hills. I sat in the pubs. I saw how people spoke to each other. They did not always get along, but there was a respect because they knew each other and each others' stories. In the country it's as basic as the weather. Everyone has to deal with this. It bonds even so-called enemies. The city is full of good people, but they are strangers to each other.

'I was drawn to this life. I did not choose it. It chose me, and so when a job came up here I applied for it. It could have been any small place, but it was here, and I have been here ever since. I could have stuck to my plan to live in the city, but I did not. I've made choices both in coming here and in choosing not to leave. The trick is learning how to do that.'

'How can we ever know we have made the right choice?'

'We stop being lonely.'

The sun rose higher in the sky. A glitter path lay on the river. The wind whispered through the grass, and when she reached home and looked up to the lion she distinctly heard, 'Listen.'

John and Soozie turned over the ground and planted. All three of them made a first-thing-in-the-morning pilgrimage to see if the potatoes were emerging from the ground. What excitement when the first one did! The same excitement the house had watched for over a century. No potatoes had been grown in this garden in thirty years, and up they were coming. Cabbages, onions, carrots, beetroot, and in Mina's greenhouse the tomatoes grew tall. The story and the plants were growing side by side. The weather was spectacular. Day after day of sunshine, the inhabitants worked in the garden, while the fourth character in this group, the house, kept its eye on what they were doing.

April and May came and went. Her tours were cancelled. Family could not come. Beth continued writing. She walked the same route every day, watching nature changing in intimate detail. She worked in the garden. She talked to people who hung over the wall for a chat. It was an entirely new way of life, and once she had left behind the terror, one she was adjusting to relatively well.

One day Beth was very excited. Her grandmother had had a rose bush. It had been there since Beth was a child, but in the previous year it had become covered in greenfly. Estimating the bush was probably well over seventy, Beth had reluctantly asked Alan on his last visit to dig it out. Her gran's bush had to go. He had cut it right back, but a little part of the root had escaped his notice. Now the bush was coming up again, its white roses shaped like camellias, clinging to the wall of the house. Soozie tied it onto the hooks which Jeanie-from-over-the-wall had thought may have been for the washing lines. Whatever they had been designed for, they were now helping this old rose to climb. Her excitement was not just that the rose bush was growing again. How the old lady had loved it! Each spring when she came to her holiday house, looking after it had taken a great deal of her time. Without human intervention, the old house had protected the root through the storms of the winter. If that could happen, the old house would take good care of her.

As she approached the end of her writing, she reflected on how she might have felt if she had not done it. For decades the dream of writing had surfaced every now and again, but in her busy life it was always for tomorrow. One day... perhaps. And now she had done it. Not doing it was a bygone world. It was a first draft, and there would be months of work ahead, but that tiny seed had blossomed.

She had seen no one for days, and as she prepared to write the ending, she unplugged the phone and switched off her mobile. She wanted to be alone with her words and her characters. She was isolated and alone, but she was not lonely.

Later that day she went up the hill, and along came William.

'I think from your smile that you have finished it.'

She nodded. Their eyes met, and held. They sat in companionable quiet. This was a new beginning.

One week later, lockdown was partially lifted, and in some trepidation, she set off to Glasgow for the day. She had not gone more than five miles in thirteen weeks. As she set off up the path, she turned and looked back to the house.

It was a bright sunny day. As she closed the gate, the sun touched metal flashing on the roof and, as her eye caught the sudden light, she looked upwards. Blue sky, the golden orb, the light; she had seen this combination before.

And just below the glancing light, the lion definitely winked.

Chapter Thirty-Six

The visit to Glasgow was a return to a former life. Except it wasn't.

She met a friend in a cafe, and then off they went for a walk. The conversation had a familiar feel to it, but when they began walking, their mood changed. The city was all wrong. Cities should be full of people, and this one was deserted. Offices lay empty, shops were closed. They could walk, not just on the pavement, but in the middle of the road. The city had been extinguished.

She was glad to go home.

As July stretched into August, her writing lay in a drawer. Like good wine, it might just mature in the darkness. By then Beth's autumn tours had been cancelled. Going into the long dark winter without the variety which came with the summer tourists was not appealing, but as it was out of her control, in her pragmatic way, she saw no point in dwelling on it. By then too, surely life would be going back to normal, and Glasgow, Edinburgh, London would once again be bursting with energy.

As travel began to open up, Beth was excited. She had spent so many months cooking for one and eating alone that making nice meals, chatting over the second cup of coffee, or a glass of wine was a delight to be rediscovered and savoured.

When she visited friends in the summer, what she enjoyed most was that they cooked for her. Someone else chose the food, someone else made it, and together they shared it. After the months alone, making human connections had never been more vital. She thought of Mrs Leitch visiting the Misses Cook, and wondered if it was not just to see the house of her youth, but that she was actually reaching for companionship over the scones.

The garden was a joy. How could she have ever thought of it as housework outside? The irises particularly drew her. The green leaves grew daily taller, and then from between two of them a bud appeared. It too grew on, and when it opened the colour was startling. Purple and white set against the green leaves – her favourite colours, the blossoms delicate as silk. The hydrangeas came in mixed colours from pink to pale blue to navy blue sometimes on the same bush, and the peonies in a bold crimson flourish. Beth spent hours looking at these flowers and as the months passed and they began to fade, they did so with a grandeur about them. She could not cut them back. They had to live out their time.

August slid into September and the virus was once again on the rise. For a second time the population were instructed to not visit any other house, although this time they could meet friends in cafes. The coffee culture became a lifeline.

Walking was also permitted, and so Beth continued her daily four miles. By then the leaves were turning to golds and russets, and once they fell, she crunched her way through the carpet they created. In the garden she began the final weeding of the year, and the annual lifting of the leaves, always leaving a thin layer for the animals to burrow under for warmth. While autumn had its beauty, it had always been her least favourite season. She thought of it as the death of the year, but this year she saw a beauty she had previously swept past. The garden, it seemed, had chosen her. Winter she liked, because while the earth lay still, under it the bulbs were preparing to stir.

As the days shortened, it was time to go back to her story. She was as afraid of this as she had been when she started. Gone was the euphoria of having written it. She set herself a chapter a day, weighing every sentence, reading it aloud, searching a better way of expressing it.

How she had underestimated this task! A chapter a day was impossible. This was slow, slow work. It was much harder than the initial writing. She had not been prepared for this, but once she grasped that this is what had to be done, she set herself to the task. Not a chapter a day, not a set number of hours, but the maxim she had worked to on the first draft. Stop when she was getting tired and beginning to make mistakes, even if in mid-sentence.

This she realised was the process, with its own order. The potatoes begin as seed, then up come the shaws, and finally they are pulled out of the ground. The irises in the garden begin as seeds, and then are shoots and only in the last stages are flowers. So also in the human world. Sculptors begin with stone hewn from the rockface, and once they have carved an outline shape, then comes the real craft, chiselling the veins on the hands, the expression on the face.

She watched Soozie. It was a sheet of silver one day. Then it was a plain circle. Eventually it was a brooch of the finest design, its beauty in the crafting.

Thus Beth worked on. She was crafting. Individual phrases were written and re-written, sometimes for days. Scraps of paper with different versions of the same half sentences lay all over the table. The mornings were dark as she set off walking, re-drafting as she went. Back home, fire on, laptop at the kitchen table and steadily once again it developed, chapter by chapter.

On a day-to-day basis, she was busy. She had her writing. She had work to do for organisations she was involved with. She enjoyed these activities in themselves, but instead of just being part of her life, they had become the totality of it. For hours she sat at a computer. This was not the lifestyle she had carved out, not the lifestyle she had chosen. There were days when it was a struggle to stay cheerful and optimistic. October, November drew on. The days became ever shorter. By December it was dark before 4 o'clock. The storm doors were closed and Beth was inside, knowing she would see no one for sixteen hours, until once again she met the morning dog walkers.

How had it come to this? Alone night after night, how had this happened? Was it the result of choices she had made, or a simple twist of fate?

It was easy to blame the pandemic, but not everyone was as isolated as she. Had she brought this on herself? She felt certain she could not have done, as her life had been so rich until this disease had struck, but without rigorous self-examination, she could not be sure. She found herself going back over her life, decade by decade. Slowly as she progressed through some very painful self-truths, she knew she was preparing a blueprint for her future, once this second terrible lockdown was over.

With the same forensic scrutiny that she was applying to her writing, she turned to look inward. What choices had she made, and why had she made them?

Her life had been directed by her parents and her grandfather. Going to university had been driven by her mother, but after that, she had made the choices. She had become a teacher, and no amount of Beth trying to upturn that bore any success. She had not chosen it. It had chosen her. It had felt natural. That, she realised, was the nub. Every other career choice she had considered was a 'brain choice,' not one formed in the depths of her being. How glad she was to have not taken a different route. She could look back on the years in a classroom with quiet pride at a job well done.

She thought of the years of travelling. Did she regret not being more conventional in her choice of holidays, going with friends to comfortable locations, rather than the excitement of the unknown? She shuddered at the idea, just as she had at the time. It was the very difference that had always been the pull.

Both her work and her holidays had forged her life view. This she interrogated next. She tried alternative choices she could have made in her thirties and forties. So many words and actions in classrooms and in remote corners of the world had shaped her, that she could not deny her view of the world without denying the people who had been part of this process. They were part of her.

Next it was the turn of her interests. What had the theatre given her? The answer was easy. The simple and difficult joy of crafting a speech from a page to a spoken reality. She had done it for the words, the visuals, and the ideas. She had not done it to be part of a social group. The valued friendships had followed on. For nearly twenty years she had spent countless hours going to the theatre and directing amateurs. When one company she was with was fifty years old, a decision had been made to mark this with songs from the shows. Instead of it simply being a concert, Beth suggested writing a mystery in which a detective moves from the clue in one show to the next clue hidden inside a song. She wrote the dialogue and moved the characters across the stage to build the narrative which of course ended with Happy Birthday! That had been great fun. No regrets about these years.

Sitting night after night as the shortest day drew on, she turned to relationships. She had friendships going back decades, built on shared values and shared interests. With these friends she could really talk. Imprisoned by the virus, they spoke on the phone, each supportive of one another.

When she came to considering her marriage and subsequent relationships, she could see the mistakes she had made. In trying to make these relationships fit, she had at various times given up her theatre, and her travelling. In the end they had not worked, because they had run counter to who she really was. When the relationships foundered, the truth was she was happier back on the boards, and on the road.

She was alone in the pandemic, because of the choices she had made. Had she taken a different route, would she have been happier? Without the choices she had made she might not have been alone, but she could have spent desperately lonely decades of her life disconnected from who she really was. She could have managed it by filling it with people and activities which shored it up, but questioning it would have been far too dangerous. In this locked-down world with all the distractions taken away, how would she have coped face to face with a life that was empty of her soul? Beth thought of the unfulfilled relationships she had been in, and in the firelight's glow she sat alone, knowing it was better so.

Thinking this through in isolation had too many hallmarks of keeping her deepest thoughts to herself. The moment would come. On a bitter day in January, she climbed the hill. There was no one there. The land lay still in its icy grip. At the top she could see in all directions – an unbroken vista in which nothing stirred. She thought of all the people in the centuries past who might have stood there turning over their own lives and the choices they had made. She thought of the constraints their times had made on the choices available to them. She was the lucky generation, but, she wondered, how many constraints are actually self-imposed?

During the brief period when travel was permitted, Beth had visited her niece Kate who had had a baby. With heavy heart Beth prepared herself once again for the half-century-old agony. She would politely hold the baby, she would smile, and she would conceal the scorching anguish.

And then the impossible happened. As she looked at the tiny bundle staring at her from deep blue eyes, Beth felt what she had never felt before, and she smiled, she really smiled. Without advance warning, her internal wall had collapsed; Beth glimpsed a new adventure ahead, just loving her great-niece.

An old gnarled tree provided a seat at the point where the trunk breaks into branches. How many years since she had climbed a tree? Up she went driven on by the knowledge she had the freedom to climb a tree, wondering only briefly what would happen if she got stuck.

She settled herself into the tree-seat and returned to her thinking. This time she spoke to the land.

'All over the world there must be couples locked down together, diversions removed, in superficial silence, wondering how has it come to this, how has this happened. Was it the result of choices they had made, or was it a simple twist of fate, the virus? Could they be honest, or were they too afraid, and if so what misery will lie ahead, once they can no longer deny the knowledge which has come to them unbidden? Many a marriage survives for half a century after the relationship is over. In some it never began.'

Once this pandemic had become history, Beth knew that in her remaining years, her life choices ahead would not waver. There was no place for fear, for not listening to what her inner truth was telling her. There was only the sunlight on the roof flashing.

~

In early December, her Christmas tree went up. She liked a real tree. The smell, and then the needles lurking for months to come were all part of it. This year it also provided a much longed for normality.

Christmas was a busy day with phone calls to and from all parts of the globe; an international community coming down the earpiece. A world sharing both Christmas and a global pandemic.

January brought full lockdown again. No cafes. No garden chats. Exercise and essential visits only. The daily walk continued. In the first lockdown an oft repeated remark had been, 'Thank goodness this didn't happen in the depths of winter.' Now it was the depths of winter, and all outside life had stopped. There was no novelty value this time; just weeks of sameness stretching ahead. Some days she met William, and, standing two metres apart, began to tell him bit by bit what she had been thinking. Sometimes she called her closest friends in the city. As she listened to herself speaking, slowly, very slowly, the last links in the chain of self-imposed silence born in uncertainty broke apart.

Night after night she sat by the kitchen fire where so many had sat before her. They too were her community bound together by their lives in this house. They too were her community bound together by dreams and fears. Sometimes she sat in different rooms. Sometimes she walked in the garden; sometimes she touched the stone wall. Everywhere she looked there were stories. The old house had known those who had loved it whose lives had been altered by global events, by village life and by their own choices. Her home wrapped itself round her as it had them.

Back to working on the rewrite, and, it being January, the armada had arrived, and Beth descended on the supermarket shelves for Seville oranges and sugar.

As she carried these beautiful fruits home, she thought of how they came to be. A tiny pip in the earth grew into a tree. Sometimes as many as fifteen years in the growing before it produced fruit, and then year after year, it grew its orange blossoms which then delivered its fruit. This could go on for fifty years and more. Some trees became centenarians.

A pip, planted at the same time as the house had been built, was producing oranges for the first time when Hugh Weir was growing vegetables in the garden. By the time the Misses Cook were making jam, the yield of that tree was stronger; there could be as many as three hundred oranges on a single tree. Regardless of what was happening in the human world, that tree drew from the earth, year after year through the wars and into Beth's lifetime.

The oranges Beth was looking at had come from a younger tree, perhaps grown from the seeds of the original as it neared the end of its life. Generations of people and generations of oranges inside the walls of the solid old house.

Once again, she began the process; this time it was not a chore. Andalucian music added to the atmosphere as she peeled and cut and minced. Tenderly she separated the pips to allow them to swell in readiness for their vital work ahead. The hours of steeping passed, and the boiling began.

'Are you at your marmalade?' came the voice of the postman. 'I can smell it on the road. Great for a cold.'

Mary Queen of Scots would agree.

'Any chance of a jar when you're done?'

'Of course.'

That was another part of the pleasure of the whole process. It was not just the community of marmalade makers. It was the community of marmalade consumers. Visitors asked for it even before they arrived. Jars were given to friends, who carried it back to all corners of the country.

Her brother had always liked it, and had feared there would be no more marmalade after Mina died. Little did he know the recipe would be brewed by a different hand. When he had come home the following year, two jars had been put in front of him; one of his mother's and one of his sister's. To Beth's delight, he had agreed they were equally good. Furthermore, he could not determine who had made which. That was the test; the recipe had truly passed to the next generation.

Windows open, heating off, coat and hat on, the tortured joy of the Spanish guitar, the contents of the old pot bubbled along. Beth was fascinated by the change of colour. The bright orange was darkened when the sugar went in. Amber, and then the glow of the sunset the oranges had known when they had been growing on their branches. Outside the day darkened; inside the Mediterranean glowed.

Eventually it was ready, poured into jars and cooled. Next day the jars were conveyed to the cellar.

Beth loved the cellar, although it was not a place she often made time to sit. Today she did, in the big chair used by Soozie's clients who came to view her jewellery. She looked round. There was Soozie's workbench with a myriad of pliers and hammers. At one end was a small chest of drawers full of stones awaiting their turn to become the centrepiece of rings or kilt pins, chains or earrings, brooches or penannulars.

Beside them sat Beth's books. Her travel library was located in the cellar, and beside it the non-fiction she had written. She took up one of her own texts and began to read. Soon she was drifting into her memory of what a struggle that too had been at the beginning. There was the same uncertainty about whether she could do this, the same drive to do it, the same effort. In the end it had become easy, but that had taken time.

She looked at the walls hung with posters from her theatre, education and travelling days. Tucked in a corner was an offcut of carpet and cans of paint. The Christmas tree decorations hibernated in their box under the table. Many a cellar contained pieces of carpet, paint and Christmas decorations, but this one was distinctive with its art gallery walls, its books, its jewellery and its marmalade.

Shelves of jars of the orange and amber nectar lined one wall. With the door open on sunny days, they glowed. Close up, the smell wrapped round every occupant of the big chair.

Behind the bookshelves had been the chimney, its fireplace the only place in the building wide enough for boiling in large pots. The unknown architect had created this as the nerve centre of the whole building. Mary Weir, Sarah Robertson, Miss Margaret and Miss Ruth – they had all been here, boiling water or making jam.

The men too had been in this space. The hooks on the walls had held the gardening implements used by the Weirs and David McLean. Beth's own father had used the space to create a chopping block for the kindling, the pile of which grew to the left of the door.

How many cellars have windows? This one does. As Beth could look in and see Soozie hard at work, so generations before could have gauged what was happening in that space, and decide if the moment was ripe for going in.

The hours slipped by in memories, as Beth hoped for a flick of velvet, a grey cap, a young man in military uniform, her grandfather, her father to come and join her. Deep down she was sure they would not come. They only did so in times of distress.

But that too might change. Perhaps they would come at a time marking a new beginning, following a human disaster. Some of them had lived through the Spanish flu, others typhoid and cholera epidemics. They had known the terror, and they had dared to hope. Perhaps they would choose to come for a different reason. The previously impossible can happen.

William appeared at the door.

'I don't think they'll come,' she said.

'Oh they will. They'll come to hear their story.' He smiled and took a seat.

She went back to the computer, beside which sat her work, printed out. She picked up the pages and returned to the cellar, opened the door and the window, settled herself in the chair beside the marmalade, and began to read aloud.

Stillness cloaked the land, and then the silence began to shiver;

a tiny sound of footsteps on the gravel path, the gentle brushing of velvet against stone, whispers of laughter weaving through the tinkling of breaking glass. The aromas of baking and of pipe smoke jostled amidst the sounds.

The old house had never felt so proud. It watched and listened; it remembered and dreamed.

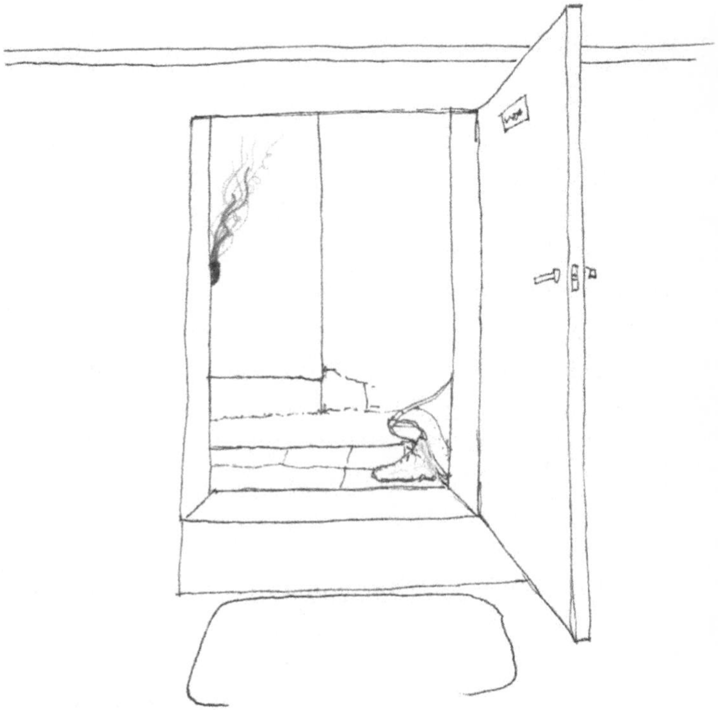

Who Lived Where?

River View House
The Leitch family
Hugh Weir, Sheena, Mary and Peter McIntosh, Jack Weir and Catherine
Isabella Thomson
Sarah and Neil Robertson, their son Douglas and Feudail
The Commandos
Mina, Eddie, Ian, Beth, Sooty and Geordie and many members of their family

River View Coachhouse/Cottage
Walter the coachman
George and Adela Keddie
Mrs Fulton
The Commandos
Mrs Enn and her family
Beth
John and Soozie with Max

The Little Hidden House down below
The Leitches
Miss Margaret and Miss Ruth Cook
Francis, Martha and David Mclean
The Connell Family: John, Maggie, Wee John, Jean and Mina
Mark and Brenda
Soozie
Beth

The Cottage-over-the-Wall
Old Mrs Paton
Johnnie the plumber, her son
Jeannie, his sister

In the interest of simplicity, characters referred to only in passing are not included in the list of residents of the houses.

The Author

Margaret Hubbard can be contacted via her website, which is www.scotlandsstorywithmargaret.com

This is her first venture into creative nonfiction. She hopes you enjoyed reading it as much as she enjoyed writing it, and would very much welcome your thoughts via an online review.

Acknowledgements

I wish to thank my 'readers' who gave me the constructive criticism and positive feedback I needed to keep going. Without their encouragement I might well have decided this was just too big a challenge.

Alan, Caitrin, Fiona, Iain, Jacqui, Joanne, Karen, Kate, Liz, Lynne, Neil, Nicola, Ros, Steven, and Stuart...thank you.

To the many friends and family who have not read the script, but who also encouraged me to keep going I also sincerely say thank you.

To Carol H Dunn a thank you for fifty years of friendship and your photograph of the gate.

I would also like to thank Claire Wingfield for her professional support as a literary editor, and then for guiding me through the whole intimidating process of production.

Thanks to Kieran McLoughlin for typesetting and cover design.

For Susan M Turmeau a very special thank you for her illustrations, her photography on the front cover and her patience.

To the people who can be identified, and who permitted me to write about them, I thank them with immense humility for their trust.

Milton Keynes UK
Ingram Content Group UK Ltd.
UKHW012126010124
435287UK00004B/16

9 781739 423704